William Minet

Some Account of the Huguenot Family of Minet

Their Coming Out of France at the Revocation of the Edict

William Minet

Some Account of the Huguenot Family of Minet
Their Coming Out of France at the Revocation of the Edict

ISBN/EAN: 9783337292553

Printed in Europe, USA, Canada, Australia, Japan

Cover: Foto ©Lupo / pixelio.de

More available books at **www.hansebooks.com**

SOME ACCOVNT OF THE
HVGVENOT FAMILY OF MINET
FROM THEIR COMING OVT OF FRANCE
AT THE REVOCATION OF THE
EDICT OF NANTES MDCLXXXVI
FOVNDED ON ISAAC MINET'S
'RELATION OF OVR FAMILLY'
BY WILLIAM MINET, M·A· F·S·A·
OF THE INNER TEMPLE

'NE SOMMES POINT VENUE DE RACE ILLUSTRE ET NOBLE. SY EST CE QUE NOUS SOMMES VENUE, DIEU MERCY DES GENS CRAIGNANS DIEU'

           J. SAUCHELLE

PREFACE

IN accordance with a custom sanctioned by long usage, I preface the work which follows with a brief account of the motives which have prompted its undertaking, and of the methods which have been adopted in its execution.

As to the methods, I would first say (with Sir Henry Wotton), 'I am but the gatherer and disposer of other men's stuff.' There has come into my hands a large quantity of papers and notes relating to our family, but in that condition of most admired disorder in which the accidents of time have left them. The first task was to arrange them in the order of the generations to which they belonged, that each might, so far as possible, tell its own story; the next, to supply connecting-links between one passage and another.

I am, therefore, responsible for the right ordering of what is original. Of my own additions this much may be said: I found, as must always be the case in a work of this nature, that a little research would enable me to add considerably to the materials already in my hands. And here I was beset by a temptation experienced by all who have embarked on genealogical inquiries—the temptation to continue research, not so much for the sake of making the story fuller and more living, as for the sake of adding date to date and name to name; the result of which, not unfrequently, is to produce a mere genealogical skeleton, perfectly articulated it may be, but still a skeleton only. With what measure of success I have avoided this pitfall I hardly know. But, while availing myself of such records of the past as I have been able to discover, I have, in my use of them, tried to keep this principle before me—that the object of my research should be, not so much the addition of another bone to the skeleton, as the making the dry bones to live. As to method, let this suffice.

It remains to speak of motive. And here, at the outset, let me disclaim any that should seem based on mere 'ostentation of ancestry.' Granting that what we are depends much upon ourselves, I hold it also true that we are to a great degree what our fathers have made us; in other words, we are the creatures of environment as well as of heredity, though what part each of these factors has played in the building up of our character, time and a fuller science must more nicely determine. To speak from my own experience of what we owe to heredity: over and over again, as I have gathered from the past some fresh trait in the character of some ancestor, it has flashed in upon me that what I found was nothing new—was but the reflexion of myself.

I have, then, collected and ordered these records, partly that our children may learn what their fathers have done in the old times before them, and partly that they may take pleasure, as I have done, in finding in the lives and characters of these the key to some part of their own.

We Huguenots are proud of our descent, with a pride which need not be personal, but should rather be based upon the part our origin has enabled us to play in the country of our adoption. Year by year we are more and more being merged and welded into that great whole, the English people; but of the various foreign elements which have from time to time added new forces to its character, ours is assuredly not the least important. It may, then, not be entirely idle to have placed on record, ere yet it was too late, the story of a Huguenot family for which it may be claimed that it exhibits in no slight degree many of those qualities which have worked for the best in the building up of a sound national life.

But one more task remains, and that is to thank those who during the progress of my work have given me their help and the advantage of their experience. To name all would be too long, but especially would I mention my old college friend, W. C. Waller, F.S.A., whose assistance has been constant and varied; while to Mr. G. H. Overend, F.S.A., whose knowledge of Dover Huguenots is evidenced by his writings, I owe both valuable suggestion and practical aid; and I am particularly indebted to Monsieur V. J. Vaillant, of Boulogne-sur-Mer, and to Monsieur C. Landrin, of Guines, for much of the material which goes to make up the chapter entitled 'The Family in France.' Nor would I omit mention of my sister, whose interest in our family is as great as my own, and who has shared with me the pleasure of compiling much of what follows.

W. M.

FOUNTAIN COURT, TEMPLE, LONDON.
June, 1892.

CONTENTS

CHAPTER		PAGE
	PREFACE .	v
I.	ISAAC MINET'S BOOK .	1
II.	THE FAMILY IN FRANCE .	7
III.	THE PERSECUTION AND THE ESCAPE	13
IV.	THE FAMILY IN ENGLAND	37
V.	ISAAC MINET .	50
VI.	THE SAUCHELLES .	77
VII.	ISAAC MINET'S CHILDREN .	95
VIII.	THE BUSINESS.	118
IX.	HUGHES MINET .	154
X.	HUGHES MINET'S CHILDREN .	176

APPENDICES

I.	FACSIMILES OF AUTOGRAPHS	197
II.	GENEALOGICAL TABLES .	198
III.	WILLS .	211
IV.	INSCRIPTIONS TAKEN FROM MONUMENTS OF THE MINET FAMILY	218
V.	DEEDS RELATING TO LA TRÉSORERIE	221
VI.	THE CUPS OF THE CHURCH OF GUÎNES	224
VII.	UNIDENTIFIED MINETS	228
	INDEX .	231

LIST OF ILLUSTRATIONS

ISAAC MINET . .	*Frontispiece*
	PAGE
SEAL OF THE TOWN OF DOVER, OBVERSE .	. . viii
SEAL OF THE TOWN OF DOVER, REVERSE	x
SEAL OF THE TOWN OF CALAIS, 1228	. . xii
HOUSE IN THE PLACE D'ARMES, CALAIS .	*To face* 12
ARMS OF CALAIS, 1570	17
FACSIMILE OF 'RECONNAISSANCE' .	*To face* 51
PIER HOUSE, DOVER	,, 151
HUGHES MINET .	,, 168
ISAAC MINET	,, 184
JOHN LEWIS MINET .	,, 189
JAMES LEWIS MINET	,, 190
FACSIMILE AUTOGRAPHS .	. 197
ARMS	*Genealogical Tables*

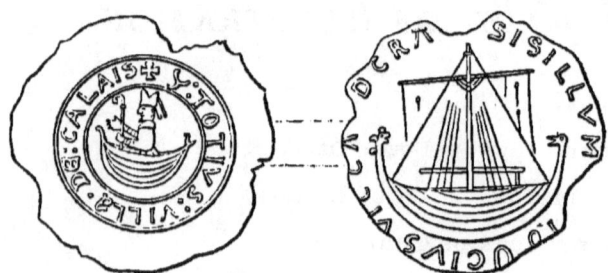

THE

HUGUENOT FAMILY OF MINET

CHAPTER I

ISAAC MINET'S BOOK

A good book . . . embalmed and treasured up on purpose to a life beyond life.—MILTON.

THERE are but few to whom the past history of their own family would not be of interest. When that family is of Huguenot origin, and when, moreover, in writing its history, it is possible to draw largely from contemporary records, such a history seems to become of more than individual or family interest. The family whose annals we propose to record is peculiarly fortunate in having had preserved to it a manuscript book containing, with much other information, a narrative in his own handwriting of the persecution and escape of Isaac Minet, who fled from France on the Revocation of the Edict of Nantes. How this book, after lying hidden for more than a century, came into the possession of the great-great-grandson of its original owner, it is the purpose of this chapter to explain.

This book came into the possession of James Lewis Minet on May 10, 1867, previous to which date its existence was unsuspected. So far as it can be traced, its history is as follows: it first belonged to Isaac Minet, and its original use, to judge from the words 'Receipt Booke' written on its rough calf cover, as also from various entries scattered through it, was that of a book of personal accounts of a heterogeneous description. Gradually, however, it seems to have become a memorandum-book, in which its owner noted public and private events, mixed up with fragments of biography and autobiography relating to his family. To disentangle this patchwork would have required some patience, even at the hands of its venerable author. Nor has the task been rendered easier by the subsequent proceedings of his son William, who (actuated, as he himself says, by the best motives to make what he found therein clearer) has torn out and renumbered pages, and carried on and elucidated what his father had written, by means of notes and remarks inserted in the blank spaces.

However, this much is clear—only three hands have ever written in the book: Isaac Minet, the father, William, his son, and a clerk employed by William to copy some of the notes relating to the Sauchelle family; there is no entry earlier than 1705, and none later than 1751. The book itself thus covers a period of forty-six years; but in the form of recollections and traditions it goes back to the birth of Isaac Minet's father, Ambroise, in 1613; and in the form of copies from much older notes relating to the Sauchelles (Mrs. Isaac Minet's family), it extends as far as the fifteenth century, though 1553 is the first actual date cited.

Isaac Minet does not seem to have written much beyond cash-entries until the year 1722 (he was then sixty-two years of age), when he gives the first, and shorter, account of his escape from Calais to Dover with his mother, and of some of the events preceding their flight. In some respects this narrative, incomplete as it is when compared with the longer one, written fifteen years later, is the more interesting, and in two particulars especially: first, it contains the story of the death and persecution, even after death, of his mother's sister, at Ardres, in June, 1685; secondly, he mentions in it the duration of his own and his mother's imprisonment—a period of about six weeks, from the middle of November till December 31, 1685.

Later, we find him entering notes on his father, brothers and sisters, his own children, and their marriages and occupations; while in parts of the book he inserts a medley of accounts and memoranda, such as the expenses of the induction of his son John to the living of Eythorne, in 1723, and of providing him with a horse, saddle, featherbed, wig, &c.; a peculiarly graphic note on some Havana snuff, of which he seems to have been extremely careful; notes on the death of Louis XIV. of France and of the declaration of the wars against France and Spain; of the youth of Lord Chancellor Hardwicke, a native of Dover; of the going ashore of some Dutch East Indiamen; of his being appointed a member of the Corporation, with the details of the cost of his gown, &c.

But all this is of slight interest compared with the narrative, which occupies sixteen pages of the book, and which (being then seventy-seven years old) he wrote in 1737, fifteen years after the shorter account, and fifty-one years after the events it describes. The next year he added an account of his wife's death, and of his own subsequent illness; and in April, 1744, occurs the last entry in his hand—a note of the declaration of war against France.

In connexion with his escape to England, and the feeling with which he always regarded it, it is interesting to quote here from a note made by Peter Fector, his clerk at Dover, who, succeeding him in the management of the business there, died in 1814; in this he says: 'With God's blessing they came safe to Dover in an open boat they had ordered f^r thence to take them on the shore near Calais, whi. brought them to Dover aforesaid the 1st Aug. 1686, with a constant sense of the goodness of the Allmighty. Amen. Mr. Isaac Minet kept that day as a fast, in Peter Fector's memory, to the 1st Aug., 1744. He died 8th April, 1745.'

We now reach William Minet's additions to the book. In February, 1745, Isaac was taken ill, and on March 11, William, his youngest son, came down from London to Dover to see him. In the account he gives of his father's last illness he says: 'He told me of his will, recommended me sundry things.' Among them must have been this book, for on the inner side of one of the covers William writes:—

12 *March*, 1745.—I took this book in my possession, as my d^r father, in my journeys to Dover, when I used to lament y^t at his spare hours he had not wrote an abs^t of the history of his life which to me, who since am come to mature age have had little opportunity of conversing with him, the time in my several journeys being chiefly taken up in less serious talk than old family affaires, redressing one or other grievance or complaint.

From this date until April 15 (Isaac died on the 8th) William, while still at Dover, seems to have looked over the book and papers which accompanied it, and during the month to have had the notes on the Sauchelle family copied into it. Besides these notes, he also wrote at this time the sort of preface to the Sauchelle entries which will be found at page 78.

At the end of July or beginning of August, 1745, Peter Fector brought the book to William Minet in London, and he, in 1749, revised the whole, as he himself tells us :—

1749. *Sunday*, 17, 7ber, 1749.—I, Will. Minet, youngest son of Isaac and Mary Minet, do make the following remarks and observations for the satisfaction of myself and family y^t will survive me.

I am sorry my d^r father and mother never thought it worth their while to have a separate volume in which they should or might have wrote what annalls or memoires of their owne family and ancestors, family memorandums, receits and other choice or pleasing subjects. It is—as above I noted, 1745—that my father did not make a book of remarks and observation on men and manners, and a sort of a sketch history of his times. It had realy been worthy and curious, and well pleasing to his family, for he had opportunitys of seeing, hearing, and knowing the sentiments of men of all sorts of degrees and qualitys, and he was a free, easy, pleasant companion, and to whome men of all degrees would and did resort and like to spend their time, from princes to a comon man asking charity. He often used to look on most affaires of Life as vanity, and all passing away and hardly worth notice ; at other times he used to be very thoughtfull, and subject to vapours and melancholy, for w^h he had at times subjects and causes, which the living part of his family are and were sensible of, and which posterity has not to do with. The chief of his own hand writting family memo. are in this book, which before he wrote in it was aplyd to other uses. I have, therefore, in order to make it more concise and more adapted for the use, taken out some leaves, w^h I have faithfully folded up, and will be found in the family bundle tied up with this book, viz. fr. fol. 54 to 69,[1] and I do declare on my honour, and will deposit my oath if required, y^t I always acted as a faithfull friend to the family, and sacredly executed the trust of my d^r father's executor.

The foregoing remarks are written on the inside of the cover, and, space failing, William writes in the margin : ' Read on w^t I have wrote in this book, this is N° 1, vide N° 2.' No. 2 follows in the first available blank space, which happens to be in the middle of folio 3, where he begins again :—

N° 2. Continuation of W. M. memoires in this book of his late Father.

This book I examined and lookt into at my father's death

---

[1] Now, unfortunately, not to be found.

perticularly, and at 1 or 2 more journeys to Dover, where it remained till July and begin̄g Aug*, y* Mr. P* Fector brought it up; and with several other small manuscript book of my mother's writting I this day, 17 7b* 1749, examined 'em all over on purpose, and tore blank leaves, and folded up loose papers, and culled and examined the whole, to have 'em ready at hand to peruse, or to be found here-after by those of my heirs or executors as may have a liking to 'em, recommending 'em, however, if they take no pleasure therein them-selves, they will at least bundle, tye, and seal 'em up, to be del⁴ in trust to the nearest akind to yᵉ family, or to such as will either promise care of 'em, and not expose 'em out of the family at any rate, because wᵗ may be curious and worthy keeping of ones owne may appear rediculous to strangers. They had better be burnt than fall into strang hands.

After this we find nothing further till 1751, when William chronicles the marriage of Peter Fector to his niece Mary, daughter of John Minet, the rector of Eythorne; and this is the last entry ever made.

The further history of the book is chiefly founded on surmise. It must have returned to Dover, and remained there in the possession of the Fectors when, in 1770, Hughes Minet retired from the partnership, leaving the Dover business to be carried on by Peter Fector; nor does it seem to have been returned to the Minets when, in 1783, the partner-ship was resumed. Peter Fector, who lived till 1814, could not have been unaware of its existence, for, as we have seen, he had taken it to London in 1745; still, he cannot have known its interest, for in 1799 he made out a sort of pedigree (now in my possession), in which he makes no sort of allusion to the book, and falls into errors which reference to it would have prevented. He speaks, too, of giving a copy of his notes to his brother-in-law, Hughes Minet, who would hardly have wished for them had he been aware of the existence of the fuller record. The succeeding generations never speak of or notice its existence, and this positive fact remains—that since William's last entry, in 1751, no one has added a single line. We may, then, safely infer that it returned to Dover some time after 1751, and remained there, unnoticed and forgotten, till 1867.

In the year 1842 the Fectors disposed of the business in Dover, from which the Minets had previously retired, to the National Pro-vincial Bank, and the book must have passed, with other old business papers, into their possession. In 1867 the Bank, desirous, on a change of premises, of looking through and destroying as far as possible this accumulation, requested Mr. Boyton, one of the former clerks of the Fectors, to look through the papers, destroying or preserving as he might see fit; it was while doing this that he came across the book, and, recognising its real nature, called the attention of the Bank managers to it, who at once handed it to James Lewis Minet, the then representative of the family.

Thus, at the close of more than a century of oblivion, these memories of the past have been awakened for us, the descendants of old Isaac; and while the main interest of the manuscript centres in the story of the escape from Calais, linked with this are incident and detail, sometimes graphic, often insignificant, but all and each helping to restore the picture of a past humble in its shortcomings, steadfast in its well-doing; of a life, in short, of piety and integrity, which, in many of its aspects, and under altered conditions, it may still be ours to win from the present.

CHAPTER II

THE FAMILY IN FRANCE

The greater part must be content to be as tho' they had not been – to be found in the Register of God, not in the record of man.—SIR THOMAS BROWNE.

THE fulness of detail with which Isaac Minet has told us of his escape to England, and the care with which he has recorded the history of his own children, make us regret all the more the slenderness of the information he gives us respecting his parents and his own early life in France. Twice only (in 1717 and in 1737) he enters a few short notes on the families of his father and mother. These it will be best to give first, adding to them what little information it has been possible to collect from other sources. The notes of 1717 are as follow :—

MEMORANDUM by me Isaac Minet; a relation of the familly of my father Mr Ambroise Minet.

My father Mr Ambroise Minet was borne at Clermon in Boullenois, he had a brother Jacques Minet who was post mast' at franc near Montreuille in Boulenois whose son James suceeded him in same imploy and whose grandson is now actually postmast' there in 1717, he is also James and hath a brother.

S^d Jacques brother to my father had a son Ambroise who was kild, being cornet of horse in ye french service and 4 daughters Mary, Anne, Suson, and Ester, who all four dyed in England.

My mother was Mis Susanna de Haffrengue, daughter of Peter Haffrengue, borne at a house called La Tresorery near Huitmille in the boullenois. She had two brothers, Daniel who dyed at Ardres, and Peter who maryed at St Vallery in Somme.

My father and mother lived at Calais and keept shopp of grocery druggs liuors etc^{ra}—my father was buryed at Calais out of ye town being a protestant in ye year 1675 aged 70 years.

My mother did come over to England & dyed at London in ye yeare 1687 & was buryed in S^t martin churchyard, I then lived at London wth my brother Ambroise.

The notes of 1737 are fuller, and are as follow :—

My father Mr Ambroise Minet was born at Cormon in the Boulonois & had a brother James Minet who was postmaster at franc in the same County, whose Son James succeeded him, and the Son of s^d James succeeded him, who being dead his widow keeps ye post office there at present 1737.

S^d James Minet ye first had 4 daughters who all came to England for ye sake of ye prottestant Religion.

My mother was Mistris Suson Hafrengue born at a farm called La tresory neare boulogne, belonging to her father—my father was inhabitant & Bourgeois or freeman at Calais and keept a shop of grocery, druggs etc^m, was a distiller, hee sold more tobaco than was sold besides in france within a hundred miles, and was ye first, and I believe ye only man in france who had from London an ingin for cutting tobaco square ; hee did furnish Boulogne, Etaples, Montreuill & all the country about with grocery goods wch hee had from Zealand, there not being at that time any body in those places y^t understood anything of trade ; hee dyed at Calais in 1675; my father was 70 years of age when hee dyed and my mother who fled from Calais to England dyed at London and was buryed in St Martins Churchyard in the yeare 1688 aged 67 years.

My father had six Sons & 3 daughters (viz) Thomas, Ambroise, Daniel, Elizabeth, Suson, Isaac, Jacob, Stephen and Mary who all fled out of france for ye sake of the protestant religion.

Several sources of information enable us to add to, and in some particulars correct, the information supplied by Isaac. First among these must be placed the 'Transcript of the Registers of the Protestant Church at Guines from 1668 to 1685,' recently published by the Huguenot Society of London,[1] which enables us to fix the date of Ambroise's birth in 1613, and to correct the date of his death from 1675, as given by his son, to 1679.[2] Another entry in the same registers[3] enables us to add the name of a sister—Martha—to the brother James mentioned by Isaac ; for in 1672 we find the record of the marriage of Jonas du Riez and Marie le Turcq, 'fille de deffunt Pierre le Turcq, et de deffunte Marthe Minet, natiue de frens en Boullonnois et dem^{te} à Calais.' It is somewhat strange that Isaac

---

[1] Publications of the Huguenot Society of London, vol. iii. Lymington, 1891.
[2] Guines Registers, p. 181.   [3] *Ibid.* p. 61.

nowhere mentions such an aunt; but seeing that she was already dead in 1668,[1] and may, indeed, have died some years earlier, Isaac, born in 1660, very probably never knew her; in another place, however, he speaks of 'Jonas Duriz's wife, our relation.'

But the fact that there is not a single Minet entry in these registers which does not relate to our family is conclusive evidence that there was no other Protestant family of the name in this district; and this, coupled with the statement that Martha came from Frencq, a village closely adjoining Cormont, makes it almost safe to assume that Ambroise, James, and Martha were all children of a Minet who lived at Cormont, and whom we claim as the ancestor of all the Minets with whom we shall deal in these pages.

Cormont [2] and Frencq are two small villages, lying close together, about ten and eight miles respectively from Montreuil. At the former Ambroise was born, and at the latter Martha lived, and James was postmaster. The office was not hereditary, but was obtained by purchase, and was often continued from father to son on payment of a fine to the State; its duties were the supplying of horses for the king's use, as also for that of ordinary travellers.

James had four daughters, who all came to England, where the only trace I can find of them is the admission of a Susanne Minet in 1670, and of an Ester Minet in 1671, as members of the Threadneedle Street Church, both 'par tesmoignage de Calais.'

James himself, or his son, if, as was probably the case, the father was already dead in 1685, must have in some measure conformed on the Revocation, since he not only remained in France, but also retained his office of postmaster. This we know from Isaac's note, and it is confirmed by a document of 1697, discovered by M. Vaillant, and given in his work, 'La Révocation de l'Edit de Nantes dans le Boulonnais.'[3] The document is headed: 'Estat des Familles D[e] L[a] R[eligion] P[rétendue] R[éformée] du Boullenois,' and among the names occurs 'Frenq.—Minet, tenant la poste, 2 garcons, 1 fille.' One of these two boys must have been the James who, as Isaac tells

---

[1] She is spoken of as dead in 1672, and I find no entry of the death in the registers, which begin in 1668.

[2] Isaac, in the notes of 1717, quoted above, gives Clermon, but corrects this in the later note of 1737 to Cormon.

[3] Page 17, where M. Vaillant suggests that the date of this document should be read 1679; but from internal evidence it is clear that the date 1697, given in the text, is correct. See p. 14, note 5.

us, was still postmaster in 1717, and who died before 1737, in which year his widow held the post.

There is evidence, to be adduced later,[1] that William, son of Isaac Minet, continued his father's interest in this French branch of the family, and kept up some communication with it, as late as 1767; but there is nothing to enable us to connect the Peter of that date with the earlier James, or to bridge over the interval between 1737 and 1767.[2]

It is with Ambroise Minet, then, that the record of our family must begin. Born at Cormont in 1613, he removed to Calais, where he gradually built up a considerable business, the nature and extent of which can be best gathered from the notes given above, as well as from further remarks of Isaac which we shall have occasion to quote in the next chapter. The date of his marriage is not known, but Thomas, the eldest of his ten children, was born in 1648. His son Isaac gives the names of nine children only; but in the Guines Registers[3] is the entry of the baptism, in March, 1669, of 'Pierre, fils d'Ambroise Minet et de Susanne Affringhue, baptisé le 3e. Parrain, Pierre Sauchelle. Marraine, Judith d'Hoye. Naissance à Calais le 19e Feurier dernier.' There is no other mention of this child, and even though we may be surprised not to find his death recorded in the registers, we may, from the absence of any mention of him by his brother, infer that he died young.

Of Ambroise as a man of business and as a citizen of Calais we know practically nothing; of his connexion with the religion to which his children remained so faithful, it is possible to speak with somewhat more of detail. Guines, some six miles from Calais, was the religious centre of the Huguenots in this district of France. Here stood their church; and with this church, the only one tolerated under the provisions of the Edict, Ambroise was closely connected. Of the church itself, and of its beginning and of its end, I have dealt fully in the preface to the Transcript of its Registers; of its organisation, and of the nature of its services, I may perhaps be permitted to say something here.

[1] Page 115.
[2] Robert Minet is given by Lefebvre (*Hist. de Calais*, 1766, ii. 515) as principal of a college in Calais in 1640. He was a Catholic, and I cannot connect him in any way with the family. In the archives of the town of Boulogne-sur-Mer (No. 1015), so M. Vaillant informs me, a Robert Minet, probably the same, is entered as presented to the Chapellerie de la Madelaine et de l'hôpital in 1655.
[3] Page 12.

Side by side with the registers has survived the book in which the accounts of the church were kept.[1] This book, now in the possession of M. Landrin, of Guines, is called 'Régistre de la Recette et Dépense faitte pour les pauvres du Temple de Guisnes, depuis 1660 jusqu'en 1681,' and contains at the beginning a list of the officers of the church; among them is Ambroise Minet, described as 'diacre assistant.' 'Le mot de Diacre signifie icy,' the book itself tells us, 'des personnes chargées de recevoir et distribuer les aumônes, et de faire les fonctions de Marguilliers [churchwardens] sous l'inspection des Pasteurs, Ministres, et Anciens.' The accounts, which form the chief contents of the volume, are in some instances authenticated by signatures, and in this way has been preserved to us the actual autograph of Ambroise Minet.

Of the services, which Ambroise must have often attended, we have the account of one who was himself present at them in the Diary of White Kennet, preserved among the Lansdowne Manuscripts in the British Museum.[2] Kennet was born at Dover in 1660, and ultimately became Bishop of Peterborough; in 1682 he spent three weeks at Calais and Ardres, and records his experiences at length in his Diary, from which the following extracts are taken:—

1682. Tuesday October 3rd. Went to Dover in compliance with an invitation to France.

Friday. Embarked in Barretts boat for Calais 10 o'clock, night tide.

Saturday. Arrived at Calais at 3 in the afternoon; the imposition for each person landing 3^d.

Sunday, October 8th. Went up by boat to Guins. A custom for the protestants formerly at 1 mile distance from Calais to sing psalms in the severall boats till they came to Gaine, but of late forbidden by authority. The freight for each person 1^d. The town of Gane formerly walled and well fortified and a distinct town of itself. The protestant church in the form of a trapeze with double galleries round. Two ministers (beside a reader) with 100l. salarie apeice; the one Mr Troulier,[3] resident at Gane, the other M^r [Simon de Vaux], at Calais.

---

[1] This must be one of the books referred to in the extracts given in Appendix VI.

[2] I am indebted to Mr. F. Bayley, F.S.A., for calling my attention to this Diary. It is No. 937 in the Lansdowne Collection.

[3] Pierre Trouillart, minister from 1673 to 1685.

The reader, at some distance from the pulpit reads the lessons and sets the psalms; their sermons set off with very eager repetitions, and very vehement expressions. The sacrament administered after sermon, the table placed under the pulpit, fenced off with seats for persons of better rank. The bread divided in a dish, and the wine poured out into 2 large cups; the ministers assisting, the one consecrates the bread and administers to himself and then to the other, and the same with the wine. Then the communicants are admitted singly by order, and at the entrance of each the minister distributes to each a piece of bread. When the table is filled round, at the pronouncing of a prescribed benediction they all eat; and soon after the minister that consecrated the wine takes the 2 cups and delivers them to 2 persons in the middle, so they pass round without any genuflexion. After which with another short benediction they depart, and give room to new successive sets till all have received.

That Sunday on which the sacrament is administered no sermon in the afternoon.

Returned to Calais on horseback, called to drink at a publique house on the road, and room next to highway filled with severall companies at cards.

The Diary continues until October 23, when the writer returned to Dover. Its entries until that date are of great interest, but, with one exception to be quoted later, contain nothing more bearing on the Huguenots, and therefore need not be further reproduced here.

This, then, is all we know definitely of Ambroise. He married Susanne de Haffrengue, a daughter of a distinguished Protestant family, and his ten children were born between 1648–69. The sixty-six years of his life were spent in the management of his business, the education of his family, and the performance of his duties as a citizen of Calais and a churchwarden of the church at Guines. He lived in a house still standing on the north side of the Place d'Armes at Calais, of which an engraving is given on the opposite page. Such, at least, has been the abiding tradition of his race, and the stone 'minet' which still looks down from the centre gable of this house would seem to give it considerable support.[1] He died on July 16,

---

[1] It is but right to state that there is another legend, which gives the cat a more venerable origin. 'At the present day, a house may yet be seen in the "Place d'Armes," at Calais, surmounted by the effigy of a cat in stone; the legend running that the building, or, rather, in

HOUSE IN THE PLACE D'ARMES, CALAIS

1679, and was buried in the Protestant cemetery outside the town.[1]

Whatever of Huguenot principle Isaac inherited from his father, he must have owed at least as much more to his mother, for in all the records of Protestantism in the North-eastern district of France the one family which stands out as 'chef des Huguenots' is that of de Haffrengue, and from this family Susanne de Haffrengue sprang. Pierre de Haffrengue, her father, was a yeoman living on his own estate of La Trésorerie, near Wimille;[2] and here, in 1626, his daughter was born.[3] The place is said to have derived its name from the fact that it had at one time belonged to the Chapter of the Cathedral church at Boulogne, by whom its revenues had been allocated to the support of the Canon having the care of the treasury. It stands on the brow of the sharp hill which rises above the village of Wimille, and about six miles out of Boulogne, close to the high-road leading to Calais.[4] Of the original house, which dates from the sixteenth century, only a portion remains; but this is striking and picturesque, reminding one of the farmhouses with their peel towers so common on our Northern border. The centre, a plain and massive stone construction, now grey with age, is flanked at each end by large semicircular towers; the interior has been almost completely modernised, and only a portion of the ceiling and the fireplace of the kitchen can claim any antiquity. It now forms part of a group of modern farm-buildings; but the sixteenth-century portion is used as a summer residence by the present owner, M. Bourdet, of Paris, himself a connexion by marriage of a de Haffrengue.[5]

---

strict truth, the site of the one now standing, was sold and conveyed in consideration of receiving the animal in payment during the famine created by the siege of 1347' (R. B. Calton, *Annals and Legends of Calais*, p. 11. London, 1852).

[1] 'Le cimetière des Huguenots de Calais était situé sur une extrémité de la grande Commune, auprès du pont Thierry, au bout du quai de l'Est. La découverte toute récente (Juillet, 1888) d'un nombre considérable de squelettes permet d'en déterminer l'emplacement. Ce cimetière fut supprimé en 1685. Un état de recettes de 1706 provenant des fermes des terres nouvellement réunies à la ville de Calais, comprend entre autres locations celle de cinq mesures de terre au lieu dit le *Cimetière des Huguenots* près le pont Thierry' (C. Landrin, quoting E. Brullé ; *Notes pour servir à l'histoire de Calais*, p. 120).

[2] Isaac writes Huitmille, but Wimille is obviously meant; curiously enough, the same spelling occurs in the Guînes Registers, p. 233, *s.v.* Ballin.

[3] This appears from the entry of her death in the Registers of St. Martin's-in-the-Fields ; it does not, however, agree with what her son states in the note quoted above (p. 8), that she died in '1688, aged sixty-seven years' ; this would put her birth in 1621.

[4] *Dict. Archéologique et Historique du Dept du Pas-de-Calais*. Arras, 1882, ii. 43.

[5] Another instance of the survival of old names in the district may be cited. The wife of the present farmer, M. de la Hode, was a Prudence de Haffrengue. Neuchâtel-en-Boulonnais is the present headquarters of the family.

The family of de Haffrengue[1] was an old and important one in the Boulonnais, and at this period seems to have been represented by two branches: the elder, fixed at La Converserie, a small village near Boulogne; the younger, at La Trésorerie. It is with the latter that we are alone concerned; but seeing the position held by the former as 'chefs des Huguenots,' and the connexion existing between the two branches, I may perhaps be pardoned if I turn aside for a moment to speak of the Converserie branch. 'Sur la rive gauche de la Liane, au sommet de l'abrupte colline qui domine le hameau si connu de Pont-de-Briques se dresse la petite église de St. Etienne. A peu de distance de St. Etienne, dans les dunes, s'abrite le hameau de la Converserie, qui était un fief à Jehan de Haffrenghes avant 1480,' says M. Landrin; a later Jehan must have been of the New Faith, for in 1626 we find 'Jehan de Haffrengues, Sieur de la Converserie,' witness to an inventory of the goods of Simon Coquet, farmer and brewer of Guines, who bequeathed 300 livres Tournois to the poor of the Reformed Faith.[2] At the time of our story Jehan was dead, and had been succeeded by Philippe, his son, who married in 1684 Anne de la Croix, of Boulogne,[3] daughter of Pierre de la Croix and Anne Flahault. We must suppose that at the time of the Revocation Philippe to some extent conformed; for on February 4, 1690, 'Philippe de Haffrengues, sieur de la Converserie, et Anne de la Croix sa femme obtiennent concession des biens de feu Pierre de la Croix et d'Anne Flahault sa femme fugitive.'[4] But this relapse cannot have been a very complete one, since seven years later we find him called 'chef des Huguenots' in the 'Estat' already referred to. Among the names of Huguenots of the parish of St. Etienne, in Boulogne, in which parish La Converserie was situated, occur, 'Le Sr Haffrengue, chef des Huguenots, de la Converserie: sa femme, fille de la Croix; a 5 enfans dont les deux plus vieux de 12 ans et de 10.[5] Il a son neveu nomé Souchey (?) dont le père est venu à Calais et a abjuré, une servante opiniâtre Susanne Latteux, et Madelon Haffrengues, sœur dud. Haffrengue.' Later on, in the same list, we find the name of one Jacob Gueule of La

---

[1] I have adopted this spelling as the most usual; but, as was commonly the case at this period, the name occurs in very many forms, frequently without the H.

[2] C. Landrin, *Tablettes Historiques du Calaisis*, iii. 254. Calais, 1888.

[3] Guines Registers, page 269.

[4] *Les Huguenots et la Ligue au Diocèse de Boulogne*, p. 232. F. Lefebvre. Boulogne-sur-Mer, 1855.

[5] It is this entry which fixes the date of the document as 1697, for we know from the Guines Registers that Philippe married in 1684. See above, page 9.

THE FAMILY IN FRANCE

Haye, 'qui a épousé une catholique qui fait ses fonctions : ce mary ferait son debvoir, s'il n'étoit retenu par le Sieur Haffrengue.' Was it on account of the influence he is here accused of exercising that he was thrown into prison? for in the following year Philippe was shut up in the Castle of Boulogne,[1] where, however, he could not have remained long, as in a deed of February of this year (1698) he is spoken of as 's'étant évadé du royaume.' Where he fled to I have been unable to discover.[2]

It seems more than probable that his wife remained behind, and that her courage failed her for the second time: indeed, this must be so if the following entry in the Boulogne archives refers to her :—' 1700, 12 Avril. Nous Pierre Framery chanoine théologal et vicaire général, avons reçu à la grille du chœur des religieuses Ursulines l'abjuration d'hérésie, faite en présence de témoins par dame Hafrengue.' An entry which follows this, and is dated November 6, 1703, clearly refers to Anne de Haffrengue, and confirms the inference drawn from the former, and shows further that Philippe de Haffrengue, her first husband, was dead, for we are told that on this date 'Anne Haffrengue de La Conversiere' married, according to the rites of the Roman Church, Joseph Herbault, a merchant.[3]

The de Haffrengues of La Trésorerie, however, interest us more nearly, for it was from this branch that Susanne was descended; and here, if we neglect an apocryphal 'Etienne,'[4] it is Pierre de Haffrengue who must be our starting-point. This Pierre was Susanne's father, and she

---

[1] *L'année Boulonnaise*, p. 602. Ernest Deseille. Boulogne-sur-Mer, 1886.
[2] The following table, drawn up from the Guines Registers, shows the Converserie Haffrengues, so far as it has been possible to make them out :—

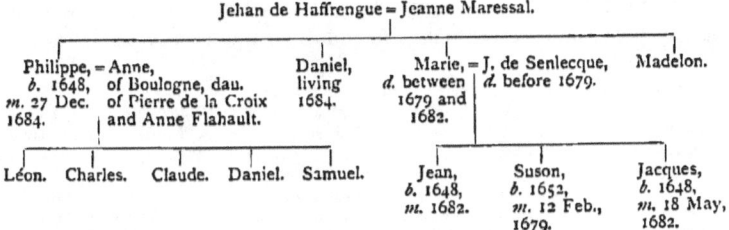

[3] *Archives de la ville de Boulogne-sur-Mer*, Nos. 1700, 1828.
[4] L. E. de la Gorgue-Rosny, in his *Recherches généalogiques sur les comtés de Ponthieu, de Boulogne, de Guines, et des pays circonvoisins* (Boulogne-sur-Mer, 1875, *s.v.* Haffrengue), gives a list of Haffrengue ancestors, some clearly wrong, and others not to be depended on.

herself was one of a family of four. The date of her father's death is not known; but as in a curious and interesting deed of 1668,[1] which I owe to the research and courtesy of M. Landrin, Daniel and Pierre, her brothers, are spoken of as landlords of La Trésorerie, at Wimille, then leased to one Pierre Coze, it would seem clear that at that date the father was no longer alive.

What the connexion between the two branches was I am unable exactly to make out, although the existence of the relationship is clear from two sources. In one of the endorsements on the deed just mentioned, dated October 26, 1669, the tenant of the Trésorerie is credited with a payment of fifty livres 'baillé à notre aquy à la Converserie,' a payment clearly made to Daniel and Pierre, Susanne's brothers, who had succeeded to their father's property. Again, Daniel of the Trésorerie had married a Jeanne Latteur,[2] and Philippe and Madelaine of the Converserie appear on several occasions in the Guînes Registers as *parrain* and *marraine* in the baptisms of Latteur children. Further, we may again call attention to the list of Protestants in 1697 quoted above, where a Susanne Latteux, a common variation of Latteur, appeared as a 'servante opiniâtre' of Philippe de Haffrengue; this, added to the fact that relations were always, if possible, chosen as godparents, makes it highly probable that the de Haffrengues of La Converserie were related to the Latteurs, as the latter were, we know, connected by marriage with the Trésorerie branch.

Ambroise Minet of Cormont and Susanne de Haffrengue of La Trésorerie[3] are, then, so far as we can discover, the root from which our family sprang. Apart from any question of genealogical interest, one would wish to be able to penetrate yet further into the past, if only to learn how and when the two families came to be adherents of the New Faith. But we must be content to come upon them when we do. Of one thing we may be certain—that Ambroise and Susanne were each born of a

---

[1] See Appendix V., where I have given this deed at length.

[2] This Daniel lived at Ardres, where he died May 1, 1681 (Guînes Registers, p. 214). Among the abjurations at Ardres we find that of his son, '11 Decembre 1687. Daniel Haffringue, 22 ans, né et élevé dans la réligion Calviniste par défunts Daniel Haffringue et Jeanne Latteux, ses père et mère' (Ern. Ranson, *Histoire d'Ardres*, St. Omer, p. 694).

[3] See Table *II*, where I have given all the information respecting the Trésorerie branch of the de Haffrengues that the Guînes Registers and Isaac's notes supply. The only instance of the name I have been able to find in England is the admission, on December 18, 1687, as a member of the Church at Dover, of 'Jean Haffrengue agné de quinze ans ou environ fils de Pierre Haffrenghe et d'Elisabeth Desbionuille de l'eglise de Calais recueillis à Guisnes auant cette dure persecution.' Jean may have been a son of Pierre de Haffrengue, Susanne's brother; but born in 1673, this hardly seems probable.

race well-tempered for everyday duty, and yet able on occasion to rise above commonplace ideals and personal interest; and, further, we may surely say that the mingling of the two families in this marriage added such strength to the Huguenot fibre of the sons and daughters born of it that they were, one and all, content to venture the loss of goods and land, and to risk the perils of the unknown, rather than ensue peace and prosperity by a surrender of the faith in which they had been reared.

CHAPTER III

THE PERSECUTION AND THE ESCAPE

> Yet these and their successors are but one ;
> And if they gaine or lose their liberties,
> They harme or profit not themselves alone,
> But such as in succeeding time shall rise.
>
> And so the ancestor and all his heires,
> Though they in number passe the starres of heaven,
> Are still but one ; his forfeitures are theirs,
> And vnto them are his aduancements given.—SIR JOHN DAVIS.

THE events of 1685–6 must have burnt themselves deeply into Isaac's memory, but it was not until 1722 that, so far as we know, he attempted any record of them. In that year he writes the first of the two narratives which form the substance of this chapter. It occurs on folio 3 of the book whose history has been already given, and would seem to have been meant for little more than a memorandum ; it has no title, follows without a break on an entry of the cost of a corporation gown, and, together with some notes on his father and mother and brothers and sisters, occupies only five folios. In 1737, Isaac would seem to have re-read this sketch. Struck, perhaps, by the last sentence he had penned, fifteen years earlier, 'To write all ye particulars, and especially of our whole familly, would make a great volum,' he determined to attempt a much fuller and more formal account. This second narrative stands by itself in the book, being separated by blank leaves from other notes, and has the title, 'A Relation of our familly' ; it begins on folio 17, and is more than three times as long as the first, occupying seventeen folios. In plan and arrangement it follows the first so exactly that it is clear the writer must have had the previous record in his mind when writing it, though, curious to state, he nowhere refers to it. There is little or no contradiction of statement between the two, but a few incidents which occur in the first are left out in the second.

When we remember that over fifty years had elapsed since the events recorded took place, we may well be surprised at the accuracy of Isaac's memory whenever, by independent evidence, it is possible to test it. Wherever possible, this test has been applied, and the results are given in the notes appended to the narrative. Both accounts are written in English, though we know that the writer was equally at home in French; witness his account of the French Church at Dover, written in 1731, of which a transcript is given (Chap. V.) later on.

Of the policy which culminated in the Revocation of the Edict of Nantes, and of the means by which that policy was carried out, this is not the place to speak; the main facts must be sought in the history of France, of which they form so sad a chapter; but some slight account of the application of the decree in the 'Calaisis' will not, perhaps, be an unfitting introduction to Isaac's own narrative.

In 1681, Claude le Tonnelier de Breteuil was appointed Bishop of Boulogne, and to his zeal was due the severity of the persecution in this district. In 1683 he begins the crusade against the Huguenots by the publication (May 18) of a 'Mandement au sujet du conversion des hérétiques,' the tone of which will be best gathered from an extract:—

'Nous gémissons et considérons dans toute l'affliction de notre cœur que ces citernes dissipées (comme les appelle Isaïe) ont pris la place des eaux vives et salutaires de la grâce qui découlaient autrefois avec abondance dans nos villes de Guînes et de Calais, et parce que cette dernière, comme la plus grande, peut être appelée à bon droit la Babylone de notre diocèse, d'autant plus qu'étant très voisine de la Hollande et aux portes de l'Angleterre (pays où il semble que toutes les ténèbres de l'église se soient ramassées et conservées), elle a de funestes ressources pour se tenir ferme dans son erreur; c'est aussi principalement en cet endroit que notre zèle pastoral doit agir avec plus de force et de vigueur.

'Malheur à eux' [*i.e.* the Huguenots] 'si, continuant à marcher dans la route de Coré, et voulant toujours nommer la lumière les ténèbres, et les ténèbres la lumière, ils méprisaient d'entendre la voix du pasteur; s'ils nous obligeaient malgré nous d'avoir recours au bras terrible de cet invincible Josué qui fit tomber les murailles de Jéricho.'

This 'Mandement' was followed in the next year by the issue of an 'Avertissement Pastoral du clergé de France.' This was communicated to the Consistory of Guînes by the King's Intendant de Justice, François le Tonnelier de Breteuil.

'L'an mil six cents quatre vingt trois, le dimanche onzième jour de juillet, nous François le Tonnelier-Breteuil, conseiller du Roy en ses conseils, maistre des requestes ordinaire de son Hostel, Intendant de justice, police, finances, et des troupes de sa Majesté en Picardie, Artois, Boulonnois, Pays conquis et reconquis, en conséquence des ordres de Sa Majesté nous sommes transportez au bourg de Guisnes.'[1]

The object of the visit was to meet the ministers and elders of the congregation, and deliver to them the 'Avertissement pastoral' which his Majesty had issued to the Huguenots. The first part of this 'Avertissement,' which was addressed to 'Nos frères toujours égarez et comme perduz dans l'affreuse solitude de l'erreur,' was an exhortation to repent them and return to the true fold, but its conclusion was somewhat threatening:—

'Si vous refusez de reconnoistre votre erreur devant Dieu après de si pressantes exhortations de notre part, et si vous ne voulez ni vous laisser vaincre par nos prières, ni gagner par nos tendresses, ni vous rendre à nos avertissements, sachez que les Anges de paix en pleureront amèrement. Et parceque cette dernière erreur sera plus criminelle en vous que toutes les autres, vous devez vous attendre à des malheurs incomparablement plus épouvantables et plus funestes que tous ceux que vous ont attirez jusqu'à présent votre révolte et votre schisme.'

Early in 1685 the Temple at Guines was closed, as we learn from a report of the Bishop of Boulogne made to the general meeting of the clergy on June 30, when he adds a request to the assembly to assist him in obtaining its destruction. He had not long to wait: on October 17 was signed the Revocation, the first article of which runs:—

'Voulons et nous plâit que tous les Temples situez dans notre royaume pais terres et seigneuries de notre obeissance soient incessamment demolies.'

The issue of this edict armed the Bishop with fresh powers and renewed his energies. Signed in Paris on October 17, it was published on October 25 in Calais;[2] but already, on the 23rd, he was

---

[1] Vaillant, *Notes Boulonnaises: La Révocation de l'Edit de Nantes dans le Boulonnais*, p. 19.

[2] Pigault de l'Epinoy (b. 1726), author of a manuscript history of Calais in six vols., now in the library of that town, writes: 'Révocation de l'édit de Nantes du 22 Octobre publiée à Calais le 3 Novembre, et suivie de la démolition du temple de Guines fermé par ordre du Roi dès l'année précédente. Par le traité de Nérac [1579] les Calvinistes qui avoient un temple à Marcq, le transfèrent, comme je l'ay avancé, à Guines à cause de la situation du lieu plus commode et plus étendue que Marcq. Guines était alors le Genève non seulement du pays, mais encore du Boulonnais, de l'Artois, de la Flandre et d'une partie de la Picardie; ce temple n'était pas d'une construction magnifique ny apparente, mais il était spacieux et au moyen de

at Guines, consulting with the curé Raoult as to its enforcement, and practically enforcing it himself by standing as godfather to a Huguenot child baptised in the Catholic church. On October 27 we find him at Calais, and on the next day he himself baptizes the child of Jonas Duriez and Marie Cassel, 'faisans profession de la R.P.R.'

Thus to gather the children into the true fold was an easy task; but to persuade their parents to abjure was more difficult, and the preaching of the Bishop's chaplains proving ineffectual, means which had been used too largely over the rest of France were adopted, and soldiers were quartered on the recalcitrants. At this point Isaac may fitly take up the tale :—

NARRATIVE OF 1722.

I Isaac Minet was borne at Calais the 15th September 1660, and was brought up at my fathers house till I was 14 years of age, and then I was sent over to Dover to learn the English language, and there lived 21 months at ye house of Mr William Richards at ye greenhouse in ye room of Elizabeth his daughter who was at my fathers house, and afterwards Patience her sister. After I had beene at Dover 21 m^o I went back to Calais and stayed there, managing ye buisseness of my mother, my father being dead in ye year 1675.[1]

I manag^d my mothers buisseness at Calais untill ye year 85 w^n by order of the french king, ye protestant church wch was at a place called gaines 6 miles from Calais, was demolish'd; and the percecution increasing great number of protestant famillyes from townes and vilages fled and made theire escapes into protestant countreys as england, holland, brandenburg, or prussia, to geneva, Switzerland, etc.

Most of my Brothers and sisters got out of france, I was left alone at Calais wth my mother; in June 1685 my mother went to

---

galeries où se mettoient le sexe, il pouvait contenir plus de trois mille personnes ; la maison du ministre qui existe encore était contre ce temple, convertie actuellement en grange et cour de ferme, et dont les matériaux ont servis à la réparation et à l'augmentation de l'église paroissiale de ce bourg.' After speaking of the former glory of Guines, he concludes ; ' La Révocation de l'Edit de Nantes, l'émigration qu'elle a causée d'un grand nombre de riches familles protestantes, qui se sont retirées en Hollande a occasionné le dépérissment et l'annéantissment de cette ville réduite en bourgade.' The date he gives for the publication is wrong ; it took place on October 25. He is also mistaken in stating that the church at Guines had been closed in 1684 ; it was, as we have seen, not closed till 1685. For a fuller account of the 'Temple' at Guines, see the Preface to the *Transcript of the Registers of Guines* (vol. iii. of the Publications of the Huguenot Society of London).

[1] 1679 ; *cf.* p. 8.

arders where she had a sister in law who was sick and dyed, and because she did not receive ye Sacrament of ye Romish Church her dead body was caryed to prison and her estate confiscated,[1] and three days after she was dragged by ye feett by horses about the streett, ye mobb stoning ye body in such a maner y^t her head was broke in pieces of from her body, and was so drag^d out of ye town and stakt on a crossway.

Abt. ye begining of octob. ye same year every protestant house had one or 2 gards wth armes to take care none of ye familly should goe away, and a strict gard was keept at ye gatts of the towne to prevent any protestants going out of ye town. Abt. ye 15 of November, being advised dragoons were coming to persecute us, we gave our gard plenty of wine, and he fell a sleep by the fire, my mother and I took y^t oportunity at 10 of ye clock at night to gitt out of our house, and we went to ye house of one fournier, a dutch man who keept a chandlers shopp near ye prison; w^n our gard wackt and mist us he was very much concerned and immediately cald ye main gard who did make a strick serch and enquiry for us in ye neighbouring houses, and 3 or 4 of our friends being protestants who happened at y^t time to come to our house were taken and caryed to prison on pretence y^t they knew where we was; we herd and saw them goe to prison from a little garett where we was and we were very much concerned at it. The next day we heard by beat of drum a publication made about ye towne of a reward of 100 Livers to such as would inform where we were and of 1000 Livrers fine for whoever should conceal us. We did continue in s^d house from Wednesday till ye Satterday following and finding y^t my mother nor I could neither eate drink nor sleep because of ye great uneasyness and fear we were in, we fearing to fall sick, resolved to venture in trying to gett out of towne. Y^e Satterday many country peeple coming and going out of towne I thought was a fitt day, I sent for a man y^t keept a sluce out of town towards ye seaside, and agreed with him to harbor us at his house, for wch he

---

[1] Susanne Minet had a brother Daniel living at Ardres, and his wife was Jeanne Latteur. M. Vaillant, at page 63 of the work cited above, mentions as having been treated in this cruel fashion a Madame Valla, who must be the person referred to in Isaac's narrative, and for this reason:—there is in the Guines Registers (p. 80) the marriage of a Marie Vatta, 'assistée de Daniel Haffreingue, beau-frère.' Marie Vatta was therefore sister-in-law to Daniel Haffrengue; and Isaac is only slightly stretching the relationship when he speaks of Madame Vatta as sister-in-law to his mother. M. Vaillant informs me that the name he reads 'Valla' may well be 'Vatta.'

was to have 30 french crowns; I sent for a porter whom I could trust, he brought his wifes clothes and my mother putt them on, and wth an earthen pitcher in her hand, towards evening she went out and followed our future landlord who was to cary her to his house. Soon after I putt on an old fur capp, a leathern apron, a rule under my arm, my face blakend and my shoes in slipers.¹ I went also out and gott out of the gates, having rusht by the gard who knew me very well, but not in y^t dress; it was very dusty, just out of ye town one of my slipt shoe stuck fast in ye dust. I did not think fit to stay to take it out, w^n I was a little further in ye fields I took ye other shoe in my hand and walk without shoes about ½ mile to ye house, very joyfull till I came there, expecting my mother was there before me, but when I found she was not I was under great concern, and more a quarter of an hour after, w^n ye landlord came and told me my mother was taken coming out of ye gates having lost time wth a popish woman who had known her in the street and to whom, after pleading, she gave 4 crowns to lett her goe free wch occationed her coming to late, ye furthest gate of ye town being shutt before she came there, and some of ye gards having known her, she was sent to prison, our landlord who conducted her having got through ye gate before, heard ye noise and told me ye misfortune, wch made my lodging in a little hay garrett as little pleasant as the other, but ye nexte day I took a little courage and did eat and drink, and I writt a letter to my brothers² at dover to send a boat over to fetch me and was in great hope to escape, but ye day before I expectd s^d boat after having bene there 4 nights my landlord went to town, gott drunk and betrayd me. Ab^t 4 afternoone I was much surprizd to see a sergant, 6 soldiers and 2 of ye govern^t gards coming to ye house wch was out of any road and remote from any other houses; I soon concluded I was betrayd, I buryd myself in hay and heard a great noise below, and at last they came up and said 'trust y^r swords in ye hay its noe matter if ye kill y^t heretick' I layd wist till they moved some hay and found me. They caryed me to Calais where I was sent to prison. Y^e nexte day the president came and examined me and said if I did not sign to be a Roman Catho^k I should be burnt. We were 140 Protestant prisonrs, men women and children, I was putt

---

¹ Perhaps sabots.
² Stephen was then in Dover, and probably Ambroise.

in a dungeon with my mother, we laid on dung a very stinking hole, and could have noe victuals for mony, we were there 6 weeks,[1] my mother sick; we were very often solicited by ye prists and threatend by ye intendent, very rudely as if we had bene doggs, at last we were one night ye 31 xber caryed by dragoons to Church and there prevaild on to signe and swear abjuration tho we protested with tears in our eyes y^t it was aganst our consciences; at 11 at night we went home and found 4 officers who had made away wth w^t we left. After having tryed severall times before our imprisonm^t and since to gitt away we did at last embarque at night ye 1 Agust 1686 and gott to Dover at 8 in ye morning, for wch I shall ever praise the goodness of God whom I begg to forgive me my faults for ye sake of Jesus Christ.

To write all ye particulars, and especially of our whole familly would make a great volum—1722 I write this.

SECOND NARRATIVE, OF 1737.

I, Isaac Minet, was born at Calais ye 15 Septemb: 1660. In 1674 I was sent to dover to learn English to the house of m^r Willm Richards, in ye room of his daughter patience; and sometime after I went to m^r Willm Eaton then merch^t at dover to copy his letters and did sometime goe to doe buissness for him at ye Custom house. After having bene at dover about 21 months I went back to my father's house, & after my brother daniel was maryed,[2] & ye death of our father[3] I did take care of all ye buiseness under my mother till ye time of perceeution wch was at Calais in ye yeare 1685, our church wch was at gaine 6 miles from Calais being the last protestant church wch was condemd & demolished in france; & soon after the Edict of nantes by wch the protestant of france enjoyed theire liberty was anuled & broken wch was done by ye president & the others officers of justice by sound of trumpet[4] in ye market place at Calais & ye Edict of Cassation Read, by wch it was said y^t althought our grandfather and our father did grant & promis to maintaine s^d Edict of nants, as well as ourself, yet it being done in time of troble when it could not be preventd, wee being now in peace, wee have thought fit to breake & annul ye same (and saith

---

[1] From November 22 to December 31 (thirty-nine days).   [2] October 25, 1682.
[3] July 16, 1679.   [4] October 25, 1685.

alsoe) and whereas before yᵉ making of the sᵈ Edict of nants, our subjects of yᵉ pretended Reformed Religion were exposed to mercy of our Roman Catholik Subjects, wee have of our gracious favour taken them under our protection untill such time as it shall have pleased god enlightened them. Some time after our church at gaine was demolisht & puld down to about seven foot of yᵉ wall left & I am told it is now a garden.

Sometime after I with 4 protestant friends went to gaine & seeing the remainder of our Church it was soe sorowfull a spectacle to us yᵗ wee all shodd teares. Such is the zeal of persons in time of percecution more fervent.

Abᵗ Septemb 1685 yᵉ Bishop of boulogne[1] came to Calais & with him 3 or 4 of theire best prechers in order to instruct & convert yᵉ protestants, & on a Satterday afternoon the head of every protestant houses were somond to be at yᵉ presidents house, my mother sent me being left alone with her all the Rest of our family being gone out of yᵉ Country. There did apeare about 25 of us & having found all the govenors gard in armes at yᵉ entrey & in yᵉ yard wee were surprised not knowing wᵗ was to bee done, wee were caryed in a large roome were yᵉ govenor,[2] Lieuftenᵗ,[3] major[4] & others came in & told us yᵗ hee had orders to order us in yᵉ Kings nam to goe yᵉ nexte day being Sunday to heare the Sarmon yᵗ one of the Bishops doctʳˢ was to preach, & noe body making answer hee asked every one in particular if they would goe, none did promiss, then hee said if wee did not goe wee should repent for he should be obliged to put yᵉ Kings ordʳˢ in execution wᶜʰ wee should find to bee sever, & after hee had made a discourse representing yᵉ Kings goodness in his using such myld meanes to save yᵉ souls of his subjects etcʳᵃ hee went out & his company, then came in yᵉ president[5] and lieuftenant of justice yᵉ Kings proctor etcʳˢ and made yᵉ same sommation in yᵉ Kings name & having obtained no promiss hee & compy went out after wᶜʰ came yᵉ mayor[6] of yᵉ towne wᵗʰ yᵉ vicemayor & echevins etcʳᵃ & made the same sommation, to wᶜʰ noe promiss being

---

[1] Claude le Tonnelier de Breteuil. Upon the Revocation of the Edict this active prelate took instant steps to enforce its provisions. He went at once to Guînes, where he baptised a Huguenot child on October 23; and on October 28 he performed the same office at Calais for a son of Jacques Cassel and Sara Pilart, 'de la religion prétendue reformée.'

[2] Armand, duc de Charost.   [3] Marquis de Courtebourne.

[4] Claude de Bussavent.   [5] F. de Thosse.   [6] Etienne Carrel.

made they went out after wch ye govenor came in againe & said yt if wee did not goe the day following to hear ye sermon hee would putt ye Kings orders in execution & that wee should have cause too repent and soe wee were suffered to goe each one to his house. The nex day being Sunday wee had resolved not to goe to church & about 10 in ye morning wee were informed yt ye gates of ye town were shutt, wch did make us feare yt wee should be molested, but at noon ye gates were opend & nothing did hapen. In our company at ye presidents house there was Mr John Hays who behaved like a protestant hero, and spoke with a great deale of prudence and courage Mr James Hays,[1] Mr Adrien Lernoult the father, Mr Abram le Maire, Mr Isaac Sigart, Louis Delebecque, Jonas Duriz, James Sauchel etca.

About ye begining of October[2] one of ye govenors gards whose nam was Le Duc orderd in our house wth orders to take care yt my mother nor I should not make our escapes; hee was six weekes in ye house did eat & drink with us & laid on a matras in my mothers room wth his armes & baricaded our back door & winders; and being informd that dragoons were coming in order to bee quartered at all ye protestant houses at discretion in order to oblige them to change theire Religion wee, I say my mother & I resolvd to leave ye house & endeavour our escape[3] & having prevaild wth on fournier a dutch shop keeper to receive & conceale us in his house wee made our gard at super drink plentifully, hee fell a sleep by ye fire side as did alsoe Jonas Duriz's Wife our relation[4] who wth her husband supt wth us, on wch I told sd Duriz our design & advised him to take his wife home wth him, but hee said it was noe mater & yt hee desird to bee sent to prison to shun ye dragoons, hee went to his house & my mother & I gott out of ye house & gott to our Rendesvous & gott up in

---

[1] James Hays had married in 1677 Marie Sigart, sister to Sara, wife of Jean Sauchelle, who was later to become Isaac Minet's mother-in-law. Jean Hays, son of Claude Hays, who married Marie de la Croix in 1680, was probably his brother (see p. 89, note). Adrien Lernoult was a 'diacre receveur' of the church at Guines, and had married Madelaine Pilart. Isaac Sigart was brother to Marie Sigart, wife of James Hays. Louis de le Becque, a Calais merchant married: first, Jacqueline Beurre, in 1669; second, Marie Aimery; he was an 'ancien' of the church at Guines. Jonas du Riez married, in 1672, Marie le Turcq, a daughter of Martha Minet of Frencq, Isaac Minet's aunt. James Sauchelle may have been connected with the Sauchelles of Flushing (Chap. VI.), but I am unable to trace the relationship.

[2] From this it is clear that the persecutions began at Calais before the actual Revocation as we know they did at Ardres.

[3] About November 15. See First Narrative.

[4] Isaac's first-cousin. See note 1, above, and page 9.

a garett, soon after our gard awackt & not seeing us he went in all ye rooms & having waked m^is Duriz & asked her where wee was, who said shee did not know & indeed she knew nothing of ye matter, hee went to enquire at ye nighbouring houses & not finding us he cald for ye main guard wch came & sercht ye nighbouring houses & stopt m^is Duriz pretending shee knew where wee was & her husband being come to fetch her home hee was stopt alsoe as was m^r Isaac Emmery[1] a friend of ours who cald to bid us good night as hee was going home, m^r Duriz's maid servant came to see for her master & m^is, shee alsoe was stopt & they were all caryed to prison wch was just over against ye garet where wee were, soe y^t wee could heare ye women cry & ye men excusing themselfs, my mother then proposed our going back to our house but I made her sensible y^t if wee did wee should alsoe be sent to ye prison. The nex day wee did heare it publisht by beate of drum that whosoever shoud declare where wee was should have a hundred Livers reward & a thousand Livers fine to whoever harbourd us at wch our Landlord was a little startled but I assurd him hee should never suffer for us & there being only him & his wife in ye house hee had nothing to feare. Wee were there thursday, fryday & satterday during wch time wee could neither eat drink nor sleep I then considerd y^t if wee should bee sick it would be very badd, & soe I sent for one Banse[2] who keept a sluce ab^t ½ mile out of towne neare ye sea with whom I agreed to bee at his house from where wee could enbark & I sent for a porter who brought his wifes clothes wch my mother putt on & took a pitcher in her hands & I putt on an old coate of our landlord fournier & an old capp without wigg a leathern apron & a carpenters rule under my arm. My mother went out first ab^t 5 afternoon & banse ye sluce man walkt before who was her guide, I went out soon after & when I came to ye gates where two men were posted to hinder the protestants from going out of ye towne I rusht close by one of them & got by & gott to ye sluce house very joyfull expecting my mother was there but to my great sorow shee was not. Banse came soon after & told me that my mother not having followed him fast enough the gate being just shutting hee had time to go through, but she was stopt and known so shee was

---

[1] Aimery, or Aymery, is the form in which the name appears in the Guines Registers.
[2] A name still to be found in Calais.

caryed to the prison & putt in a dungeon. The reason of my mothers coming to late to y⁰ gates of y⁰ town was that going along Banse her guide having percevd y' a woman followed her did lead my mother into another street thinking to shun s^d woman but s^d woman perceiving it came up & told my mother y' shee knew her design & y' if shee gave her something she would not betray her. Shee gave her foure crownes & shee parted but y⁰ loss of time caused y⁰ misfortune.

I sent y⁰ next day for James Lingo one of y⁰ paket boat men & gave him a letter for my brother Stephen at dover desiring him to send over a boat to cary me over wch I expected but y⁰ day before s^d boat was to come Bance went to Callais got drunk & betrayd me; that same day the dragoons were coming to Calais & I could see them from a garet where I was & looking y' way I spyed a Sergant six soldiers & two of y⁰ govern^s gard coming to y⁰ sluce house wch made me conclud y' I was betrayd, however I buryed myself in hay y' was there, I heard the s^d soldiers making a great noyse & swearing at y⁰ woman of y⁰ house and shee crying. At last they came up in y⁰ garet & I heard them say—the heretick dog must be here trust y^r sword in y⁰ hay its noe mater if hee bee kild—and they pulling the hay away, found me took me & handed me down & being put between y⁰ soldiers was caryed to the comandant on y⁰ market place[1] who sent me to prison, having been followd from y⁰ towne gate to y⁰ prison by all y⁰ mobb. I was putt in a room under that where my mother was & y⁰ bords being broken wee could speake to one another; shee told me what shee had declard on her examination & I declard accordingly when I was examined by y⁰ president etc^ra, after wch y⁰ president told me I was a heritick & smelt stong of fagots & y' I should be burnt etc^m and m^r James de Cashel & his wife having that day bene betrayed & taken going out of towne in a cart under straw were brought to y⁰ prison & putt in y⁰ room where I was and I was putt in y⁰ dungeon wth my mother where we remaind till y⁰ 28 of Xber soe much neglected by the geoller y' y⁰ door of our dungeon was not opened for severall days together but there being a hole in a wall y' parted y⁰ dungeon from a publick room where were severall prisoners & amongst them one J^n Buck of Dover who was prisoner for having

---

[1] The guard-house was under the old lighthouse which still stands on the Place d'Armes. It is said by Lefebvre (*Hist. de Calais*, vol. ii. p. 466) to have been built by the English.

sold tobaco, hee was of good service to us by procuring us some provission as bread, butter, wine, water, linnen, etc^{rn}, his making a formal abjuration of the protest^{t} religion hee was released & came to dover where hee was a protestant as before.

The 28th of Xber 1685 the Intendant Chauvelin came in ye prison with ye govern^{r} ye major & ayde major[1] etcra, and demanded of ye prisoners in particul^{r} if they would abjur theire religion & become Roman Catholighs & on refusall threatned them very severely & cruelly, among others m^{r} Samuel D'hoy of Chaussée[2] neare Calais who was Lieuten^{t} of a comp^{y} of ye horse mellitia aged ab^{t} 70 years who having bene about 6 weekes in a dungeon under ground from where hee was taken & apearing before ye Intendant who on first sight said in my hearing 'This is D'hoy for hee lookes like an obstinate Heretick' and having asked him if hee would abjure & m^{r} D'hoy answering y^{t} his concience could not permit him to doe it, on wch ye intendant told him y^{t} ye King was to good & y^{t} wee all deservd to bee destroyed & told s^{d} d'hoy y^{t} hee should bee sent to his own house next day wth 12 dragoons & y^{t} when hee would desire ye favour of receiving him to abjure hee would leave ye dragoons a month longer with him for the punishment of his obstinacy wch made D'hoy silent wch was taken for consent,[3] after wch ye Intend^{t} told mee that hee was Informd I was a you[ng] Heretick who perswaded my mother not to abjure but y^{t} I should pay for it for my mother & I should bee sent home ye next day wth dragoons & hee would give ord y^{t} I should not want for blowes etc^{ra}, & I had on ye other hand one M^{r} desofre[4] who was ye Major of ye towne & who pretended to bee my friend having severall times

---

[1] L'hermite de Lenty.

[2] La Chaussée, a small village near Calais, on the road to Coquelles.

[3] M. Vaillant (*Notes Boulonnaises: La Révocation de l'Édit de Nantes dans le Boulonnais*, p. 63) gives the following entry of the death of Samuel Doye, taken from the registers of Neufchâtel:—

'L'an 1686 et le vingt cinquiesme jour de Septembre est décédé en la maison de Pierre Senlecque, un nommé Samuel Douye nouveau converty de la paroisse de la Chaussée-lez-Calais estant arrivé chez ledit Senlecque le vendredy vingtiesme du présent mois revenant de Paris lequel Douye n'a receu aucun sacremens pour n'avoir ledit Senlecque ny autre de sa maison donné aucun avertissement de ladite maladie ; nous avons pourtant mis le corps en terre dans le cimetière de Neufchastel, veu le certificat comme [quoi] il avait esté confessé et communié ès prisons de Calais. En foi de quoy j'ay signé.   N. LE ROY Pre.'

M. Vaillant adds : 'Son cadavre, exhumé de sa fosse, jeté sur une charrette, fut transporté à Calais et là s'exécuta la sentence d'une incroyable horreur.'

[4] René de Joffré had been Mayor from 1679 to 1682, when he was succeeded by Claude de Bussavent. See above, p. 25, note 4. The Major and the Mayor were two distinct officials.

before bene at our house & conversed with me, who represented to me yt my mother was sickley & if wee went home and shee saw mee beaten it would cause her Death & yt it was but trying & if I did not like to bee a Roman Catholick I could at any time git away, so yt being threatned by ye Intend{t} on one side & flatered or tempted on ye other I stood mute & said nothing on wch ye major told ye Intendant yt I would signe ye abjuration, I was then fully convinced of ye greate weakness of man by my own and other person's woefull experience, & I say lett no man boast of his strenght or constancy for without a particular assistance from god man is altogether vanity.

On ye 30 of xber ab{t} 9 at night came an officer wth a comp{y} of solders & took out of ye prison such as had consented to signe wch was about 34 persons & conducted them to ye great church[1] of wch number my mother & I were—in sd church wee mett severall of our protestant friends whose patience being wore out by the hard usage of ye dragoons came to make also abjurat{n}. There wee all shedd teares lamenting our sad conditions. Wee were ledd to a Chapell where the form of abjuration was read to uss (as falloweth or to yt porpos)—Wee whose names are underwritten do acknowledge before God the father etc{ra}, the holy virgin mary St petter St Paul etc{ra} the church & the holy father the pope yt wee were born & have heitherto lived in an Heretickall & Damnable Religion and that by ye inspiration of ye holly ghost, without any force or constraint wee do believe the Catholick apostolick & Romish Religion to be the only Religion in wch is Salvation & I do hartyly embrase the same & promise to live & dye in the same & do abjure & detest the Religon in wch I was born etc{ra}—and although wee protested yt wee could not in our conciences signe nor aprove ye same & in shedding teare declared it was contrary to our will & inclination, to wch some there present said—'Its noe matter, come sign your name'—so yt wee did all sign yt were there and after that all our hands were layd on a booke & an oath was reade by wch we promised to perform wt had bene signd,[2] after wch wee were conducted to ye great Altar where the

[1] Nôtre Dame.
[2] In confirmation of this I may quote from *Les Protestants du Calaisis*, by M. Landrin, of Guines, the following passage he has extracted from the Registres de l'état civil de St Pierre-lès-Calais :—' Le 30 Dec. 1685 cinquante cinq personnes, hommes, femmes, enfants, confessent avoir fait abjuration de la Religion Prétendue Réformée entre les mains de Maitre André Mareschal, curé, pour embrasser la Religion Catholique, Apostolique, et Romaine.' I have

chief prest[1] was in a suplice who made a discourse giving thankes for our conversion, & y^t as hee was perswaded y^t wee were cincer & harty in w^t wee did hee receivd us into ye bosom of ye church & y^t as wee were new born babbes hee would inflict us an easey penance wch was that every one of us should before wee went to bed say three paternosters & y^t such as could not say it in Latin may say it in french & about ½ past ten wee were dismist & came out of church.

When wee came to our house wee found 3 persons who had bene ordd^d there to look after w^t was there who had burnt eaten & drinkt all y^t was found there & wee could not come in possestion without an order from ye president wch I went for, but ye presd^t told mee I must have a certificat from ye prest of my abjurat^n. I went to ye church again & got a certificat & then an ord. from ye president & between 12 & one at night ye 3 men left our house & wee were in possession of w^t little was left, wee did gitt some linen from a neigbour where wee had caryed it before wee left ye house. Wee were obligd to pay s^d 3 men 30 Sous a day each for ye time they were in our house, from y^t time wee were free at home but on Sundays wee went to Church to ye sermon but did not stay to heare the latter part of ye mass but came out so soon as ye sermon was done as did alsoe all the old Roman Catholick who had bene at mas y^t morning it not being requird of them to assist at 2 mases in one day. Sunday morning messrs. Isaac Sigart, James Hays, Jn. Hays, Adrien Lernoult, Abraham le Maire, Jonas Duriz etc^{ra} those persons came to my Mothers house and I went with them to heare ye sermon wch sometimes were very good.

I was left alone of ye familly wth my mother and wee continued there till ye month of Augt 1686 when I did order my brother Stephen who was at dover to send a boat to fetch my mother & I and Brother & Sister Destrier & familly s^d boat to bee ab^t 2 miles eastward of Calais at midnight Sunday ye 31 July old stile & to make more sure I agreed to give ye ryding officers 30 Louis d'or for attending ye coming of ye boate, giving us notice of it & seeing us on bord. I had agreed with a man to bee ready to bring from

---

found the following form of abjuration in the same registers, which is very similar to the one given above :—'Nous confessons avoir fait abjuration de la religion prétendue réformée pardevant André Mareschal curé de la paroisse, pour embrasser l'apostolique, catholique, et romaine dans laquelle nous voulons continuer ; en foi de quoi nous avons signé.'

[1] André Ponthon was curé in this year.

mark about 2 miles distance from yᵉ seaside my sister Elizabeth & her husband Jⁿ Detrier & his mother & 2 children to whom I sent advice to bee ready, all yᵉ night I did dream yᵗ I was betrayed & yᵗ my design was known wᶜʰ affected me soe much yᵗ I rose early & about 7 in yᵉ morning I went to yᵉ harbour & talked with one of yᵉ custom officers asking him wᵗ newes & found he knew nothing of my designe and soon after I mett mʳ Sollomon Lafarce a protestant wᵗʰ whom I went to a publick house where wee brakfasted so hearing nothing I was better satisfyed & went home & some time after my mother and I went to church & after sermon wee came home & took our diner, and soon after I desired my mother to go in yᵉ church by one door & out of it by yᵉ other & to goe out of yˢ town & yᵗ at yᵉ Crucifix[1] there would bee a man who shee knew yᵗ would conduct her to yᵉ Rendezvous which was done, soon after I went to yᵉ harbour & there saw a vessell wᶜʰ was come from dunkirk & was to goe to sea the next tide to cruise for yᵉ boats yᵗ caryed over protestant which made me uneasey, and I was more soe when I came back to yᵉ market place where I saw a detachment made of 25 soldiers & an officer to goe along the sea side to guard yᵉ coast & prevent protestants from going away, yett by gods grace I had courage and considering yᵗ all things were disposed & my mother gone I took a Resolution to go through, & sent for 4 paket men to whom I gave wᵗ money I had in yᵉ house, Bookes & wᵗ I found more valuable of small volum yᵗ could go in their great pokets wᶜʰ they caryed on bord their vessel two severall times & after that I went to a tavern & gave them 2 quarts of wine & took 2 or 3 glaces of it myself & I took wᵗʰ me James Lingo one of sᵈ paket men and desired him to walk wᵗʰ me out of town, it was then abᵗ 8 oclock when many people yᵗ had been walking out of town were coming back. I went along carelessly talking with Lingo,[2] taking up smal stones and tosting them in yᵉ aire, an aquaintance asked me where I was going soe late I told him not far & yᵗ we should be soon back—being got out of yᵉ gates we walked softly till we mett but few people & taking towards grauelin[3] rood Lingo asked whether I designed to go further, I then told him my designe & asked if hee thought a boat could come from

[1] Near the sluice-gate to which it gave its name, and close to the Hospice St. Pierre.
[2] James Lingo, who has been mentioned before. He and his wife Bridget appear several times in the Registers of St. Mary, Dover.
[3] Gravelines.

dover as ye wind was, he said they must row for there was but little wind, I desired him to go back & if anybody enquird for me he may say he left me going for marke to see my sister.

Soon after I left him I got to our Rendezvous, a house about a mile further where I found my mother, & ab^t 11 oclock at night 4 Riding officers came to y^t house, at wch I was some thing started having expected but 2 of them but ye chief of m̅ tould me it was ye same & y^t I had nothing to fear from m̅. I borrowed a horse of ye man of ye house & went with s^d officers by ye sea side, to look out for ye boat, till abt 12 & seeing nothing coming, the s^d officers advised me to Ride from them & keep behind sand hills about ½ mile from ye sea & y^t so soon as ye boat apeard they would come & give me a signall with a wissell, wch signall I hurd soon after & being mounted againe (for I had lighted) I gallopt to ye sea side & saw ye boat, & spoake to J^{os} Dunstan on of ye seamen; now my sister & brother Detrier not coming I went to mett them, to hasten them & after ridding above a mile I found them & ye wagoner mending a wheele of ye wagon with Roaps I desired him to make w^t hast he could & came back to ye boatmen & told m̅ the wagon was just coming, for they were in hast to bee gone it being then past one & they would not stay for fear of daylight, I ridd again to hasten the wagon wch was then at hand & coming back to ye boate I did see two farmers their wifes & six children in ye boate, I asked ye boatmen who they were & who ordd^d them there, they answerd they did not know & did think them to be of our company & said the boat could not cary us all, I asked s^d farmers w^t made them be there with their wifes & children & severall bundles of clothes wch they had brought on horses backs, they said y^t they were told y^t a boat was to be there y^t night & they came there in hopes to find room to gitt over to England. I told them I should bee glad if there was room for them but as the s^d boat was come for my mother etc^{ra} wee must have room first & ord^d them to gitt out wch the 2 men did tho much ag^t stomack. My mother gott in ye boat & also my Sister, her husband, his mother[1] & their 2 children & I.[2] It being faling water ye boat was aground, the six seam̅ & ye 2 farmers who

---

[1] Catherine Vanthune.

[2] There were thus twenty-three people in all in the boat. Isaac has told us the exact spot where the embarkation took place: 'off of petite wall' (see p. 46). This was La Petite Walde, *i.e.* the small wood, and was in the Commune of Marcq; near it is La Grande Walde, and in the English plans of 1556 it appears as Wayle Mill. Its exact position can be well seen in

were still on shore got in yͤ water to yͤ middle & gott yͤ boat over 3 sand banks & at last to sea when the 2 farmers begged for god sake to be suffred to git on bord, yͤ men told them yͭ if any wind did rise they would be obliged to throw them over bord & their wifes & all their baggage, to wᶜʰ they answered that if it was god's will they wold submit to it, but hoped that god in his mercy would preserve us all. The riding officers had of m̄ 40 crownes that is 20 crownes of each familly & soe by yͤ grace of god we set saile & yͤ seamen rowed sometimes; about 2 houers after we Left yͤ shore we spyed a Sloop & fearing yͤ dunkirk cruser, they spread a saile over all yͤ passengers heads who layd down in yͤ boat, & yͤ fine wind & wather being favorable we landed at dover on yͤ shore about 8 of the clock yͤ same morning[1] for wᶜʰ mercy I shall ever give thanks to God, it being a very great deliveranc. we were mett on yͤ shore by brother Ambroise Jacob & Stephen & sisters Suson & Mary full of tears of joy in our eyes & many more of our friend who recᵈ us as bretheren saved from yͤ great percecution.

It is now fifty years since we landed at dover & I doe find that time doth wear out matters after such a manner yͭ all yͭ is past is now as a dreame, whereas at yͤ time of our being in prison & percecuted by dragoons or otherwise it is a very terible thing wᶜʰ makes people promiss yͭ if god delivers them they will mend their wayes, & live more like true Christians than ever they did before, but yͤ generallity of Christians even yͤ reformed ones are like yͤ Israelites, noe sooner past yͤ sea but they forgett their deliverance and goe a Stray.

It did happen yͭ about 15 days before, a gard of yͤ governͭ came to be at our house, a rumour being spread that we did designe to make our escape, all our creditors came & demand payment & such as wee had bought goods to pay in two monthes, or given bills payable in a monthe or six weeks came & demanded paymͭ or to give them good security of Roman Catholick persons, or else they would obtain sentences to compell us to do it, & my mother not being willing to part wᵗʰ wᵗ money we had I was

---

a map preserved in the Cottonian Collection in the British Museum, and of which a reduced facsimile is given in the *Chronicle of Calais*, published by the Camden Society in 1846. In this map it appears as 'Wael,' and is on the sea-coast, close to Marck.

[1] The landing was effected on the Bulwark Rock, removed in 1844, when the South Eastern Railway Company's station was made.

obligd to give them goods for security, such as brandys, hard & soft soap, Lead, oyle, tallow, sugars etc^m wch they caryed away & I was buysy two days about delivering goods & paying of small debts & I never was more tyered & vexed than during s^d two days.

During the time we were in ye prison severall prists capuchins & minismes came severall times to ye prison & did endeavour to perswade ye protestant prison^{rs} to abjure and turn Roman Catholick but to no porpos for even ye Country people were better instructed in theire religion than most of s^d pristes were in theirs.

The manner of being dragoond was thus m^r Pillart [1] a merchant had 8 men & horses at discretion in garison at his house for about a monthe who were soe kind as to suffer him & wife to take rest, but by reason of their being to casey they were discharged 20 foot soldiers putt in their place who being told y^t they should be relived in 24 houres soon gott drunk & abused their Land Lord & Lady who were old persons, did not suffer them to sleep, sent for ye fidlers, forced them to dance, sold all y^t they found in ye house, & spoiled all ye goods, ye lady made her escape out of ye garet window & gott to a nighbours house who out of compation conceald her, ye man was struk on his side by one of ye souldiers & layd as dead & a surgeon being sent for he was lett blod & recoverd, one need noe more than consider w^t a sober person is exposed to when he is left at ye discretion of 20 drunken souldiers, s^d m^r Pillart being tyred & not being able to suport any longer the cruell usage of the souldiers he submited to make his abjuration which was in feby 1686 ab^t 8 at night, I was desired by m^r Adrien Lernoult merch^t at Calais (neveu to s^d m^r pilart) to go with him to s^d m^r pilart's house & I did go in order to prevent ye souldiers caring goods away, but being there we found nothing worth carying away for every thing was soe broken & cutt & destroyed y^t it was a lamentable sight, in a room up stairs was spread 5 or 6 bedds & blankett in such a dirty condition as if beastes had layen there.

That is ye methode y^t was made use of by ye popish church to make converts to theire religion by wch meanes they could show the abjuration of many hundred thousand persons under their hands, I pray god to preserve all people who call themselves

---

[1] Daniel Pilart, 'ancien' of the church at Guines ; his wife was Catherine Lamens.

Christians from the spirit of persecution wch hath bene so long prevalent among them.

Severall other famillyes in Calais were used after ye same maner (viz) m^r Louis Delebecque a worthy gentleman who had a numerous familly who had a daughter maryed to a Captn of a Company of Suisses of 200 men etc.[1]

m^r Isaac Sigart, Abrah^m Le Maire, Adrien Lernoult, James Hays, Jacob Dehane,[2] Jonas durier, all merchant and severall other famillys by wch on may judge w^t a terible desolation it caused in all parts of france.

---

[1] ' Le 24eme fevrier 1683 a esté beni le marriage d'Isaac Russillon, agé de 33 ans, fils de feu Pierre Russillon et de Suzanne Jovet, native Dyvedon au canton de Berne en Suisse, lieutenant de la c^ie du s^r de Besenval cappitaine au regiment Suisse de Salis ;—et Jeanne de le Becque, Agée de 24 ans, fille de Louis de le Becque et de defunte Marie Evrard, née et demeurante à Calais' (Guines Registers, p. 244). Louis Delebecque was a 'diacre receveur.'

[2] Jacob de Hanne, who was a 'diacre' of the Church at Guines, married, before 1670, Anne de la Marc.

CHAPTER IV

THE FAMILY IN ENGLAND

Behold! the world is full of troubles; yet, beloved, what if it were a pleasing world? How would'st thou delight in her Calmes, that canst so well endure her stormes?—QUARLES, after ST. AUGUSTINE.

OF the nine surviving children of Ambroise Minet and Susanne de Haffrengue, eight had now escaped to England; one, Daniel, was at Flushing. In what way they escaped, how they fared in the new lands, and what has become of their descendants, so far as it has been possible to trace them, I propose to speak in this chapter. And here, again, we have to depend mainly on the notes which Isaac has left us, and which he seems to have jotted down on two occasions—in 1722, and again in 1737; though in one or two instances he has added still later notes.

1. Thomas, the eldest son, was born in 1648, a date we are able to fix from the record of his marriage, which reads as follows:—

> 1681. Aoust. Le 31ᵉ. A Esté beny le marriage de Thomas Minet, marchand, agé de 33 ans, fils de feu Ambroise et de Susanne Haffrengue nat. de Calais et y demᵗ assisté de sad. mere et d'Ambroise Minet son frere: et Marie Goubart, agée de 28 ans, fille de feu Jacques, et de defᵗᵉ Marie Pilart, nat. dud. Calais et y demᵗᵉ, assistée de Jonas Goubart son frere, et de Daniel Pilart son oncle maternelle.[1]

When Thomas escaped to England we do not know, but it would seem probable, from the following evidence, that it must have been shortly after his marriage. His eldest child, Susan, must have been born in 1682, but no record of her birth is contained in the Guines Registers, where, had Thomas remained in Calais, we should expect to find it. The birth of another child, Ambroise, is, however, recorded in the Canterbury Registers in September 1683; and between that

[1] Guines Registers, p. 219.

date and 1695 there are entries of seven other children born to him at Canterbury.[1]

Evidently, then, Thomas was in Canterbury from at latest 1683 until his death in 1698; and this is confirmed by the note of 1722 which Isaac has left us, in which he says:—

> Thomas maryed Mary Goubard at Calais, he dyed at Canterbury 29 May 1698 left two sons 4 daughters, Thomas who is established at London and Peter who went to sea and suposed to be dead.

The note of 1737 repeats the same statement, but gives some further details:—

> Thomas was maryed at Calais to Mis Mary Goubard and did come over to Canterbury where he dyed in ye yeare 1698 hee left 2 sons and 4 daughters, his eldest son Thomas is now living at London, the other son peter tooke to the sea and dyed yong, 3 of ye daughters are maryed, and live one in prucia and ye other at Rotterdam, the eldest Suson maryed one albert and lives at Canterbury as also Elizabeth her sister unmaryed and those two are

---

[1] The following are the entries in the Registers of the French Church at Canterbury relating to these children:—

1. 1683, Sep. 23. Ambroÿse fils de Thomas Mine et de Goubar sa feṁe.
   Tem. Ambroÿse Mine ; Ellyzab Stanly.
2. 1684, Sep. 14. Thomas fils de Thomas Minet & Marie Goubard sa feṁe.
   Tem. Jean Peltier, serugien ; Marie Coppen.
3. 1686, Aug. 9. Marie fille de Thomas Minet & Goubart sa femme.
   Tem. Jaques Casel ; Mad^e Marie Regnier feṁe de Monsr Deprez. Nasq^t le 2 de ce mois.
4. 16$\frac{88}{89}$, Feb. 3. Elizabeth, fille de Thomas Minet.
   Tem. Jacob Minet ; Susanne de Fays.
5. 16$\frac{89}{90}$, Feb. 1. Isaac, fils de Tomas Minet & Marie Goubart sa femme.
   Tem. Isaac Minet ; Susanne Minet. Nasq. le 24 Jean^r.
6. 16$\frac{91}{92}$, March 20. Pierre, fils de Thomas Minet and Marthe Goubard sa feṁe.
   Tem. Pierre Le Mestre ; Marie Sauchelle, presenté en sa place par Marie Minet, feṁe de Pierre Le Mestre. Naq^t le onzieme de present Mars.
7. 1693, May 21. Judich, fille de Thomas Minet & Marie Goubard sa feṁe.
   Tem. Jaques Delemar ; Madam Susanne Renier femme de Monsieur Trouillart.
8. 169$\frac{4}{5}$, Jany 21. Madilainne fille de Thomas Minet & Marie Goubart sa femme.
   Tem. Baptize dans sa maison par Monsieur Trouillart qui en est le parain, et Mademoiselle Susan Deprez la Maraine.

The Registers of the French Church at Canterbury are now in course of publication as vol. v. of the *Publications of the Huguenot Society of London*; but only the first of the above names will be found in Part I. (the only one published so far), at page 303. These registers also show us (page 300) some Goubars at Canterbury, and this may have been one of the reasons that attracted Thomas thither.

poor, but by gods blessing I Isaac Minet have been able to assist both theire mother and them.

Thomas was, it would seem, a grocer and distiller, a trade for which his early training in his father's house at Calais had no doubt fitted him. As, beyond these few facts, there is nothing known of him, we may pass on to his eldest surviving son, Thomas, from whom is descended the eldest branch of the family as now represented in England.

Thomas the younger was born at Canterbury on September 14, 1684. Of his early life nothing is known, and the first trace to be found of him is an entry in the minutes of the Corporation of Dover, which runs as follows :—

6 *Nov.* 1711. Thomas Minet, a freeman, by marriage with Rebecca, daughter of John Winter.

He perhaps resided at Dover for some time after his marriage, but in 1743 he was settled in London, where, in 1746, a letter was written to him by Peter Fector, his sister Mary's son, who was then paying his addresses to his kinswoman, Mary Minet, but whose suit had not been received favourably. The letter itself I shall have occasion to refer to more fully in another connexion,[1] but the fact of its being written to Thomas, shows that he must have been intimately connected with the negotiations. The really interesting point about the letter, for our present purpose, is an endorsement made on it by Hughes Minet, Mary's brother, into whose hands the document fell. This endorsement may, of course, have been touched by prejudice, as Hughes was strongly opposed to the marriage; but it is certainly not at all flattering. 'This Thomas,' he says, 'was a sort of a muddling, puddling, smuggling merchant, who broke twice, and was always under difficulties and prosecutions for smuggling, etc.; he was Peter Fector's mother's brother, consequently his uncle.'

In 1747 Thomas was living on Tower Hill, and in a directory for 1754 there appears a 'Thomas Minett, merchant, Mincing lane,' which may refer to him, though he would be seventy years of age at this date. The date of his death is not known, but he left surviving him four children—Thomas, James, Susan, and Mary—who were all alive in 1767, as appears from the fact that legacies were then paid them under the will of William Minet. The eldest, Thomas, is

[1] Page 136.

referred to as 'late of Tetuan of Barbery,' and nothing further is known of him.

It is from James, the second son of Thomas the younger, that what may be called the Madeira branch of the family traces its descent. How or when is not known, but this James drifted to Lisbon and the Azores. Under William Minet's will he took a legacy of 50*l.*, which in the executor's accounts is entered as having been remitted to him. He is further spoken of in the same accounts as 'of Lisbon, and late of Fayal,' in connection with a debt of 110*l.* 10*s.* due by him to the deceased; which debt was never paid. He married Josepha Maria Durpont, of St. Michael's, in the Azores, where his eldest child, Mary Isabel, was born on August 26, 1762, the two later children—Joseph and Mary Ann Victoria—being born in Lisbon. His wife, from her name, may have been of French origin : but she was apparently a Catholic; at least, all her three children were baptised in that religion. There may, perhaps, have been some special reason for this; in any case, the family are now of the Reformed faith.

Joseph, his son, is said to have come to England when quite young, and it is from his two marriages with Anna Maria Barker and Elizabeth Brissault that the two divisions of the elder branch of the Minets trace their descent. Full particulars of these will be found on reference to Tables *B* and *C*. I may add here, however, a note on Joseph Minet's second wife, who strengthened the Huguenot blood already running so strongly in the Minet veins. She was granddaughter on her father's side to John Brissault, of Southampton and of Whitechapel, where he carried on the business of a sugar-refiner, and on her mother's side granddaughter of Nicolas Hebert, of Spitalfields, weaver.[1]

---

[1] The following table shows the descent of Elizabeth Brissault; the births of two of her sisters and her brother are recorded in the Southampton Registers (*Publications of the Huguenot Society of London*, iv. 80, 81) :—

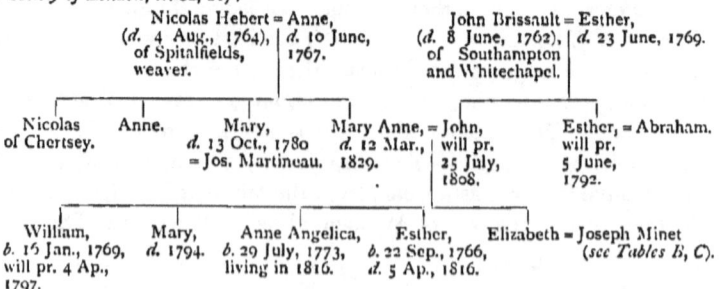

Thomas the elder, of Canterbury, interests us also in another direction, since through his daughter Mary, who married Jeremy Fector, of Rotterdam, he becomes the starting-point of the long business connexion which existed between the Fectors and that branch of the family, of which the writer is the present representative. When I come to speak of the business in a later chapter, this connexion will be more fully dwelt on; suffice it here to say that Mary's son, Peter, came over from Rotterdam as a lad, in 1739, to be a clerk in his great-uncle's house at Dover. Marrying his 'master's' granddaughter, Mary, he ultimately became a partner in the house of Minet & Fector, and survived till 1814. A portrait of him hangs in the Dover Town-Hall. His son and grandson remained on in the business until 1842, when John Minet Fector finally retired. The Fectors were well known at Dover. John Minet Fector the elder built Kearsney Abbey, near Dover, where, however, he never resided, as he died shortly before its completion. The family is extinct in the male line, but in the female line is now represented by the Rev. Sir John Robert Laurie Emilius Laurie, Bart., late vicar of St. John's, Paddington (see Table *D*).[1]

2. Of Ambroise, the second son, but little is known beyond what his brother tells us in the following notes, and in the note upon Susan, his sister. He acts as godfather to his brother Thomas's second child, at Canterbury, in 1683,[2] though of course he may not have been actually present; if he was, he must afterwards have returned to Calais, for in 1685 we have an account of his attempt to escape thence with Daniel and Elizabeth, his brother and sister. He must have succeeded in a second attempt, made the same year, as, with his sister Susan, he reached England by way of Nieuport in 1685. Isaac's notes on this brother are as follow :—

> Ambroise the second son of my father maryed at London imprudently the daughter of one jolly a Roman Catholik scotchman, his wife contrary to her promis, continued papist caused him a great deal of sorow and poverty, she died and left him a son Ambroise who is now at London wth him 1717 (and dyed since at sea, 1720).

[1] Hasted's *Kent* (vol. x. p. 63, ed. 1800) gives an account of the Fectors, which is, however, inaccurate in some particulars. They became large landowners in the county (*ibid.* vol. ix., *passim*).

[2] See p. 38, note.

S^d Ambroise the father dyed at Dover ye 2nd Octob. 1722, I subsisted him for many years.

Ambroise came out of Calais to dover in 1685, and in 1686 he and I, Isaac, went to London, hyered a house in newport street and then sett up a small shop of licors and parfumer etc^{ra}, where with dilligence and paines wee gott some practice and customers of persons of quality, and in all likelyhood wee would have done well, but being advised y^t our Brother Stephen who keep shop at Dover was sick I Isaac came downe to Dover and found him Dying in 1690, wch occasioned mee to stay at Dover, and hee remained at London and unbecomingly maryed to an irish [sic] woman who deceived him, both by remaining a Roman Catholick contrary to her promis, and her father in not giving him w^t hee had promised, she dyed and left one son who went to sea and dyed, hee being grown poor I was obliged to assist him and I had him come to Dover and payed his bord severall years, he dyed in 1722. I buried him, and I thank god y^t hee made mee capable of maintaining him severall years.

It is clear from this that Ambroise was not very successful when left with the sole management of the Newport Street business; and we have further evidence of it in an entry in the report of the French Committee for distributing relief, dated 1706, from which we learn that 'Ambroise Minet de Calais, 60 ans distilleur, et un enfant,'[1] who resided at Charing Cross,[2] received 3*l*. special relief.

It seems safe to say that Ambroise left no descendants.

3. For Daniel, the third son, we have again the Guines Registers as our starting-point, and they give us the record of his marriage as follows :—

1682. Octobre. Le 25e. A Esté beny le marriage de Daniel Minet, marchand, agé de 27 ans, fils de feu Ambroise et de Suzanne de Haffrengue, nat. de Calais et y dem^t, assisté de sa dite mere et d'Ambroise Minet son frere ; Et jeanne Flahault agée de 20 ans fille de feu Jaques et de Jeanne Burette, nat d'Andres et y dem^{te} assistée de sa dite mere, et de Jean Haudeguemp son oncle.[3]

[1] Probably the one son, Ambroise, who died at sea in 1726. The report is in the Lambeth Library.

[2] Newport Street is the continuation westward of Long Acre, and therefore not far from Charing Cross.

[3] White Kennet, whose Diary we quoted from above, was, curiously enough, an eyewitness of this marriage. Being at Ardres on Sunday, October 15, he went to Guines, apparently with

THE FAMILY IN ENGLAND

Isaac's notes on this brother give yet another glimpse into the dangers and troubles that overtook the Huguenots on the Revocation, and show him to us once more in his character of the good genius of the family :—

Daniel ye 3rd son maryed one Jane flahaut of Ardres near Calais and did live there about 2 or 3 years, but in the year 1686 he left ye country for his religion sake and went to flessing in Zealand where he lives now 1717, and hath a son and 3 daughters. (Is living in 1725—in 1732—his wife dyed in March 1732.)

Daniel maryed Mis Ann flahault of arders neare Calais where hee lived severall years, and untill ye persecution in the yeare 1686 [1] when endeavouring to make his escape hee and his wife and a daughter [2] were obliged wth Ambroise Elizabeth and her husband and child were obliged [sic] to refuge in woods neare Boulogne for severall days and nights, during wch time they were robbd of w^t they had and at last obliged to go home again, and some time after hee and his wife made their escape and got to flessing in Zealand, their child was given to a contry woman who was to cary it as her own child to newport, but was betrayed and caryed back to arders, but by a stratagem to long to relate here, and one hundred crownes pay by me to som magistrats the child was taken away and caryed to Newport out of the dominions of france and from thence to flessingue ; hee had a son Daniel Minet and one daughter more, ye son is a chirugeon in a small towne neare

the wedding-party, and gives the following account of the ceremony and the subsequent festivities :—

'*Sunday*, 15 *Oct*. 1682. Severall waggons prepared with tilts and 4 horses in coach order to carry the wedding guests to Gane. The Bridegroom cloathed in black the 1st day. 3 couples married without any repetition of the office, a list of their severall names being read the minister officiating in the pulpit. At our return to Ardres a very solemn bride supper prepared, after which they danced till bedtime.

'*Monday*. The wedding entertainment continued. The custom for the vulgar people at such solemnities to sit at table from 8 in the morning till 4 in the afternoon with supplies of fresh dishes without any rising up and with very small intermissions from eating and drinking. The poultry dressed without larding, pigs roasted with legs on, and the spit run through the brain without wiping' (Brit. Mus. Lansd. MS. 937).

There can be no doubt that White Kennet is speaking of this marriage, as October 15, the date given in his diary, would be October 25 according to the New Style, which was adopted in France in 1582 ; and, further, the Guines Registers (p. 237) confirm his statement as to three couples being married on that day. From this, as well as from other sources, it is clear that Andres in the Registers should read Ardres.

[1] This must be an error for 1685.

[2] This must have been Jeanne, who was born in 1684, as the Guines Registers tell us (p. 259) ; while Elizabeth's child we know from the same source was Suzanne, born in 1683 (p. 250).

s^d place.¹ The s^d D^l minet father having bene to cassey in adventuring wth people that wrongd him hee is not rich, so y^t I have for many since years asisted him and hee being now in 1737 very old I do allow him twenty pounds a yeare and writt him y^t soe long as it shall please god to bless me I will not lett him want and that if god takes me away before him, I will order things soe as hee may be assisted, I thank god y^t hath made mee capable of doing it.

My s^d brother dyed at midelburg ye 15th May 1740 aged 86 years, hee left only one son Daniel who is a surgeon and has no children.²

Daniel's escape to Flushing in 1685 is probably to be accounted for by the close intimacy which existed between the Protestants of the two towns of Flushing and Calais, of which we shall find striking examples when we come to speak of the Sauchelles.³

4. Of Elizabeth, the next child, we know more; born in 1657, in 1681 we find the record of her marriage :—

> 1681. Septembre. Le 21e.—A Esté beny le mariage de Jean Destriez, marchand, agé de 26 ans, fils de feu Pierre et de Catherine Vanthune nat. d'Ardres et y dem^t assisté de sad. mere, et du Sr Daniel Pilart, cousin; Et Elizabeth Minet, agée de 24 ans, fille de feu Ambroise et de Suzanne de Haffrengue, nat. de Calais et y dem^{te}, assistée de sad. mere, et de Thomas Minet son frere.⁴

After their marriage they lived at Ardres, where Susan, their eldest daughter, was born in August, 1683.⁵ Upon the beginning of the persecutions in 1685,⁶ Jean and Elizabeth Destrier attempted to escape, with their infant daughter, being accompanied by Daniel Minet and his wife and child, who also lived at Ardres, and their brother Ambroise. What befell the rest of the party we are not told, though they probably all shared the same fate; but the Destriers were caught, and imprisoned at Ardres, where in December, and in prison, their second child, Marie Françoise, was born :—

---

¹ Probably Axel, where I find the births of all his children, except the eldest, recorded in the registers.

² Added in the margin three years later. The statement that Daniel the younger had no children was true at this date—1740; but he afterwards had nine, whose descendants are still to be found at Flushing (see Table *E*).

³ Chapter VI.   ⁴ Guines Registers, p. 219.   ⁵ *Ibid.* p. 250.

⁶ In the note on Daniel given above, Isaac says the attempt was made in 1686, but this must be an error for 1685.

12 Decembre 1685, baptême a l'église catholique d'Ardres de Marie Francoise Destrier, fille de Jean et d'Elizabeth Minet, laquelle nous a été présentée par le père de la religion prétendue réformée.

Jean Destrier's mother, though she had not shared in the attempted escape, was also imprisoned, and we find her mentioned as abjuring with her son and daughter-in-law :—

29 X^{bre} 1685. Catherine Vantune, 65 ans, veuve de Pierre Destrier, marchande à Ardres, Jean Destrier son fils, aussi Marchand en cette ville, et Elizabeth Minet sa femme ont promis comme tous les autres dans les pages précedentes.[1]

The ultimate escape of the Destriers, with their two young children, Susan and Marie, furnishes yet another example of Isaac's care for all the family, for it was he who brought them to England, as he has told us above. Jean Destrier did not long survive his escape :—

Jean Destriez, natif d'Ardres est decedez le 3^e Juin 1687 age de 33 ans.[2]

ISAAC DE LA CROIX.   JACOB DE LESCLUZE.

And shortly afterwards his widow married again :—

Du 17 Feburier, 1689-90. Se sont epousez Daniel Giles, natif de Bourdeaux, aagez de 32 ans, et Elizabeth Minet agez de 33 ans, natif de Calais et veuue de Jean Destriez.

S. DE LE BECQUE.[3]

Of this second marriage one child was born, who appears in the same registers:—

Du premier Mars 1690-1. Elizabeth Dina Giles fille de feu Daniell et d'Elizabeth Minet né le 19 de Feburier, baptisez ce jour. Parain Isaac Minet. Maraine Marie Lequesne femme du Sr Jacob Delescluze et Mad^{elle} Susanne Stock.

ISAAC MINET.   S. DE LE BECQUE.[4]

After her second husband's death, Elizabeth lived on at Dover until her death in 1731, and it seems fair to conjecture was supported

---

[1] The registers of Ardres show that one hundred persons abjured there between August 21, 1685, and December 11, 1687. The names will be found in M. Ern. Ranson's *Histoire d'Ardres* (Saint-Omer), p. 691, and are almost all those of members of the Guines Church.
[2] Registers of the French Church at Dover, p. 17.   [3] *Ibid.* p. 16.   [4] *Ibid.* p. 12.

by Isaac, to whom for money, as for counsel, each member of the family seems to have applied.

One is glad to note that Marie, her daughter, who had been born in the prison at Ardres and forcibly baptized a Catholic, went after the death of her mother to live with Isaac, and took care of him till his death in 1745. Peter Fector, in his letters written from Dover, 1740–1745, often speaks of 'cousin Molly.'

Catherine Vanthune, who had come over in the boat with Isaac and her son and daughter-in-law, was admitted into the French Church at Dover on the same day with those who had enabled her to escape, as her signature testifies.[1]

Isaac's notes on his sister Elizabeth are as follows:—

> Elizabeth maryed one J^n Destrier of Arders by whom she had two daughters Susan and Mary, and her husband being dead at Dover she maryed on Daniel Gillis, a surgeon, by whom she had a daughter Elizabeth and s^d husband dyed at Dover. (S^d Elizabeth maryed James De Roussel who is reckoned a good fortune 1721) (she *i.e.* the mother, dyed at dover 1731).
>
> Elizabeth was maryed [1681] to Mr John Detriez who lived at Arders who both were making theire escapes with my brother Daniel as related before in this book and had the same fate of being robbd in ye woods, and at his coming back to arders was haprehended and putt in prison, during wch time shee was brought to bed of her daughter Mary and by intercession of friends hee was some time after released out of prison, and in order to theire more easily making theire escape, they went to live at mark neare Calais, and by gods grace and my providing a boate to come on ye french shore from dover etc^{ra} both her s^d husband, herself 2 children and his mother came in ye night in a wagon y^t I had also provided from mark to ye sea shore off of petite wall, and on ye first august 1686 landed at dover wth my mother and my self where they sett up shop keeping, her husband detriz dyed about two years after [2] and some time after [3] she was maryed to Mr Daniel Gillis of ye isle of olleron in france. She had by her firs husband two daughters Suson and Mary, Suson dyed at dover unmaryed ab^t ye yeare 1728, Mary is living now 1737 at dover also unmaryed, and by her second husband shee had Elizabeth Gillis, who was maryed to Mr James

---

[1] Page 52.   [2] June 3, 1687.   [3] Feb. 17, 1689-90.

de Rousselle in 1721 who is a man of a very good caracter and good estate whom I consider very much, and lives now neare Canterbury ; s^d Mr Gillis dyed about a year after hee maryed and his widow dyed at Dover in 1731.

5. Isaac himself was the next brother; but as I propose to deal with his life in fuller detail, I will first mention what little is known of the three youngest children.

6. Of Jacob, the sixth son, born at Calais, September 14, 1662, Isaac gives but one brief note :—

> Jacob was not maryed, he served in Oxford regim^t of horse-gards 11 years and then came and lived wth Isaac at dover and dyed there the 20th Sept. 1715, (he was born 14 Septemb 1662) aged 53 years.

How or when Jacob escaped to England is unknown. All we are told is, that he was at Dover when his brother landed on August 1, 1686. His regiment, now known as the Royal Horse Guards Blue, was originally raised in 1661, and was one of the first to join the Prince of Orange in 1688. The following year it was sent to Flanders, but was soon recalled to join the King in Ireland. In 1691 it returned to England, where it was quartered in London, as one of William's favourite regiments. In what capacity Jacob served I have been unable to discover.[1]

7. Stephen, though we know but little of him, is of more interest, as it was he who founded the business in Dover which in after years grew into the firm of Minet & Fector. He, too, had preceded Isaac to England, and, 'with tears of joy in his eyes,' was among those who received his brother on August 1, 1686, as one 'saved from the great persecution.' How and when he had made his escape to England we do not know; but in 1685 he was already established there, as in the end of that year we find Isaac communicating with him at Dover, and asking him to arrange for his escape.

However this may be, it is clear that at his death, in 1690, he had established a business that was sufficiently good to make it worth Isaac's while to leave the favourable opening he already had in London to be developed by his brother and partner, Ambroise, and to come to Dover and take charge of his brother's business, as appears from the note

---

[1] *An Historical Record of the Royal Regiment of Horseguards, or Oxford Blues* (Edmund Packe, Lond. 1834).

on Ambroise given above.¹ The only other direct information we have of Stephen is this note by his brother :—

Stephen was not maryed, he setled at Dover where he dyed 10 Sept 1690 was born y⁺ 24 September 1664. He lived 26 years.

The date given by Isaac as that of his death must be an error, for in the registers of the French Church at Dover occurs the following :—

Le 11 Feburier 1690

Est deceddez Estienne Minet, filz d'Ambroise et Susanne Haffrengue, natif de Calais ;²

while in the registers of St. Mary, at Dover, he is said to have been buried on Feb. 13, 169⁰⁄₉.

8. The two remaining children can be dealt with very shortly. Susan had escaped to England with her eldest brother, Ambroise, after sharing with him and Daniel and Elizabeth in the first attempt, which failed.

Of her Isaac tells us :—

Suson who was wᵗʰ the rest when robbd in yᵉ wood, did after that make her escape with Ambroise by way of Newport, did come to dover and was maryed to Mr. Gregory Kerr, a wine cooper of emmerick in holland and shee dyed at dover about a yeare and a half after and left no children.

The registers referred to above contain the following entry of her marriage :—

Du 21 D'avril 1690

Se Sont epousez Gregoire Kerc agez de [blanc] ans, natif d'Emerick, et Susanne Minet, natifue de Calais age de 30 ans.³

S. DE LE BECQUE.

She had apparently lived in Dover from the time of her first arrival there till her marriage, as in 1687 she is twice described as acting as godmother.⁴ Her husband, Gregory Kerr, was 'ancien' of the Church at Dover in 1691.

9. Mary, the youngest child, was twice married, and after the death of her second husband lived at Dover, which Isaac was more

¹ Page 42.   ² Registers of the French Church at Dover, p. 17.   ³ Ibid. p. 16.
⁴ Ibid. pp. 11, 12.

and more making the central home of the family. He tells us of this sister:—

Mary maryed to one Mr Peter Le maitre a chirurgeon at Canterbury, and her husband being dead she did in the year 1715 mary Mr Thomas Rooth and are now both living at dover, she had no children, they are living and well to past 1722.

Her husband Rooth dyed y^e [*blank*] of March 1726. The 2nd 9ber 1726 she came to live in a little house y^t I fitted for her near my house.

CHAPTER V

ISAAC MINET

Il faut de plus grandes vertus pour soutenir la bonne fortune que la mauvaise.
La ROCHEFOUCAULD.

IN endeavouring to reconstruct the history of the family, it is around Isaac, the sixth son of Ambroise, that the chief interest gathers. In whatever relation of life we consider him—whether as the centre and support of the family in England, or as a man of business; whether as a citizen, or as the mainstay of the French congregation in Dover—we are struck by his thoroughness, his clear-headed business capacity, and his overflowing gentleness and kindness of character.

Nor are we left to estimate his character merely from the recorded facts of his life: it must not be forgotten that it is he himself who records most of them, and who in so doing unconsciously reveals himself, most of all, perhaps, in the narrative of the persecution and escape, which in its clear and simple straightforwardness seems in some measure to reflect the mind and heart of the writer.

Let us endeavour to sketch the outlines of his life from the scattered fragments and records that are available. Born in Calais, September 15, 1660, probably in the 'Maison du chat' on the Great Square, he was in 1674, at the age of fourteen, sent to Dover to learn English at the 'Green House,' with Mr. William Richards, whose daughters, Elizabeth and Patience, took his place at Calais. On leaving Mr. Richards he went to Mr. Eaton, 'copying his letters and doing business for him at the Custom House.'

One may infer from this that the Calais business must have been largely concerned with England. Whether Isaac's elder brothers, Thomas, Daniel, and Ambroise, had also been sent to learn English we do not know, though it seems probable that, had this been the case, Isaac would have mentioned it.

After twenty-one months at Dover Isaac returned home, and he must have been for the next three years employed in learning the business

Depuis ce jour sont venus presenter
en cette compagnie Susanne
de haffengke vefue de ambroise
minet, Isaac minet son fils
Catherine vantane, vefue de
Destrier, Jean Destrier son fils
Elisabeth minet sa femme avec
deux petits enfans, qui sont de
Ladite Eglise de Calais, lesquels
ont souffert des prisons et la hors
Et auoir esté pris voulant se sauuer
auec ladite Eglise des Dragons.

Tridant Minas

J. Monguis elisabet bralesse
              qui n'a pas esté a la messe
                       P. delabecque
                           ministre
Susane de hafrengue Isaac Minet
Catherines vautgan
Jean destrier   michael de la ff
   marque
Catherine vantane que
Elisabeth de   anne O delagarre
  minet

FACSIMILE OF 'RECONNAISSANCE'

under his father, who died in 1679; from which date till 1681 the mother, with her four eldest sons, carried it on. In 1681 Thomas, the elder brother, married, and must have left Calais shortly after, as we find him in 1683 at Canterbury.[1] In 1682 Daniel, the third brother, married, and removed to Ardres. Ambroise, and Stephen, a younger brother, were also in the business, and remained on at Calais for a short time longer; but Ambroise, we know, came to England in 1685, and Stephen probably in the same year. Of Jacob we know nothing but that he also escaped in 1685; so that in this year Isaac was left, as he tells us himself, absolutely alone with his mother at Calais. The escape of all his brothers and sisters before the actual Revocation of the Edict of Nantes is probably to be accounted for by the zeal with which the new Bishop of Boulogne was entering on his duties, evidence of which we have had in the 'Mandement' published in May, 1683.[2] Why Isaac alone remained we can only conjecture. The position must have been a difficult one, as, indeed, we know from what he has himself told us in the 'Relation.' It is worthy of notice how, at the age of twenty-four, he already appears in the character of the helper of his brothers and sisters. It is he who provides for the safety of his brother Daniel's infant child; it is he who, after their first attempt had failed, carries out all the arrangements for the successful escape of his sister Elizabeth and her two children, with her husband and mother-in-law.

Of the stirring events which took place from the autumn of 1685 until his flight he has given an account in the 'Relation,' which leaves him safe on the shore at Dover on August 1, 1686. He remained there for at least a month, for we find him at the end of August, with the little company who had shared in his flight, making public acknowledgment of his error in having consented to abjure his faith in Calais, and signing as a re-admitted member of the Church in Dover.[3] The minute-book of the French Church in Dover, to which is due the knowledge of this fact, has been preserved, and is now in the possession of Mr. Frederick Arthur Crisp, to whose courtesy I owe it that I am able to give a facsimile of the entry. It is of the greatest interest, as showing us Isaac Minet's little company appearing together in the

---

[1] See page 38.   [2] See page 19.
[3] The importance attached to this ceremony may be gathered from the note, in the handwriting of M. Delebecque, which follows the name of Elisabet Brulefer; in which he says, 'Qui n'a pas esté à la messe.'

church at Dover, as many from Calais had done previously, and continued to do for some time to come, in order to be solemnly cleared from the stain of having attended mass, and to be re-admitted to the communion of the faithful. The signatures of all of them are appended; Catherine Vanthune, it will be noticed, is only able to make her mark, and Elizabeth Destrier signs her maiden name as 'de Minet,' the only instance known to me of the occurrence of the prefix.

Of Isaac's brothers, Thomas was established in Canterbury, Daniel was in Flushing, Jacob had entered the army, Stephen remained in business in Dover; Ambroise and Isaac alone were without occupation. Their resources must have been slender, but they determined to go to London, taking their mother with them; and in that same year we find them setting up a small shop of 'licors and parfumes' in Newport Street.

Newport Street still exists as the continuation westwards of Long Acre, and is in the Parish of St. Martin's-in-the-Fields. The neighbourhood of Leicester Square would seem to have been already a French centre, for in Stow's 'Survey'[1] we find Newport Street referred to as 'a very good place, with well built houses on the north side which is in St. Anne's parish. The other side being but ordinary and inhabited by tradesmen, several of which are French; it butts upon Long Acre from which it is parted by St. Martin's Lane.'

Early in 1688 their mother died, and was buried on March 29, at St. Martin's-in-the-Fields. The business would in all probability have succeeded, but before long came news of Stephen's illness at Dover. Isaac hurried down, and must have been present at his death on February 11, for on February 15,[2] 169⁰⁄₁, we find him signing the register there as godfather to the infant child of Solomon Delebecque, the minister of the church, and an old Calais friend. It would seem probable that he was at Dover during the remainder of that year, for he appears again as godfather in March[3] and October.[4]

It is evident that he had made up his mind that the business begun by Stephen was worth continuing; he therefore remained at Dover, where we find him, in August, 1691, twice signing the minutes of the Consistory as a 'chef-de-famille,' which would seem to imply a permanent residence there. Moreover, it was in this year that his marriage with Marie Sauchelle took place—a step he would hardly have ventured on

---

[1] Ed. 1720, vol. ii. b. vi. p. 68.   [2] Registers of the French Church at Dover, p. 11.
[3] *Ibid.* p. 12.   [4] *Ibid.* p. 12.

had he not felt his position and prospects somewhat assured. Of the Sauchelles we shall speak more fully later on; it is enough to say here that they were an old Flushing family who had been closely connected with Calais through the marriage of Jean Sauchelle with Sara Sigart. Jean Sauchelle, Marie's father, had died at Flushing in 1679, and his widow must have returned to Calais, her native town, where her family, the Sigarts, were still living, for on August 1, 1683, we find her acting as 'marraine' to Robert Hays, her sister Marie's child.[1] Later, she came to England, and settled, it would seem, in London, for though we find her in January, 1691, acting as 'marraine' at Dover to a de la Croix, she is described in the entry as 'demeurant à Londres.'[2] If, as is probable, Marie Sauchelle was with her mother in Calais before the Revocation, and afterwards in London, Isaac must have known his wife for some years before their marriage.

So soon, then, as he had arranged his brother Stephen's affairs, and found himself in a position to marry, he returned to London, and the marriage took place at the end of the year, as Marie herself tells us in the following words:—

Monsr. Isaac Minet et moy Marie Sauselle a esté marié par la grace de Dieu et sa Ste Benediction à Londres le 16e Decr 1691 dans l'église appellé l'artillerie ground Spittlefields, mon epoux avait 10 ans plus que moy; le Seigneur luy accorde des jours long et heureux, aussi à moy. Amen.

The marriage was solemnised by the minister, Campredon, and the young couple must at once have returned to Dover, as on January 31, 1692, we find the following entry in the Dover Registers:[3]—

Du Dimanche 31me Jan^{er} a esté Baptisé une fille née le 24 x^{bre} 1691 du mariage de Samuel Durier et de Susanne Newiar, presentée au Bapteme par Mr Pierre Fouet et par Demoiselle Marie Sausel, à laquelle a esté imposé nom Marie.'[4]

CAMPREDON Ministre.[5]

---

[1] Guines Registers, p. 250. Marie Sigart, wife of Jacques Hays, Madame Sauchelle's sister, appears as godmother October 28, 1688 (Dover Registers, p. 11). The Hays, however, had remained in Calais.

[2] Registers of the French Church at Dover, p. 11.   [3] *Ibid.* p. 12.

[4] *Ibid.* p. 13. This entry illustrates the custom, then prevalent, of a wife being known by her maiden name, even sometimes, as in this instance with the prefix 'Demoiselle.' It is obvious that this custom makes it far easier to disentangle these old pedigrees.

[5] See p. 56 note.

Isaac and Marie were now established in Dover, where he was slowly but surely building up the business that was ultimately to become the bank of Minet & Fector. Almost at once we find him taking an important part in the management of the French Church, which since the influx of refugees consequent on the Revocation had taken fresh life.[1] On January 17, 1692, he is named as a deacon, Gregory Kerr, his brother-in-law, being one of those signing the minute; and on February 14 he is publicly received and confirmed in the office. That he was held in some esteem may be gathered from his appointment, in the March following, 'pour travailler à la réconciliation de M. Jacob de Hane et du Sr de la Croix; M. Jacob de la Hane s'estant plaint à la compagnie d'une offence par un coup de canne qu'il prétend avoir receue du Sr de la Croix depuis quatre ans.'

It is pleasant to read further on of the success of Isaac's efforts as peacemaker, but seeing that it took more than a year to bring about a reconciliation, the work cannot have been of the easiest. On April 12, 1693, we are told: 'La compagnie aiant appellé les Sieurs Isaac de la Croix et Jacob Hane pour terminer leurs differences au suiet du coup de canne qu'il receut le Sr Jacob de Hane du Sr Isaac de la Croix il y a quattre ans ou plus, le Sr de la Croix a satisfait la compagnie tesmoignant avoir du desplaisir de ce quy s'estoit passé, et qu'il estoit de sentiment de charité envers le dit Sieur de Hane, desirant de vivre désormais en paix et bonne union avec luy. Apres quoy la compagnie a exorté le Sieur de Hane de vouloir estre dans le mesme sentiment d'esprit d'union et de charité envers le Sieur de la Croix.'

We may imagine that Isaac was all the more ready to undertake the office of peacemaker in this instance on account of the relationship existing between his wife's family and the de la Croix;[2] and that the connexion was still closely kept up appears, not only from Madame Sauchelle's acting as godmother to a de la Croix in 1690,[3] but also by the further fact of Isaac himself being godfather to another de la Croix child in 1693.[4]

In 1694 Isaac was appointed 'ancien'; and it is evident that more and more he came to manage the business affairs of the Church in Dover. From 1692 to 1701 we find him more than once keeping the

---

[1] For the history of the earlier French Churches at Dover, see *Proc. of the Huguenot Soc. of London*, iii. 91, 286.
[2] *Cf.* p. 89.   [3] Registers of the French Church at Dover, p. 11.   [4] *Ibid.* p. 13.

accounts of the receipts and payments made on account of the Church; and from 1701 to its final ending in 1731, the books are entirely in his handwriting. It is evident that during the whole of this period of thirty years all the business affairs of the small congregation were entrusted to his management, and if we may judge from the manner in which the accounts are kept, they could not have been in better hands.[1]

That his services in this capacity were appreciated by the members of the congregation we have evidence in the following entry in the records of the Church :—

> Nous, soubsignez, certifions que le Sieur Isaac Minet as servy la ditte église française de Douvre en qualité d'ancien pendent plus de trente quatre ans, durant lequel tems il s'est acquitté dignement de la ditte charge d'ancien en condhuissant et maintenant la ditte église en paix jusqu'à la mort de M. Paul Lescott, ministre de la ditte église, arrivé au mois de Decembre 1724.[2]
>
> JEAN FRANCOME—ancien.
JACQUES PERCHE
J. JACQUES GIROD
GABRIEL GIROD
ESTIENNE GIROD.

But we have yet further evidence of his interest in the Church, of which he was for so many years the life and guiding-spirit. When, in 1731, the congregation became so small as no longer to suffice for the support of a minister, Isaac's last act was to enter in the records an account of its history during the time of his connexion with it; and though this has no immediate bearing on his own life-history, I have ventured to reproduce it for its interest as a sketch of one of the numerous Huguenot Churches in England. It will be noticed that, though written in 1731, it is in French :—

---

[1] The history of the French Congregation can be largely reconstituted from these accounts, a task I hope to undertake before long, as the continuation of Mr. Overend's papers on the earlier French Churches of Dover.

[2] The passage quoted above, though not dated, occurs immediately after an entry dated 1727. It would seem probable, then, that it was written in that year, in which case the thirty-four years would refer back to 1693, when Isaac was not yet 'ancien,' but had been 'diacre' since the previous year. Isaac's connexion with the Church continued to its dissolution in 1731.

Relation de l'Eglise françoise de Douvre faite par Isaac Minet, Marchand, aud^t lieu et ancien de lad^{te} Eglise.

Je trouve par le Registre tenue sur quelque feuilles de papier separé que lad^t Eglise as comencé en 1642 mais que ce présent Registre n'a comencé que l'anné 1646.

Paul le Heup estoit alors Pasteur jusquà l'anné 1652.

Puis luy as succéde Mr E. Paien, quy as continué jusquà l'anné 1660 auquelle temps lad^t Eglise as discontinué et esté vacante. Cependant en l'anné 1674 moy led^t Minet estoit à Douvre pour aprendre la langue, ay^t esté a lad^t Eglise où un ministre francois estoit, précepteur des enfants de Cheu^r Oxenden de Wingham, préchoit quatre fois l'an, y ayant alors plusieurs françois habitant aud^t Douvre ; mais cela ne continua point et lad^t Eglise fut vaquante jusquà anné 1685 que la persécution de Protestants en France fut qu'il se réfugit à Douvre nombre de personnes, la plus part de Calais et pays voisin, alors lad^{te} Eglise fut rétablie dans le même lieu appellé le New Buildings par les soigns de M. Isaac de la Croix, Marchand, réfugié de Calais (ou je suis aussy née) et Mr Solomon Delebecque (fiz de Louis, March^d aud^t lieu) fut elevé Ministre de lad^{te} Eglise et as continué jusquà l'anné 1692), qu'il fut à Londre pour estre Lecture de l'Eglise de la Savoye et lad^{te} Eglise fut alors sous la Liturgie englois, n'ayant peut l'obtenir du Roy Jacques Second permission sous d'autre conditions.

Mr David Campredon,[1] proposante estant venue d'Hollande fut apellé p^r estre ministre et ay^t fait scrupule de se conformer à la Liturgie de l'église anglicane il retourna en Holland pour recevoir l'imposition des mains, et as continué ministre de lad^{te} Eglise jusquà l'anné 1709 au quel temps led^t Sieur Campredon ay^t obtenue l'Eglise de Shepardewold et Caldrige et aussy Charlton il quitta lad^{te} Eglise françoise.

Puis Mr Isaac Conilliette est venue et as esté Pasteur de lad^{te} Eglise sous la Liturgie angloise jusquà l'anné 1717 qu'il fut appelé

---

[1] 'David Campredon, propposant, retirez de France depuis l'abrogation de l'edit de Nantes en Hollande,' was elected minister on Aug. 9, 1691, but returned to Holland for two months, 'pour ces affaires,' before commencing his duties. On December 16, 1691, he was back in London (where he married Isaac Minet and Marie Sauchelle), and came to Dover early in 1692. In January, 1700, he became rector of Charlton, a village close to Dover, on the Deal road (Hasted's *Kent*, ed. 1800, ix. 474), but did not give up the French Church till 1709, when he became also Vicar of Sheppardswell and Coldridge, also close to Dover (Hasted, *ub. sup.* p. 384). He died in 1731.

pour estre l'instructeur des Nouveaux Converty et Refugiés à Londres, et consoler les malades.

Mr Gabriel Collin prosilite de Poitou, parent de Messrs Solomon Penny Esqr et de Mr Robert Miré, et par eux recommandé, as esté establly ministre de lad^te Eglise en Juin 1717, et as resté 2 ans et un cartier ; et ne trouvant point de gages suffisant, et que le comité de Londre ne payoit point, il s'en retourna en France ayant obtenue le pardon de l'Evesque de Poitier.

Il fut succedé en lad^t Eglise par Mr Paul Lescott venant de la Carolina ou il avoit esté ministre 17 ans ; il vint à Douvre et précha la prem^r fois le 27 Decembre 1719, fort brave homme et digne ministre, quy ayant esté appellé à l'Eglise de Wanswortth prèz de Londres, et estant venue p^r prendre congez et emporter ses meubles, tomba malade et mourut le [*blanc*] Decembre 1724,[1] fort regretté de l'assemblé de Douure et de tous ceux dont il estoit conue ; apres quoy Mr Isaac Roussier vint à Douure, recommandé par Monsr Degulhon de la part de Monsr l'Archevesque de Canterbury et précha la prem^r fois le 10 Septembre 1731. Se trouvant que tres peu de françois a Douure et ne pouvant l'entretenir il en est party le mois de Juilliet sans aparence que lad^t Esglise puisse rétablir.

Fait a Douure le 31 xbre 1731.

Il est resté dans lad^te Esglise la chaire et les bans quy y estoient avant et au temps du retablissem^t en 1685, comme apertenant au propriétaire du lieu, et il reste entre les mains de moy, led^t Minet, deux coupes d'argent servant pour la St Cene, pesant ensemble vinte neuf onces et demy, provenant et apartenant cy devant à l'Eglize protestant de Calais ;[2] plus aussy trois napes et deux serviettes fort usé et un table ou sont escript les dix commandements.

Isaac Minet.

Ratifié à Douure le 15^m Feb. 1736-7

N.B. Mr Ponsade a comencé lad^t Esgliz en 1641 ; je dit as esté le prem^r ministre jusquà 1646 quil as esté succedé par Monsieur Paul le Heup.[3]   Isaac Minet.

à Douure le 29me Mars 1732.

[1] His burial took place on December 2 in this year, according to the Registers of St. Mary, Dover.
[2] The ownership of these cups seems to have been disputed in 1686 between the two Churches of Dover and Cadzand. I have found two entries relating to this dispute in the Bodleian Library, which are given in Appendix VI.
[3] Isaac compiled this account mainly from the books of the Church, which were in his keep-

The records of the Consistory, with the 'deux coupes d'argent,' must have remained in Isaac's hands, and the books were still in the possession of the family in 1784. When or how they passed from it is not known. The cups have vanished altogether; the books have, happily, fallen into the hands of Mr. Frederick Arthur Crisp, who has printed the Registers, and to whose kindness in allowing me to consult the Consistory Minutes I am indebted for many of the details of this sketch.

Having thus treated of Isaac's connexion with the French Church at Dover, it is time to consider him as a citizen of the town, where he had established himself in 1690. It was not, however, till 1698 that he became a freeman of Dover, as we learn from the records of the Corporation :—

Isaac Minet, merchant, was made a freeman by order of the Common Council, February 14th, 1698.

His own account of his admission is far more graphic and detailed, and had best be given in his own words :—

MEMORANDUM.

That on ye 29th of June 1698 I did pay to Mr John Holland by order of the Mayor and common counsell of Dover three pounds wch they did order I should pay to enjoy the libertys of a freeman, they not thinking fitt to grant my freedom as to voting, tho. I was then a free denizen by King James Letter pattent, among many others.[1]

In the 3rd year of ye reigne of queen Anne, in 1705, I was naturalized by act of parliament, with david de haut and severall others as appears by a writting in partchment among my papers, and in ye said year 1705 Colonell Hollingbury gave me my freedom, and in 1706, at ye persuation of Mr Winell, I consented to be made a common counsell^r of ye corporation. I was twice putt up for ellection for a juratt but not ellected, for ye reason, I suppose, y^t I was born in france, in w^{ch}, though it seems to be slighting of me they have obliged me in the main, for it had been a prejudice to me to have bene a juratt.

---

ing. He has misread two of the names. Ponfade should be Poujade, and le Heup should be le Keux (see Baron F. de Shickler, *Les Eglises du Refuge en Angleterre*, Paris, 1892 ; pp. 102, 103). His descendant has found the same difficulty in reading these old handwritings.

[1] Of January 5, 1688. See the list of this date in Agnew, *Protestant Exiles from France* (Lond. 1874), Index volume, p. 47.

MEMORANDUM.

In September 1709 I was at London and then I had a Corporation gowne made for myself wch cost

for 8¼ yards poudesoy at 14s. of Mr petr. guerin	5.	15.	6
2 yards of valvet at 22s. 6d.	2.	5.	0
6½ yards of Shalloon	0.	13.	0
2¼ pound of silk at 21s.	2.	7.	3
16⅞ yards of lace	1.	13.	6
Making ye loopes	0.	5.	0
for durant,[1] buckram, silk and making	1.	5.	10
A true acc^t of ye cost of ye gown	£14.	5.	1

On the 28th of March 1731 I was ellected and made a juratt and was sworen in s^d office the same day, in order to oblige his grace the duke of dorset, who had before, at Dover very much prest me to consent to be a juratt, I having otherwise great reason to refuse because I had been il used by ye commoners of ye corporation who had oposed it severall times wⁿ I had bene putt in election, tho I never desired the s^d office, I haveing buisseness to do of my own and having by the goodness of God credit and reputation enough not to desire s^d office, but rather to be freed from it.

After his election as a common councillor in 1706, his name appears constantly as attending the meetings, in which it is obvious that he was as assiduous as in all else that he undertook. His election as a jurat is thus recorded in the Dover Corporation minutes:—

1731. At a Com. Council holden on Wednesday the 31st March. At this assembly Mr Isaac Minet was elected a Jurat of this Corporation, and the said Isaac Minet was accordingly sworn into the said office and took the oaths to the Government according to law.

At the date of his election as jurat he was seventy-one years of age, but he continued to attend until 1743 (September 8), when his name appears for the last time. In 1744, the year before his death, he is

---

[1] 'A stout worsted cloth, formerly made to imitate buff leather' (*Dict. of Needlework*, London, 1852). James, in his *Hist. of Woollen Manufactures*, describes it as coarse tammy, and states that it was little used in this country, but exported in considerable quantities to Spain and Portugal.

fined for non-attendance; which, unless it was a mere form, as is probable, seems a somewhat ungracious reward for thirty-seven years of service in the several offices of councillor and jurat.

But it is time to consider Isaac in his more personal character as head of his family and of his business. His married life began, as we have seen, in 1691, and was a long and happy one of forty-seven years. In 1694 his eldest child, Isaac, was born, but only lived nine months. In 1695, John was born; and to both of these 'Madame Sara Sigart, veufe de Jean Sauchelle,' acts as 'marraine.' It would seem that she was living with her daughter and son-in-law, for in 1699 she died at Dover, and was buried in the churchyard of St. Mary's,[1] under the east window, where one stone recorded her death, with that of the Isaac to whom she was godmother and grandmother, and those of Ambroise and Jacob, her son-in-law's brothers.

Between 1694 and 1703 six children, all sons, were born to Isaac and Marie. Their baptisms are all entered in the registers of the French Church,[2] from which their father made an extract (which is in his own handwriting), for the purpose, apparently, of having them inscribed in the parish registers of St. Mary's, where, however, they are not found. This extract is given here, as it is interesting to see who the godparents were:—

Isaac, filz de Monsr Isaac Minet et de Mad^l Mary Sauchelle fut né le 27 avrill 1694, baptisé le 30 d^o. Parain Mr Thomas Minet, mareine Madam Sara Sigart vefue de Monsr Jean Sauchelle.

Il mourut le 19 Janur. 169$\frac{4}{5}$.

Jean, filz de Mr. J. M. et de Marie Sauchelle sa femme, né le 24 Septembre 1695, baptisé le 30 d^o. Parain Mr Ambroise Minet, mareine Madame Elizabeth Sauchelle[3] famme de mons^r. Piere Le Gay.

Isaac Minet, etc^{ra}, née le 11 Octobre 1696, baptisé le mesme jour. Parain Mr Piere Fannet en place de Mr Isaac Sigart, mareine Mad^m Elizabeth Minet[4] vefue du Sr Dañl Gillis.

Jacques, etc^{ra}, née le 15 Mars 169$\frac{7}{8}$, baptisé le 17 D^o. Parain Monsr Jacques Haÿs filz, de Calais, mareine Mad^m Mary Minet famme du Sr Piere Le Maitre.

Daniel, etc^{ra}, née le 18 9bre 1699, baptisé le mesme jour.

---
[1] Her burial took place on March 30, according to the Registers of St. Mary, Dover.
[2] Pages 13, 14.   [3] Of Berlin, Marie Minet's aunt.   [4] Isaac's sister.

Parain Mr Daniel Minet, mareine Mad^m Jeane Sauchelle,[1] famme de Monsr. Zachary grandidier.

Guillaume, née le 8 Decembre 1703, baptisé le 11 D°. Parains Mr Isaac Lambe et le capit^n Charles Gibson, mareine Mis Mary down.

Given copy in English to Mr Macqueen[2] the 7 Sept. 1720.

That Isaac should have thought it desirable to have these records entered in the parish registers is evidence of how, little by little, the change from French to English was progressing in his case, as in that of other Huguenots—a change which led to the gradual dying out of the French Churches as their members became more and more English.

Of his personal life Isaac has left us absolutely no record. We can only judge, from the after-history of the five sons who grew to manhood, how wise must have been the home-training they received. When we come to speak, in Chapter VII, of the various professions they embraced, we shall note, too, with what a kindly interest their father followed their success, and how materially he contributed to it. It is, indeed, to his affectionate records that we owe the possibility of giving a comparatively full account of their various pursuits.

Though of Isaac as a father we can only speak by inference, of his fatherhood in a wider sense we have fuller knowledge. Already, in France, we have seen him remaining as the sole support of his mother and of the business; nay more, it is he who, 'by a stratagem to long to relate,' saves his brother Daniel's child, and provides for the escape of his sister Elizabeth. Settled in England, he alone of the family may be said to have succeeded in life; and his success he uses ungrudgingly for the helping of his brothers and sisters. Thomas, the eldest, settled in Canterbury, where, after his death, his daughters Susan and Elizabeth were evidently left badly provided for: but 'by God's blessing I, Isaac Minet, have been able to assist both their mother and them.' Ambroise had been left with the business in London, and, as we should expect from what we know of his character, was not successful; of him Isaac tells us, 'I had him come to Dover and paid his bord several years.'

---

[1] Another aunt of Marie Minet.
[2] Rector of St. Mary's, Dover, 1698-1729; but see p. 68, note 2.

Daniel had gone to Flushing, where, Isaac tells us, he had failed to do well:—

> The s^d D^l Minet having bene to eassey in adventuring with people that wrongd him, hee is not rich, so y^t I have for many years asisted him, and hee being now in 1737 very old I do allow him twenty pounds a yeare, and writt him y^t soe long as it shall please god to bless me I will not lett him want, and that if god takes me away before him I will order things soe as he may be assisted, I thank god y^t hath made mee capable of doing it.

Jacob, who had served in the army, came to Dover on his retirement, and lived with Isaac till his death. Mary, his sister, after the death of her second husband was, it seems, but ill-provided for, and she, too, he says, 'came to live in a little house I had fitted up for her near my house.' His niece Mary (daughter of Thomas Minet, of Canterbury) had married a Mr. Fector, of Rotterdam, and their son Peter was brought over as a clerk in the Dover house. From the nature of the letters written by his parents at the time [1] we may gather what a boon this opening was: the use Peter Fector made of it we shall see later on. Mary, another niece (daughter of his sister Elizabeth), born in the prison at Ardres, and brought over in the boat, came to live with Isaac after his wife's death.

These are the instances in which we know him to have proved himself a father in the widest sense of the word; there must have been many others of which we know nothing. But perhaps enough has been said to enable us to endorse what his son William said of him when he died: that he had been 'serviceable to mankind in general, charitable to poor travellers, father to french and foreigne prisoners, relief and comfort to poor and distressed townspeople, the father and giver of employ and bread to many poor familys in Dover.'

Of the nature of the business he built up, which ultimately became the banking-house of Minet & Fector, we know but little. It seems to have been that of a general merchant, commission and shipping agent; while his French connexion was evidently large and important. Hughes, his grandson, being in Paris in 1752, had an interview at Fontainebleau with Louis XV., who asked him, he tells us, 'how my grandfather at Dover did, who had sent him so many

---

[1] *Cf.* Chapter VIII.

fine English horses?' At least as early as 1721 he owned the packet-boats crossing to France, as he himself tells us in a declaration respecting the death of Mr. Pierre Porré, who, being a 'marchand à Londres, s'estant embarqué a Calais sur un de mes vaisseaux, mourut en debarquant du vaisseau dans une chaloupe et fut aporté mort dans ce port, et comme j'avoit l'hon^r de le conoitre je pris soign de son corps et en ayant donné avis à ses amis à Londres je le fitt enterez'; while in the public accounts are notes of sums paid to the house for the convoy of ambassadors and other important persons in special boats. In the same records we find notes of communications made to the Government as to the movements of French men-of-war and transports in the Channel.

Among Isaac's own notes are but few which have reference to his business. Two there are, however, which I reproduce. The first, unimportant in itself, yet shows that attention to detail by which alone success in larger ventures can be reached :—

> 1718. A barill of redd harrings well dryed the full should weigh 1.1.0. and shotten[1] 1.
>
> Memorandum. To observe to buy dryed harrings y^t were hanged new caught, and not of two nights ketching—w^n full at 20 p^r barill shotten for 16. 6 to 17, but the draw back of the salt being taken of, harrings will sell for 5 or 4 per barill less.
>
> from Lisbon 5 muys make 3 tons.
> from S^t ubes[2] 5 d^o make 3¼ tons.
> a hundred of salt at Olleron makes a^{bt} 25 tons.
> from Crossick about . . . . . 22 tons.
> S^d Croisick salt is ye weakest and smaller grain not soe much esteemed.
>
> In Norway 112 Rixdalders make about 25 ster.
> The best salt from france is from ollone, or Rochelle.

The next note is one of more general interest, and his action under the circumstances narrated would seem to have led to his appointment as agent for the Dutch East India Company.

> Memorandum, that in ye month of february 1735 there were by misfortune three Dutch East India shipps on shore on ye goodwin

---

[1] A fish that has ejected its spawn.
[2] Saint Ubes, or Setuval, on the coast of Portugal, near Lisbon.

sands, viz. the Meermont, Captn Jacob hoogstad, and the loosdregt Captn Willm Vroom of ye Chamber of Amsterdam, wch were broke to pieces and lost, except ye treasure and some small mater of goods wch were saved and brought on land and seven chestes of ye treasure were carry^d on bord of the galiot [*blank*] Captn Jons Brander, who came in dover harbour some time and went to deale to take ye rest and some riging to cary to Amsterd^m; and the shipp Buys of ye Chamber of Enchuysen, Captn [*blank*] Orsec, command^r wch was gott off by folkston and dover men, and came to anchor ab^t 2 leagues off of Dover and ridd there [*blank*] days, her dutch comp^y having left her; and the 12th of s^d febuary s^d Captn orsek came here from folkston with his chief mate and 2 other dutch person and came to my house and told mee his case and desired assistance.

I told him y^t I was extremely surprized to see y^t hee had left his shipp and left nobody in possession but English men, and I having then no order to act, I advised him to go to Mr Primrose at deale, agent of ye comp^y of Holland; hee did go to deale, and same night I rec^d ord^r from Mr primrose to endeavour to save s^d shipp, and do all I thought proper to y^t end, and would aprove of all I should do. I did immediately send for Mr John paskall, pillot, and order him to find out fifty men to go on bord with him in order to cary s^d shipp in safety either to Sherness or portsmouth, and y^t I would see them well payd for theire service, s^d paskall came ab^t 10 at night and said hee did hope ye next morning to find men enough, and I did ord^r Captn Wm. Boyket with his sloop to cary s^d men on bord of s^d shipp Buys and to tend on her till shee was in safety, but y^e next morning s^d paskall came and said y^t the men were willing to know w^t they was to have for bringing s^d shipp in a safe place, I did offer them 5 guineas p^r man, wch they did not accept of, and s^d paskall saying they would not goe under $7\frac{1}{2}$ gns. p^r man I consented to it considering there was an absolute necessity for it, Captn Orsek having told me y^t hee had left but ab^t 40 men on bord and y^t there wanted 50 more.

About 10 of y^e clock w^n I thought they were going off s^d paskall came and said y^t some of y^e men having heard y^t one of ye shipps on ye Goodwin was broke to pieces were gone and going with their boats to ye wracke, and y^t the others would not go under 10 G. p^r man, at wch I was much concerned, but not knowing how to prevent was obliged to consent to it, and they went off in ye sloop.

Captn Orsek being soon after come back from Deale with his chief mate, I sent them also on bord by a boate, but it did so hapen y^t the men on bord having bene recruted from folkston, they weighed anchor and refused to lett ye capt^n come on bord as alsoe ye men of ye sloop; and ye wind being come to ye S.W. they caryed ye shipp in ye downs and shee is since caryed to Sherness and there refitted. I was glad y^t the s^d men were not admited on bord for they would have expected the 10l. p^r man and I should have been blamed for promising it, tho I knew not how to prevent it, for if ye ship had bene lost for want of assistance, I should have been blamable. I did give ye men 5s. each for theire trouble and a g^a to Mr paskall etc.

The mater of salvage of s^d shipp hath bene since made up and settled by Collonel Marsh.

Mr Gerard Bolwerk, agent for the Honourable the East India company of Holland at London, did by his letter of ye 20th 8tober 1736 apoint mee agent for ye s^d company, with order to assist all such ships belonging to s^d company that shall be in this roade, or to ye westward of this port as far as dungeonnest and on this side of ye S. foreland; I take it to be westward as farr as Beachey head, there being no agent at Rye.

During the eighteenth century Dover was more peculiarly the gate of England than in our times of increased facilities of communication, and the foreign connexion of the house must have helped to bring Isaac into contact with many of those who passed through the town. ' He had opportunities of seeing, hearing and knowing the sentiments of men of all sorts of degrees and qualities,' his son tells us, and we may join with him in regretting that his father did not ' make a book of remarks and observations on men and manners, and a sort of sketch-history of his times.'

The only notes we find relating to public events are the following, the last of which deserves notice—written, as it was, only the year before his death—both as showing the interest he still took in public affairs, and as being also the last note we have from his hand.

Louis the 14th King of France dyed the Sunday before the 5th of September, new stile, Mr James parent merch^t at Calais gave me advice of it ye s^d day 1715.[1]

---

[1] Louis XIV. died on Sunday, September 1, 1715.

1738 [should be 1739 as P. F. was present and he came to Dover 16, 7ber 1739].¹ The war ag' Spaine was declared at London on y' 23 of Octobre with greate formality and affluance of people who were much satisfyed at it, and it was declared at dover y' 29 Do. the mayor and juratts and common counsell men in theire gowns, the collors, 8 sergants, 4 drums and y' comp' of soldiers in armes; I pray God it may soon end to y' advantage and glory of England.²

The warr of England ag' Spaine was proclaimed at Dover the 29th of October 1738 as in foregoing fo. The warr of y' king of france was declared against y' king of Greate Britain at Calais the 21 March, old stile, 1744. The warr of the king of Greate Britain against the king of france was declare'd at Dover the 9th of Aprill following,³ the dover men being under armes, and y' mayor and corporation in theire gowns—I pray God it may soon end to y' glory of God and the advantage of Greate Britain.

Local matters he recorded more frequently, but, of the notes which follow, the first only is of any general interest; it relates to Lord Chancellor Hardwicke, and will be read with interest in connexion with his life by Lord Campbell.⁴ The others are given as relating to names, some of which are still to be found in Dover:—

1737 Aprill. Memorandum of the extraord' rise of fortune of the present Lord Chancellor of England—who was born at Dover the first day of december 1690 as it apeares by its being writt in theire familly bible, and I remember him since y' years 1694 and 1695; his father was an attorney at law at dover Mr phillip york, and had only this son also Mr. phillip york, and two daughters, the eldest maryed Mr John Billingsley y' presbiterian minister at dover who about five years since took y' orders of y' church and had no living but of late, the youngest daughter maryed councellor Jones who doth not practice, nor hath hee exerted himself, nor procured the esteem and love of his brother-in-law y' now Lord Chancellor, by wch means hee could obtaine good inployes; but soe

---

¹ Correction made by William, his son.
² The Declaration was issued on October 19, 1739 (Lord Mahon, *Hist. of England*, Lond. 1839, ii. 423).
³ The Declaration was issued on March 31, 1744.
⁴ *Lives of the Lord Chancellors* (Lond. 1868), vi. 158 *et seq.*

it happeneth y' y° difference is extreame between the Lord Chancellor and his sister's husband. I have had an extra^y good opinion of y° Ld. Chan. since y° time hee was about 20 years old ; by an accident y' happened in which hee acted and behaved with y° prudence of a person of 40 years. He pleaded at y° barr at [*blank*] years of age,[1] hee was made solicit^r generall in y° yeare [1720] and attorney generall in [1723], Lord Chief Justice of England in 1734 [this date should be 1733] and Lord Chancellor of England in 1736 wch is a prodigious rise, but not more than his meritt, having gone through the severall offices with y° generall aplause of y° whole nation.

In May 1735 Captn J^n Dalglish who is deputy agent for Mr Hall for y° paket boat, who hath allowed him by the postmast^r General 5s. p^r each passenger and 2s. 6d. p^r each servant told me y' in 3 months time y' Mr hall had been absent, hee had not collected above fifty pounds wch was much less than usuall.

Memorandum y' s^d 5s. and 2s. 6. for servants was never before allowed to y° agents of paket boats before the time of Mr Cha. Lovell, it was given him as a recompence for y° service he did in examining passengers very strictly during y° time of the comotion of preston and it hath bene continued to Mr hall his successor by y° intercession of his friends and Lady Jarsey, he allowing y° annuity (100*l.*) to s^d Lovel during his life, s^d lovel being non compos mentis, he dyed in 1737.

Mr Nathanael Matson dyed at his house at Dover y° thursday morning 5th 9ber 1719 and was buryed y° Satterday 7 do. and had a very pompous funerall, the bearers were Capt Blindston, Mayor, Mr Thomas Bradley, juratt, Mr Wm Vealle[2] comtroll^r of y° customs, Mr J^n Slodden, Mr Robt Wickenden and Mr Benjamin Devinck.

Mr Henry Matson dyed at his house at Dover y° 8th of March 172½ and was buryed y° 11th do. on a Sunday ; y° bearers were Mr J^n Knott, one of y° Mayors for at y' time was alsoe mayor Mr John Hollingbury, y° bearers were besides Capt Blindston, Mr Veale, Mr Devinck, Capt Gunman, and Capt Lamb ; I say M^r

---

[1] Entered at the Middle Temple, November 29, 1708 ; called to the Bar, May 6, 1715.
[2] The Veels owned Capel-le-Ferne. See p. 98, and Table *L*.

William devinck, Mr Benjamin one of yᵉ excut. being at London, Mr Bradley yᵉ other executor.¹

The 22nd 9ber 1723 my wife and I stood godfather and godmother by ord. and in the roome of the Earle of Essex and my Lady Essex to Captⁿ Wᵐ Westfield's daughter who was named Jane, baptized by Mr John Macqueen.

15th Augᵗ 1727 Mⁱˢ Grandsire of Calais came over and the 16 went to Canterbury and yᵉ 17 do. her daughter Magdelaine was maryed wᵗʰ Mr Denis Claude Coetlogon of Ploetmell in Brittany in france who pretended to be worth 2000 sterl.

Mr John Macqueen dyed the 9th January 173¾ at night aged 82 years he had been minister of yᵉ parish of St Mary during [33] years and Mr Jⁿ Lodewick his predecessor was minister of said parish in yᵉ year 1673.²

In 1738 came the great break in Isaac's long and happy life: his wife Marie, his companion through nearly half a century, died. He has left us such a full account of her death that it is unnecessary to do more than reproduce his own words:—

1738.

My deare Wife after having been trobled for abᵗ a yeare and a half with a continuall greate noise in her head for wᶜʰ shee severall times went to Canterbury and consulted Sʳ Wᵐ Boyes phissitian, alsoe Doctʳ Gray and Dʳ Peck and severall others, and took many medicins yᵗ were ordered and purged very often, and even yᵉ day

---

¹ Henry Matson, by his will, left a sum of 150*l*. per annum (subject to a life-interest to his brother Christopher) for the repair of Dover Harbour. Isaac Minet, as administrator to Christopher, became party to a Chancery suit which arose respecting the carrying out of the trusts of Henry Matson's will. The reason for Mr. Matson's legacy is thus given by J. Lyon (*Hist. of the Town and Port of Dover*, Dover, 1813, i. 180):—' He was walking round the pier, and let a gold-headed cane slip through a hole in a plank, and left the annuity on the condition that such holes should not be suffered in future, and the Warden was to take care and have all the trunnel-holes stopped, or to forfeit the benefit of the annuity. The ceremony of stopping up the trunnel-holes was soon reduced to a farce. The mayor, with two or three of his brethren, once in a year appointed a day for driving in a few trunnels, and, the fatigue being over, they retired to a supper; and this has been considered as fulfilling the will of Mr. Matson.'

² Hasted (*Hist. of Kent*, ix. 546) says that John Lodowick was rector, 1671–1698, and that John Macquean was appointed in 1698, and dismissed in 1729. The story of this 'dismissal,' which was quashed by the Archbishop of Canterbury, is given at length by J. Lyon, *op. cit.* i. 116.

before, was on ye 14 of october 1738 seized with a fit of apoplexcy when shee was rising out of her bedd and put one of her stokings on, ye maid going up to aske someting found her mistris staring and speetchelesse, I went up immediately and found her sitting on ye bedd in y^t condition, and having sent for yong doct^r bradley hee would have bleeded her at left arm, but shee would not suffer it, and found y^t her right arm and legg were seized with dead palsy, hee did bleed her of s^d arme and it bleeded sufficiently and then aployed a blister on her shoulders wch discharged aboundantly. I sent for Doct^r Peck fro. canterbury who came that night and ordered a second bleeding, and on handling her arme ye first orifice opened itself and vented as much blood as was thought sufficient by Dr Peck. 2 days after a blister was putt on her head wch alsoe vented very much humour, and ye nexte day after mustard seed was aplyed to her inkles and her dead riste wch took of ye skin having risen blisters; ye sixth day her right part of her face sweld very much and I then feared shee would not live long, but in a day or two ye swelling went off, but shee remained speetchelesse and only pronounced some words as 'O my god, my saviour, have mercy,' wch shee repeated oftentimes in french, shee sometimes was sensible and knew me and severall others.

About 10 days after her dead hip grew sore and very raw and shee continued so till ye 9th of November; shee did from ye beginning take w^t was given her to eate and drink and seemed to relish w^t she tooke.

My son John came to dover ye 16 8tober, and hath bene most of ye time here, my son W^m came from London ye 18 do. and was here 12 or 15 days and his buisseness requiring him very much and his mother continuing in the same condition hee went back ye 4 9ber, and his sister wid^w of my son daniel arived at dover to confort mee and take care of my house, my niece mary detriez hath since ye beginning attended her ante with a grate deale of care and affection for wch I am obliged to her. Wm Minet my son did give advise to my son James at Berlin of his mothers illness before hee came from London and since, and I have writt to him myself ye 8 9ber desiring him to come to dover soe soon as was convenient for him.

My dear wife departed this world the 30th 9ber about noon and was caryed to her grave in a herse the 3rd december accompanyed with our sons John and William and ye widow of our son Daniel.

and Mary Detriez my niece in a coach; the bearers, Mrs Dalglish, mayoress, Madm. Gunman and Mrs Billingsley, Jones, Gay and Mis perche and ye servants in another coach. I doubt not of her happyness shee having bene a very vertuous pious and charitable person.

The nexte day after her death I was taken ill of a feaver and keept my bed and I did not expect to live; my son will^m sent for Doct^r Lynch twice from Canterbury and by God's grace I grew better after keeping bedd about one month, after wch my daughter in law, widow of my son daniel, who had taken care of mee and my house went back to London, and, I thank God, I was in good healthe during ye summer and during all ye very severe and cold wather of ye winter 1740 but ab^t ye 16 May I was ill of a feaver and my son willm. came to dover and sent for doct^r Lynch; I thank God after I had taken ye barke some time ye feaver left mee, but I suffered much and that hath continued, tho not soe much to ye 22nd of June. I have good apetite and hope y^t with God's blessing I may enjoy more healthe a little longer.

It would seem that this account was written, or at any rate completed, in June 1740; and it must have been about the same time that his daughter-in-law, Mrs. Daniel Minet, who had been with him at the time of his wife's death, again visited him, as he tells us in the following note:—

1740 on Monday y^e 9th June Mrs Anna Maria, widow of my son daniel, came to dover to see mee with her son Daniel Minet, who is $10\frac{1}{2}$ years of age, who I was very glad to see, being a handsome and very much promising yought, and I pray god to bless him; shee came in her chaise with her waiting woman, who was nurse to her s^d son and hath bene with her ever since, and her son came on his owne little horse and her fottman Willm. on another horse, and they went back fryday ye 20th June inst.

It is satisfactory to think that the old man was well cared for during the seven years that elapsed between his wife's death and his own. His son John, with his children, no doubt came over frequently from Eythorne, and William at rarer intervals, as his business allowed him, came down from London; while from 1739 onwards he had living with him his niece, Mary Destrier, and the new clerk, Peter Fector.

Mary, it will be remembered, had been born in the prison at Ardres, and it was to her uncle, who had brought her over as an infant, with her father and mother, that she owed her escape. Peter Fector was Isaac's great-nephew, and came over from Rotterdam at the age of sixteen. It is from his letters, written to William in London, that we get our only glimpses of Isaac's last years. In 1740 he writes, 'Your dear father, my uncle, seems really to be at a mending hand,' which must refer to the fever from which Isaac had been suffering—an illness sufficiently serious to bring William down from London. In November of the same year we have from another letter a glimpse of the life at Dover. Peter Fector writes: 'After dinner I go again to the Counting House till such time as it pleases your dear Father to go in, which is most times at 4 or 5 o'clock, and then we begin to play at draughts till 8. After supper I play again at wisk with your good father and cousin Molly [*i.e.* Mary Destrier] till 10 or 11.' The same letter adds, however, "'Tis certain your good father cannot attend business as usual.'

The old man's interest in public, as in family, matters, was evidently still keen, but his active share in business life was naturally abating, and his son, his niece, and his great-nephew united their endeavours to while away the hours of increasing leisure. And here, perhaps, we may introduce the one personal touch we have of him—his fondness for snuff. Trivial as his record of this is, it is curious as an illustration of his thoroughness and attention to detail. We can only regret that he had not enough of his favourite brand to last him all his life.

> 1732 Octob 18*th*. Memorandum that about 18 or 19 years past I had from Ostende ab^t 160 lb. of havana snuff sent by Mr Emmery of wch I have now left, in a box under ye beare celler staires 5 lb., in a broken jar in a cirecloth 3 lb. wch was keept in jarrs till now, and in s^d jarr wch was a very long time in ye Granary, and is a little musty, 4 lb.; Octob 1736 I have 2 lb. left and ab^t ½ lb.

During the next two years the same life went on; and we know that Isaac was still, until 1743, attending to his duties as a jurat. William was evidently constantly exhorting Peter Fector to interest and divert his father, as in April, 1743, the latter writes: 'I observe the admonition you give me as to playing and diverting your good father'; while the same letter shows that Isaac was still able to attend to business in some degree, for the writer adds: 'I have of late wrote a good many letters which your Father did all approve without ordering any alterations.' In October of the same year another letter says, 'I play six hours with him every day. My master holds it brave and hearty, God be praised.' The last note we cull from this correspondence shows us the old man still interested in some of the details of business. It had been a question of paying some moneys to French prisoners, remitted by their friends abroad, and the writer explains, 'Your father expressed some uneasiness at our not paying the money.' As his last business comment was connected with the country of his birth, so, as we have seen, was his last note on public matters also a French one; but both comment and note show Isaac as the thorough Englishman, so made, like many another Huguenot, by the fatal policy of Louis XIV.

Isaac was now eighty-four, and the end was not far off. From Peter Fector we hear no more, but William has left a very full account of his father's last illness and death :—

> Mr I. M. latter end from feb to 8 April 1745.
> About the [*blank*] feb 174$\frac{4}{5}$ at the time that I, W. M. was very ill of the gout in Lond°, the whole a 7 week confinement, and despatching the great concerne of the ship Hardwicke I had news of my d^r hon^d father being very ill. B^r Minet[1] wrote me melancholy letters and y^t he feared the worse.
> Dr Lynch was sent for [*blank*] times and little hopes; I waited being weake till able to get out and hoped y^t 8 or 10, in 4 or 6 days [*sic*], to be able, when on a Sunday 10 mar I rec^d express from Dover my d^r Father was near his end and that he should die at rest if he saw me, and enquired much and often for me as the family, Dr Bradly, Dr Lynch, Cozen Mary, P. F.[2] and S. P. witness; 6 hours after express Collins arrival I set out, 11 Mar. 2 Morn^g with John Bolver in a coach of Mr J. Poultny and got y^t Monday ab^t 5 afternoon to my fathers house and being under great apprehension finding him expired, according to the account on the road, which hurried and distressed my spirits, however found my dear father full of vigour and perfect in his understanding, but weak of body and teribly afflicted and in pain. He told me of his will and recomended me sundrye things. I made him easy and satisfied, had his blessing, from time to time visited him, 2 3 and

[1] John, the rector of Eythorne. [2] Peter Fector. I cannot suggest who S. P. was.

4 times a day, attended him sundry times he called on and for me, took care to say nor advance any thing or subject y^t might give him the least concerne. He suffered extremely the first 8 or 12 days by the discharge of urine, afterwards less pain and fell weaker, I dayly spoke with Mr Broadly about consulting Dr Lynch, Dr Bernard etc., discharged all the duties of a son towards the best of fathers, advised and consulted him all I could, and would have proposed a more regular forme of will but he was not in a condition at any one time to enter into perticulars of a thing of y^t consq^e, he worded on several occasions perticulars I took downe in writting in a book I may annex to this or take out abstract.

Latterly 10 or 15 days before he died he was extremely light headed flighty and delirious, and in his poor head he had infinite number of transaction of buisseness imperfectly, disturbing him constantly to the very last, with all wch there was always some intervalls of quite free and composed thought, and thro the whole illness and pain there never was a more pious patient docille man examplary to all, praying with zeal and fervency and most hartily praying God to del^r him out of this world and to ease him of his misery, wondering often why providence should retain him so long and praying for his end. He would always see us, but finding his situation grieved us he would not chose we should be witnesses to his misery. 2 days or 3 before he expired he was extreme low and bad, took little nourishment and after all on the 8 of April 1745 at 5 of the clock this dear man did expire and died in the 85 year of his age being born $\frac{8}{15}$ 7ber 1660 as much regreted and lamented and as much beloved as ever man was, and more knowne by near 60 years settlem^t at Dover, y^e greatest passage by land and sea of any in Europe; has been as serviceable to mankind in general, charitable to poor travellers, father to french and foreigne prisoners, relief and comfort to poor and distressed townspeople, the father and giver of employ and bread to many familys in Dover, etc.

He was on the 13 Ap^r buried from his house, in the grave near my d^r mother in the Parish Church of St Mary the virgin, Mr Wm Byrch min^r doing the office, and who was one of my father's friends and companions. S^d Mr Birch dayly called to see us B^r M. and self and enquire after my d^r father as did several as well at London as here, pert^y J. Chauvel and 20 more. Messrs Matson, Dalglish,

Underdowne, Gay, and the gent^n of the towne, as well as the comonalty, every one speaking well and affectionately of him. The pall bearers invited by my orders consult^s Mr I. M. were Mayor Cap. Cuthbert Hodgson, Coll. Richd. Hollingbey, Cap. John Dalglish, Goddard Gay and John Matson Esqs. and John Walton; mourners B^r I. M. his spouse myself and Coz. Mary Detrier, Pr Fector, R. Colbran, 2 maid servants, and Mis Detrier's servant, make 4 coaches and 4 horses attending the herse and 6 horses set out at 10 o'clock evening and returned home at 11½ o'clock at night.

The herse and coaches were adorned with scutchons 30 on buckram, and 12 silk over for the pall bearers, desk cloth, and the desk hung [with] 4 escutchons and black cloth and a hatchment over the door in all *l*.12. 17. od. The body was conveyed with 24 porters carrying 24 links or flambeaux who had gloves, also ye pall bearers with crapes, scarves: rings—B^r M. wife, self, M.D.^{1} Pr Fector and R. Colbran and Mr El. Veel had rings, also the 2 clarks each mourning, (5*l.*) the 2 maids mourning (50*s.* each) Mr Birch read the funeral service, Candles in ye church, rings given to friends of the deceased as per margent, the whole bill of funeral and its apendages am^o to *l.* [*blank*] as per acc^t in a bundle with those of my late d^r mother.^{2}

This is a copy of what was in the paper called The Kentish Post or Canterbury News letter from Wed. 10 Apl. to Saturday 13 April 1745. No 2862 printed by J. Abree, Cant. 12 April:—

'On Monday last dyed at Dover in the 85 year of his age Mr Isaac Minet for many years an eminent merchant, in which profession he was universaly known and esteemed not only by persons in trade but by those of the first rank in most parts of the world His excellent judgment, his integrity and openness of hart rendered him a most valuable friend, and his sweetness and cheerfulness of temper an amiable and improving companion. He was constant and devout in the practice of Religion, charitable to the poor and benevolent to all. He discharged the dutys of his station as a kind husband, a tender parent, an indulgent master, an upright magistrate, and a sincere christian in such a manner, that as few men have gone thro the world more usefully, and left it with more innocence. So being thus endowed with every amiable quality,

---

[1] Mary Destrier.
[2] There is nothing written in the 'margent,' and the accounts no longer remain.

he lived beloved and dyed lamented by his family and friends and every lover of religion and virtue.'[1]

So ended a long and prosperous life, of which it has been possible to gather out of the past sufficient to enable us to form some estimate of a character which may be taken as typical of the Huguenots who came out of France for the sake of their religion. Isaac Minet was not gifted with extraordinary abilities in any one direction—he would never have been a great thinker, a great statesman, or a great soldier—but he had combined in him those qualities which tend to success in any condition of life and under any circumstances. We must place first his uprightness in all dealings, his strict adherence to principle—qualities we should expect to find in those who have chosen to suffer for conscience' sake. Without these qualities the success he attained would be impossible; but other gifts are also necessary, and these the position he wrought for himself at Dover proves him to have possessed. Wide observation, and the power of learning from what he observed—in a word, a knowledge of the value of experience; the gift of organisation and of method; perseverance, and a great attention to, and grasp of, detail—these were the qualities which, added to his faithful uprightness, led him to success in business. Nor must we forget another element in his character. The instances of his kindness to his relatives make us feel sure that in his contact with the world he was gentle, sympathetic, and ready to help; while the modesty which is apparent in every word he wrote completes a character which, for strength and sweetness, stands as an abiding example to all his descendants. His portrait has been preserved to us, and is reproduced as the Frontispiece of this book. He seems to be wearing the famous 'corporation gowne,' and if this is so, the picture cannot have been painted earlier than 1709. The original picture remained at Dover, in the Pier House, where it had probably been hung when it was painted; but on the expiration of the long tenancy of the Fectors it seems to have been regarded as their property, and was removed to Maxwelton House, Dumfriesshire, Scotland, where it remained till 1874, when Mrs. Laurie very kindly presented it to James L. Minet, in the possession

---

[1] The following notice of his death appears in the *Gentleman's Magazine* for 1745; xv. 220; 'Mr. Isaac Minet, at Dover, aged eighty-four. He truly deserved the character of an honest and good man, and very few have gone thro' the world more usefully or left it with more innocence.'

of whose son it now is.¹ The painting is neither signed nor dated, and has evidently, at one time, been in an oval frame considerably smaller than the present square one. As a painting the picture may claim some merit, and, so far as one can judge, the likeness must be good. The scroll in the hand has written on it, 'Rappel de l'edit.'

Isaac was buried in St. Mary's Church, Dover, beneath a stone in the centre aisle, which vanished under the hands of the 'restorers' in 1840. A copy of the inscription was preserved, and will be found in the Appendix.²

A tablet erected to him has, happily, survived, but has been 'restored' from its original position, over the vestry-door, to the wall of the south aisle, where it is now so placed as to be undecipherable without the aid of a ladder. A copy of the inscription on this will also be found in the Appendix.²

---

¹ Mr. J. L. Minet attached great importance to this picture, as the following memorandum in his handwriting shows: 'On Tuesday, 5th July, 1871, accompanied by my sister, Susan Mantell, call on Miss Fector at Croydon, and ask her if she would use her influence with her sister-in-law, the widow of late John Minet Fector Laurie, to induce that lady to let me have the Portrait of my Great Great Grandfather, now in her possession. On Monday, 17th of July, Miss Fector calls on me in return, and states that Mrs. Laurie, whom she has seen, will let me have the Portrait in question (Isaac Minet), now in a panel in one of the rooms at Maxwelton House, Dumfriesshire, Scotland, on applying to her, and stating that I have a house in which I am prepared to hang it up. J. MINET.'

'18th July, 1871.'

² Page 218.

CHAPTER VI

THE SAUCHELLES

Thus may you know by whom they were, and what they were long agone.
W. LAMBARDE.

THE present chapter can, in the main, be of interest only to lovers of strict and minute genealogical accuracy. Those, however, whose tastes lie in this direction will study with some interest the ancestors of Marie Sauchelle, who form its subject; for, thanks to the care with which the Sauchelle records were preserved, we can reach back to 1553 as a definite date; while behind this, again, stand three undated generations which carry us back to the middle of the fifteenth century.

The task of unravelling the Sauchelle genealogy has not been an easy one, and this for several reasons. The notes have been made by at least four hands, and it is difficult in all cases to assign them to their proper authors. Moreover, after the death of Marie Sauchelle (1738), who was the last to add to them, they passed into the hands of her son, William Minet, who had them copied into the book whose history has been related in the first chapter. The intention was as praiseworthy as the result has been disastrous, for the order in which they now are, as well as the errors due to the copyist, have but added another difficulty to the task of disentangling them.

Consisting, as they do, almost entirely of mere entries of births, marriages, and deaths, it has been a serious question how far it were worth while to reproduce what are but the dry-bones of genealogy, otherwise than in the tables given on page 206, of which they form the foundation. Here and there, however, these dry-bones become clothed upon with some touch of diction or of sentiment which makes the past age live, and this, added to the wish to preserve to future generations the *ipsissima verba* of the old book, which is the foundation of all our story, must be the excuse for giving them in full.

The arrangement of these records in any definite order has been a task of considerable difficulty, and, even grouped into families and arranged in chronological sequence as they now are, the reader will find it no easy matter to follow them; the only hope of mastering them will lie in a constant reference to Tables *H* and *I*. The collection of the records was, we have seen, due to four persons, and a few words of explanation on this head will help to make their story clearer. Jean Sauchelle the elder (1595–1673) began the task, which after his death was continued by his son, Jean Sauchelle the younger (1639–1679), to whose hand most of the entries are due. His sister Elizabeth, who survived her brother forty-four years, took over the papers her grandfather and brother had collected, and added to their contents, and on her death, in 1723, left them to her niece, Marie Minet, who added the final entries to her father's, grandfather's, and aunt's work. To Marie succeeded her son William, whose share in the work was touched upon above; and from his day till now they have remained as his copying-clerk left them. To William we owe one addition, in the form of a preface, which, though given here as the introduction to the Sauchelle story, should be read in connexion with the remarks upon William himself which follow later. This preface reads as follows:—

> Here followeth a true copy of 10 small leaves in a very old manuscript book wrote by our grandfather Mr Jean Sauchelle father to our late d^r mother Mrs Mary Sauchelle Minet wife to our late d^r father Mr Isaac Minet of Dover which I, William Minet, his youngest son have had inclination to copy out and preserve for my owne and our familys satisfaction and handing it down to such of the family as may like or take pleasure in such innocent recreation, and at the time of any great and sudden change in familys, calls to mind many epochs passages of births marriages deaths funeralls, which are often times the occasion of serious and mature reflections tending to a thought of ones latter end, the vanity of the too much building on the things of this life, making ones wills, altering them, and other things of serious contemplation as I have often experienced; and do believe the care of preserving to ones posterity such annalls is quite lawfull and a recomendable thing, and were to be wished more time was by many people employed that way rather than in other idle loose and frivolous discourses, all wch tho wrote on and at the time of my ever dear fathers decease yet am I, and was I of that oppinion, at all the times of my life

See fol. [*blank*] the history of my owne times and transactions [1] and amongst my papers are sundry papers writtings and memo. of this sort, but being engaged in much buissnes from 12 May 1730 my d^r Br D. M. died in London I have not had so much time or opportunity to do it, tho there is not a little of my writtings at my house in London.

My acquaintance being large, my buissnes prety much in detail and divided in many articles have not had the proper assistents in writting clarks as I could expect, some being idle sots as Dowse, Edes, and T. G. Border; some not able as young Edes, T. Bod, A. D. etc. and some whose healths would not permit 'em as M. H. D. E. T. etc. I have great and good reason to bless and thank God for infinite more mercys, pleasures, advantage, than I deserve, and was it not for my very bad fits of gout and rather too much occupation for want of proper help, and the difficulty of putting 'em off for others on acc͞t of their wanting me, and out of gratitude for faithfullness, I might live and be one of the most happy men in Lond^o having no ambition y^t would lead me to disturb my life nor not minding *le quandira ton* when I think I've done nothing to deserve it on which footing I am lookt on by my friends and acquaintance in London and who like my d^r d^d father.

By an error of William's clerk, the records were not copied after this preface, but in another part of the book, where we find another short preface :—

Here follows the copys of some old scattered books handed downe in the family of my dear father and mother, wch as more than one in the family may be glad to have 'em, and that they will be better preserved I, W. M. one of my d^r father's executors thought proper to copy 'em in this book for my owne and others satisfaction 13 April 1745.

W^t follows is out of a longish parchm^t cover book, very old, wch I marked in the inside of the vellum covert as in margent 'W. M. 1745.'

On this second preface follow William's copies of the original entries. These refer chiefly to the Sauchelle family, but partly also to the Dela-

[1] This history does not seen to have been written, at any rate it is not contained, in the old book, where there is ample space for it.

portes, from whom Jean Sauchelle's mother was descended, the two families being connected, as was so frequently the case in the Protestant society of this district, by more than one intermarriage.

The earliest document is a letter written from Calais by Jean Sauchelle the elder, which strikes for us the keynote of the Sauchelles' love of recording their family history. The 'tableau' mentioned in the opening sentence must have been some sort of family tree, illustrated heraldically and possibly with portraits, such as were common in Germany at the time :—

Mon cousin, par memoire, j'ay achete a pris d'argent le tableau de nos ancestres provenant de la maison ma tente Jenne Sauselle.

Nos Bysayeuls	{ Baudar Pieman { Antoinette sa femme, du ponsue
Nos Ayeuls	{ Jean Sauchelle { Antoinet Pieman sa femme, fille de Baudar Pieman
Nostre grandpere	{ Jacques Sauchelle { Caterine Maquet sa femme, fille de Christofle Maquet

Lesquels engendrerent

Mourut	Naquit	
1616	1553	Marie Sauchelle
1625 pentecote	1555	Jean Sauchelle
1626 25 Fev^r	1558	Jenne Sauchelle
1619 18 Juliet	1561	Gilbert Sauchelle
1625 Janv^r	1567	Joos Sauchelle
	1569	Catherine Sauchelle

Mon Cousin, vous me feriez plaisir sy en cas vous me pouvez ecrire le nom de la feme Baudar Pieman nostre bis-ayeul et le nom de leur fille la feme [de] Jean Sauchelle nostre ayeul, et les poser sy dessus ; le pintre quy a fait la painture estoit un moyen fils de Baudar Pieman ; et frere de nostre ayeuls. Je vous prie sy pouvez avoir aussy nom et le poser aussy sur le papier et me les renvoyer a loisir, je vous prie et vous seray et demeure aussy oblige a toujours. Encore mon cousin que ne somes point venue de race illustre et noble sy est ce que nous somes venue, Dieu mercy, des gens craignans Dieu, nayant point fait tort a personne par banqueroute ou autre lache et meschant tours. Courage mon cousin ! je voy encore fleurir les Sauchelles come le cedre au Liban ; cherchons devant toute chose le regne de Dieu.

Vostre a comandement.

jean Sauchelle cousin et amis.

Cest une copie qu'on a envoyé a mon pere et moy à Calais de Mildelb^g apellé j. S. sy dessus.

Unfortunately, this letter is not dated, a circumstance which adds to the other difficulties raised by it. It was clearly sent by Jean Sauchelle the elder to a cousin at Middelburg, and returned to the writer with the required information filled in. It must have been written before 1661, as certainly by that date the writer had migrated with his family from Calais to Flushing. The note added at the end by Jean, the writer's son, would seem from its wording to be contemporary with the document, but Jean the younger was only born in 1639. Jenne Sauchelle, from whose house the 'tableau' had come, died, as the letter itself tells us in 1626. On the whole, but not without considerable hesitation, I am inclined to think that the final note was added by Jean the younger when the letter came into his possession with his father's other papers, and that its date is much earlier. It establishes one fact, namely, that whatever its date may be, there were Sauchelles established at that time both at Calais and at Middelburg. This question of the settlement of various branches of the family at Calais, Flushing, and Middelburg, and their migrations between these towns, remains a constant difficulty in disentangling their story.

The information asked for was supplied, and the pedigree returned to its writer with the names of Baudar Pieman's wife and daughter filled in; and thus we have the pedigree of the Sauchelle family for four generations, down to Jacques the younger, though it will be noticed that his name—which should come in the list given in the letter between those of Gilbert and Joos—is for some reason omitted. We are, however, able to supply the omission from notes of Jean the younger, who tells us of his grandfather Jacques's birth, marriage, and death, adding a list of his children:—

> Mon grandpere jacques Sauchelle fut née le 13 jour de fevrier 1564 entre 7 heures du matin, son parain jaques Blanet.
>
> Mon grandpere jacques Sauselle sy dessus épousa le 20 janvier 1587 Marie Dumon fille de p^{re} Dumon, sa mere Marguerite Planquielle etc.
>
> Mon grandpere Jacq^t sauselle et ma grandmere Marie Dumon, pere et mere de mon pere jean Sauselle sont mort savoir, 30 janvier 1625 deceda mon grandpere de cette valée, 24 Fev^r 1626 deceda ma grandmere.
>
> Mon grandpere et grandmere sy hault engendrer les enfans

quy sen suivent, tiré extrait du livre de mon pere jean Sauselle, savoir

26 Fev^r	1589	est nee Jacques Sauselle, mon oncle.
9 Mars	1591	est nee pierre Sauselle, oncle.
23 Oct^r	1592	est nee Marguerite Sauselle, tante.
18 Julliet	1594	est nee Anne Sauselle, tante.
Oct^r	1595	est nee jean Sauselle, mon pere.
16 Nov^r	1597	est nee Noé Sauselle, oncle.
26 Dec^r	1599	est nee Catherine Sauselle, tante.

After giving this notice of his grandfather and grandmother, and of the births of their children, Jean deals with three of his uncles and aunts, children of Jacques :—

Mon oncle jacques Sauselle espousa a Calais la fille de Louis de les Bec[1] le [*blanc*] jour de Nove 1619 age de 20 an, sapelez delebec.

Mon oncle pierre Sauselle epousa en amsterdam la fille de joos falbier apelé Caterine falbier le 22 May 1622.

Mort du frere de mon pere. Le 1er de Juin 1645 deceda de cette Valée noe Sauselle, et il laissa des enfans noe, jean, jacques, pierre, marie, anne, catherine Sauselle mes cousines et c. germain.

These three entries throw some little light on the difficulty referred to above, namely the settlements of the Sauchelles. Of this generation, the Guines Registers enable us to prove that Jacques, the eldest son, remained in Calais. They do not, it is true, give us the date of his death, probably for the reason that this occurred before 1668, but they tell us that his widow died at Calais, September 26, 1670; and to the daughter Marie, to be mentioned by Jean Sauchelle presently, they enable us to add the names of three more children:—1. Jacques, b. 1621, d. at Calais December 20, 1678; 2. Jean, b. 1625, d. at Calais May 15, 1675; 3. Jeanne, d. at Calais September 18, 1669. Pierre, the next brother, removed to Amsterdam, where the registers show us the births of two of his children [2]; while as to Noé, it seems probable that he remained in Calais, though his son, another Noé, removed to Flushing at a later date.

[1] The de le Becques were a Protestant family of Calais. A Louis de le Becque is spoken of twice in Isaac's Narrative (see pages 26, 36), where we are told that he was 'a worthy gentleman who had a numerous familly who had a daughter maryed to a Captn of a Company of Suisses of 200 men'; though this must have been a son of the Louis whose daughter Jacques Sauchelle married. Solomon de le Becque—perhaps a brother of the Louis spoken of by Isaac—came to Dover, and was minister of the French Church there from 1685 to 1692.

[2] The Amsterdam Registers contain many entries of Sauchelles. On June 3, 1630, is given the baptism of Joost, son of Pierre Sauchelle and Catryna Felbier, here mentioned, and on July 27, 1640, another son, Johan, is baptised.

Having thus spoken of three of his uncles and aunts, Jean follows with the story of his own father, and of his mother, Catherine Delaporte. The Delaportes were a Lille family, with which the Sauchelles became connected by other marriages, and about them Jean has much to say; first, however, he tells us of his father's birth and marriage :—

Mon pere son nom estoit jean Sauselle, fils de jacq' Sauselle, quy fut nee l'an 1595 en oct' le lundy a 10 heures du matin, il epousa ou il prit a femme une jeune fille nomme Catherine de la porte, natif de lille age de 18 an environs ; je dit l'espousa le 29 Sept' 1630. Elle estoit née le 10ᵉ d'Aoust 1612, ses pere et mere estoit otto de la porte et Madeline Deschamps a nostre mere.

Before dealing with the notices of his brothers and sisters which Jean the younger gives, it will be well to collect those relating to his mother's family, the Delaportes. The first is a notice of the death of Nicholas Deschamps, who is described by Jean as his uncle, but who must have been his mother's uncle, and his own great-uncle :—

Mort de mon oncle Nicholas deschamps, il est decedé le juin 1663 a Mildeb., il nous a laissé par testam' chacun *l*. [*blanc*], jay copie du testament, et a mon grand l[ivre].

Next we have notices of the deaths of two of his mother's sisters. The Noé Sauchelle whom Jacqueline married in 1649 must have been, not Jean's brother of that name, who died in 1645, but his son, another Noé :—

Mort de ma tante Jacquelinne Delaporte soeur de ma mere, elle est decedé 9 Mars 1655, elle avait esté marié l'an 1649 avec noe Sauselle le 4 aoust, neveu de mon pere, elle a laisse un fils.

Mort de mon oncle Beurse et sa femme Madelaine Delaporte soeur de ma mere, savoir—

L'an 1660 le 19ᵉ Octobre est decedé Arnoult Bourse.
L'an 1666 le 20 juillet est decedé sa femme ma tante.

Ils on laisse divers enfans, Arnoult, Gab¹, Madelaine, Francois, et Mary Beurse.

Bateme de l'enfans du cousin francois Beurse d'un garcon apellé Guillaume donc je suis parain en place de son frere Gabriel Beurse. Batise le [*blanc*] Fev' 1676.

Following on this is a notice of the family of Gabriel Delaporte.

another brother of his mother's. We are not told who this Gabriel married, but it would seem from these entries that his son, also named Gabriel, lived in London: and this is further supported by the fact that, at the baptism in Flushing of one of the Wanbeck children in 1676, Noé Sauchelle stands godfather, in place of Gabriel Delaporte of London :—

> Mariage de Susanne delaporte niece de mon pere, ma cousine germaine, elle a este marie le 15 Fev^r l'an 166[*blanc*] a Mildel^g avec un nomé Maximilian van Wanbeck, secretaire de ostcapel vilage de Mildel^g.[1]
>
> L'age de Susanne Delaporte sy dessus et de ses freres et soeurs engendré par gabriel delaporte; cette en Engleterre tiré du livre de l'oncle jan.[2]
>
> Susanne est née le 1 julliet 1641.
> Gabriel delaporte son frere est née 26e Sep 1642.
> Marie delaporte sa soeur est nee 2e Fevrier 1645.

This Susanne Delaporte, who became Madame Wanbeck, had two children, whose births are next noticed, and to one of whom Jean Sauchelle became godfather, three years before his death :—

> Bateme de 2 enfans de Suzanne porte ; le 3 Mars 1676 je suis temoin du garcon ou parain de l'enfans du cousin Wanbech et de susanne delaporte, il a nom Johan, Dieu le benie.
>
> Le cousin Noé Sauselle fils et [est] parain de fille apelle Sara en place de gab^l delaporte, de Londres.

Two more of his mother's brothers, Jean and Otto, appear in the following notices :—

> Mariage de l'oncle jean delaporte en Amst^m a esté le 20 Nov^e 1674 avec une fille apellé piternel groundich come l'oncle ma dit luy meme icy. A esté icy a flesingue avec sa feme le 21 Aoust 1675.
>
> Mort de l'oncle delaporte a Midel^g il deceda de cette valée de misere le Vendredy 3 de juin l'an 1678 apres avoir esté 8 a 10 jour malade, il passa doucement avec conoisance ou j'estoit present ; il a fait un testament le 28 May lan 1678, par notaire Wm Cramers du

---

[1] The Middelburg Registers give February 26, 1664, as the date.

[2] This 'oncle jan' I cannot account for as being in England ; the only Jean I am aware of married at Amsterdam, and, as we are told almost immediately, was on a visit to Flushing in 1675, though he may, of course, have been in London at some time.

dit Mildelbᵍ par ou il nous dona la demy de ses biens a moy et a mes trois soeur Marie Elizabeth Jenne Sauselle, et suis second executeur apʳ le testament en ma casse aux long.¹

Mort de la feme de l'oncle Otto delaporte a Midelb. elle se nome Anne pÿl Van Ameide, estoit de gorcome,² elle estoit une feme riche de 100,000 ecus quand l'oncle l'epouza, elle est morte le lundy 2ᵉ juillet 1679 et enterré le 11ᵉ juillet a l'eglise francoise a Midelᵍ.³

Finally, he chronicles for us the death of his mother's father and mother (Otto and Madelaine Delaporte), and tells us the cost of the tomb which his grandfather had bought, and in which some of the Sauchelles themselves seem to have been buried.

Mort de nostre grandpere Otto delaporte a flesingue, pere de ma mere, et de ma grandmere, savoir le 20 xbʳᵉ 1650 est decede nostre g̃pere Otto delaporte ; le 23 janvier 1652 est decede nostre g̃mere Madelaine deschamps fem̃e de mon grandpere Otto delaporte.

Memoire, que le tombeau quy est dans l'eglise francoise de flessingue a couté a mon grand pere laporte 14*l*. degros, les pierre son No 12 et 13 apartient aux cornent encore [*sic*].¹

Evidently the Sauchelle-Delaporte connexion was very close, but here again the difficulty is to know when the Delaportes came to Flushing from Lille. The Delaporte entries which Jean Sauchelle gives us, and which have just been quoted, are all connected with Flushing, Middelburg, and the Low Countries, and the earliest in date of them is 1650, the date of the death of Otto Delaporte, who must have come to Flushing, with all his children, some time after 1612.

Having finished with the Delaportes, we may now return to the main line of the Sauchelles, and deal with the minute but somewhat uninteresting catalogue of his father's children which Jean has preserved for us. Unfortunately, we are not told where the births of these children took place, and therefore this list throws no light on the problem when Jean Sauchelle removed from Calais to Flushing ; we may, however, infer that he was drawn there not only by the presence of his wife's

---

¹ *i.e.* at full length.
² Gorinchem, or Gorkum, a town in the province of South Holland, on the river Waal.
³ This entry must be by Elizabeth Sauchelle, as Jean Sauchelle, her brother, had died on June 30 in this year.
⁴ Clearly a copyist's error ; ' cornent ' should, perhaps, read ' caveau.' The vault must have been a large one, and perhaps extended under both stones.

family, but also by the fact of his uncle and cousins living there, as appears from the entries of the births at Flushing of six children of Joos Sauchelle, 1593–1608 :—[1]

Mon pere jean Sauselle et ma mere Caterine de la porte engendrer les enfans quy sensuivrons come jay tire du livre de mon d' pere, savoir—

8 Sepr 1631 est nee gabriel Sauselle par un lundy aux matin, son parin fut grandpere Gabriel deschamps, et marine feme de jacques Sauselle, M. Becq.

Ma mere accoucha d'une fille a 2 heures du matin le 20 Dec. 1632 son nom fut Catherine Sauselle, son parin fut Noé Sauselle frere de mon pere, et marine Madelaine Deschamps mere de ma mere.[2]

Ma mere accoucha dun fils a 2 heures du matin le 1er de fev^r 1634; son nom fut nomme jean, son parin fut jacq^s Sauselle frere de mon pere, et marine Madeleine de la porte soeur de ma mere.

Ma mere accoucha d'une fille a $2\frac{1}{4}$ heures du matin le 2 Novr 1635; son nom fut Caterine, son parin fut Nicholas deschamps,[3] et sa marine cath. Sauselle soeur de mon pere.

Ma mere accoucha d'une fille a $12\frac{3}{4}$ d'heure de la nuit le 12 Octr 1637; son nom fut Marie, son parin Michel heusch,[4] et marine la feme de p^{re} Sauselle frere de mon pere.

Ma mere accoucha d'un fils a $8\frac{3}{4}$ heures du matin le 1er Aoust 1639; son nom fut jean Sauselle, parain thomas l'Aoust, sa maraine la feme de Nicholas Deschamps oncle. Le jean Sauselle sy dessus et [est] moy quy escrit sesy.

Ma mere accoucha d'une fille a 2 heures du matin le 8 Fev^r 1642; son nom fut Madelaine, son parain Otto de la porte [5] et sa marine Madelaine Marischal feme de jean Eyghs d'Amsterdam.

Ma Mere accoucha d'un fils a 6 heures du soir le 1er Sept 1643;

---

[1] The Flushing Registers contain two more curious Sauchelle entries: on October 10, 1661, is the admission, as a member of the Church there, of a Noé Sauchelle, 'venant de Cales,' who was, perhaps, the Noé Sauchelle who married Jacqueline Delaporte; and on December 13, 1664, occurs the entry of the admission of Jean and Gabriel Sauchelle, whom I am quite unable to identify.

[2] Note the care with which the exact hour of birth is recorded; perhaps an unconscious survival of the habit referred to by Mr. A. Lang in his *Books and Bookmen* (London, 1886), p. 27, where he says: 'Sometimes the time of a birth was recorded with much minuteness, that the astrologers might draw a more accurate horoscope.'

[3] Great-uncle.   [4] Husband of Jeanne De la Porte.   [5] Uncle.

son nom fut jacques, son parain jean l'Aoust, marine jacqueline de la porte soeur de ma mere.

Ma mere accoucha d'une fille a 8 heure du soir le 3 Decr 1644; son nom fut Catherine, son parain jean Delaporte frere de ma mere et marine jenne de la porte fem̄e de M. heusch.

Ma mere accoucha d'un fils a 5¼ d'heure du soir le 9 Sepr 1646; son nom fut Jacques, son parain Arnoult Beurse et marine Jacqueline delaport.

Ma mere accoucha d'une fille a 2½ heures du matin le 25 Janv^r 1648; son nom fut Elizabeth, son parain fut Jacques Delaporte frere de ma mere, et sa marine Marie Sauselle niece de mon pere fille de jacques Sauselle son frere.

Ma mere accoucha d'une fille a 10½ heures du soir le 14 Mars 1651; son nom fut Jenne Sauselle, son parin fut Cornils deglarge, sa maraine jenne Delaporte fem̄e du cousin heusch.

Having given the entries of the births of his brothers and sisters and of himself, Jean next sums them up in the following table:—

Courte explication des noms et ages de mes freres et soeurs, savoir—

1	8	Sept	1631 est née Gabriel Sauselle
2	20	Dec	1632 est née Catherine Sauselle
3	1er	Fevrier	1634 est née Jean Sauselle
4	2^e	Nov	1635 est née Catherine Sauselle
5	12	Oc^{re}	1637 est née Marie Sauselle
6	1er	Aoust	1639 est née ma personne Jean Sauselle
7	8	Feb^r	1642 est née Madelaine Sauselle
8	4	Sept^r	1643 est née Jaques Sauselle
9	3	Dec^r	1644 est née Catherine Sauselle
10	9	Sept^r	1646 est née Jacques Sauselle
11	25	Janv^r	1648 est née Elizabeth Sauselle
12	14	Mars	1651 est née Jenne Sauselle

Se sont icy les enfans que mon pere jean Sauselle et ma mere Catherine Delaporte ont procrée ensemble suivent que j'en ay tiré la copie du meme livre de mon pere de son ecriture.

Of their marriages and deaths he does not tell us with like precision; Gabriel, the eldest, is alone dealt with fully:—

Mort de mon frere Gabriel Sauselle, il est decedé le 16 du dist Aoust 1668 entre les 6 a 7 heures du soir subitement. Il estoit marié a flesingue avec une vefue apelé Riche Jan, qui estoit la vefue d'un Lambrecht avant; il se maria le 31e juillet 1663 a l'eglise de flessingue il nous a laissé par testam^t chacun 150l., nous ayant mis dehors, j'en ay testament.

Of the other members of this somewhat numerous family, all but four must have died before 1673, as appears from the entry of his father's death in that year :—

Mort de mon pere jean Sauselle, il deceda de cette valée de misere le lundy 13 de Mars 1673 entre 11¾ a 12 heures de midy a flessingue avec grand conoissance jusqua la fin ; a esté une Mort douce, estant use de viellesse. Je l'ay fait enterer avec ma mere, je dis aux meme tombeau de grand pere Laporte. Il ma laisse moy jean Sauselle, et Marie, Elizabeth, et Jenne.

His mother had died previously :—

Morte de nostre chere mere Catherine Delaporte, elle deceda de cette valée de misere a flesingue le 19e Septr 1661 entre 8 a 9 heures du matin avec grand connoissance. Elle estoit fort craignant Dieu, Dieu nous fasse la grace d'ensuivre ses traces. Amen.

We now come to Jean Sauchelle the younger himself; and first let us notice the feeling of pride with which he speaks of his family's connexion with Calais. He tells us of his grandfather, Jacques Sauchelle :—

Memoire, que mon grandpere Jacq^s Sauselle et sa femme rendire Serment de fidelité au Roy pardevant M^r le president a Calais l'an 1609 en cela nous avons franchise come un vray francois ; le president estoit lors Louis le Beaucler,[1] pierre Colin estoit le procureur ; est copy du pere.

By the following note of his son-in-law, Isaac Minet, it would seem that their franchise was still more firmly established, as the father himself had been admitted a bourgeois of Calais :—

Jehan Sauchelle fils de Jacques Sauchelle et de Mary dumont ses pere et mere as esti receu Bourgeois a Calais le 29^m Decembre mil six cent trente huit, selon la lettre de bourgeoisy en parchemin que j'ay entre mes mains ce jour 28^m Octobre 1730.

ISA. MINET.

Led^t Jacques Sauchelle nee a Tournay en Flandre.

---

[1] Lefebvre (*Hist. de Calais*, vol. ii. p. 463) confirms this, stating that Louis le Beauclerc was appointed in 1605 ; he does not, however, state who was procureur in 1609.

The connexion with Calais was renewed by Jean in his marriage with Sara, daughter of Isaac Sigart. The Sigarts were one of the leading Protestant families there, the head of it being Isaac, 'ancien' of the Church of Guines, as we learn from an entry of a marriage in the Registers of the French Church at Dover of Sept. 11, 1659 (p. 15), where we are told that the marriage took place 'par tesmoignage du Consistoire de Calais,' the 'tesmoignage' being signed by 'P. Tricotel pasteur, Isaac Sigart, Scribe Hays, Michel Poree, et Pierre le Duc, antiens.'

Isaac Sigart's brother, François, appears also in the list of 'anciens' of the same Church, 1660–1681, referred to above; while Isaac the younger, his son, is spoken of in Isaac Minet's Narrative as a merchant of Calais, and as one who 'spoke with a great deal of prudence and courage.'

The Sigarts were not a very numerous family, and the subjoined table will make them clear, and show the Minet-Sauchelle-Sigart relationship.[1]

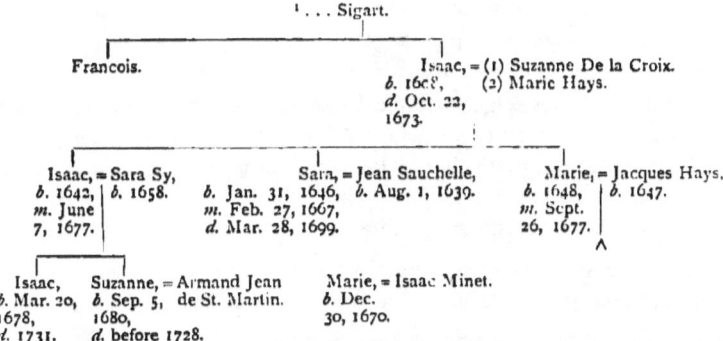

[1] ... Sigart.

The families of Sigart and Hays were as strongly Huguenot as the Minets. Witness the frequent mention of them in Isaac Minet's Narrative. It is, therefore, a little difficult to account for their remaining in Calais after 1685, as they undoubtedly did; but the friendship with the Minets was still kept up. Not only do we find Isaac Sigart and Jacques Hays standing as godfathers in 1696 and 1697 to two of Isaac Minet's children, but Isaac Sigart (the third), by his will, made in Calais, appoints 'Adrien Lernoult, merchant, living in London, and Isaac Minet, father, merchant at Dover,' his executors. Lernoult does not seem to have acted, but administration was granted to Isaac Minet on October 19, 1731. The will is recorded at Somerset House (Isham, 265), and from it we gather that the testator had no children. He bequeaths his property (presumably in England) to his nephews and nieces, children of his sister Suzanne, who had married Armand Jean de St. Martin, Sieur de Fréthun. Two of these only are named:—Henri, Captain of Light Horse in the regiment of the Prince de Conty, and Suzanne Louise, who were both twenty-five years of age at the date the will was made.

The relationship existing between the testator and Isaac Minet appears from the table given above. What relationship existed between the Sigarts and the Lernoults is not ascertained.

It is at this point that Jean Sauchelle's notes, dealing with matters with which he was personally acquainted, become fuller and more interesting. First, he tells us of his marriage; and from the fact of his being at Calais as a young man, and from his reference elsewhere to his father-in-law as the 'patron,' it may be suggested that he was engaged in some business capacity in his father-in-law's house:—

Moy Jean Sauselle ay pris a feme a Calais la fille du Sr Isaac Sigart et de suzanne delacroix ses pere et mere, et somes marié a l'eglise de guisne par le ministre nome tricotel[1] le 27 Fev^r 1667. Je dit que suis marie avec la fille Sigart nommé Sara Sigart age de 21 an, Dieu veuille que se soit pour sa gloire et nostre bien, Dieu veuille nous benir, Amen.

Ma feme Sara Sigart est née le dernier jour de janvier 1646, son parain a este Charles de la croix,[2] et Marine anthoinette de jormeaux, suivant un escrit que ma baillé son oncle franc. Sigart come ancien de l'eglisse. Je dis a este batisé le dernier de janvier l'an 1646.

Memoire, apres estre marié le 27 Fev^r 1667 j'ay demeuré a Calais chez mon beau pere Sigart j'usquau 2e juin l'an 1667 que je suis party pour flessingue pour y faire ma demeure, Dieu nous y veuille benir; et somes arrivé a Flessingue le [*blanc*] juin chez mon pere, ou jay demeuré jusquau 19e Novr l'an d^o que suis sorty pour demeurer a mon particulier, et la soeur Marie Sigart qui estoit venue avec nous, a demeuré toujours chez mon pere jusqua son partem^t pour Calais quy a esté le 23e xbre 1667 party pour Vlerchamernoire.[3]

The young couple were now established in their own home at Flushing, and Jean proceeds with an account of the birth of his chil-

The latter were a Calais family, Adrien Lernoult the father being mentioned more than once in Isaac Minet's Narrative. His wife was Madelaine Pilart (d. May 11, 1680); and he perhaps came to England, though it was his son Adrien, in all probability, who was executor to Isaac Sigart. This son married Margaret, daughter of Herman Olmius, and it was to his three children that Olmius left his house in Austin Friars, where, as we shall see later (page 152), Hughes Minet lived, partly as tenant and partly as owning one-sixth of the freehold. Adrien Lernoult the second died in 1755, and left three children: Adrien (d. 1755, leaving Mary and Elizabeth), John Drigue (d. 1782), and Elizabeth (m. Henry Evans).

[1] Pierre Tricotel was minister of the Church at Guines in 1659. See Registers of the French Church at Dover, page 15, where he signs a 'tesmoignage' for a marriage.

[2] Her uncle. The Delacroix were a very numerous family. The Guines Registers contain thirty-three entries of the name. One branch of the family came to Dover in 1685.

[3] Clearly a copyist's error; the latter part of the word may be 'à memoire,' a favourite phrase with Jean Sauchelle; the first part (if she returned by sea to Nieuport, and on by land through Furnes, as the Sauchelles did on a subsequent journey to Calais) may be Bergues, a town between Furnes and Calais. The word would then read, 'Bergues à memoire.'

dren, giving us with great minuteness the godparents, a custom which is a great help in fixing relationships in these old pedigrees :—

Moy jean Sauselle et Sara Sigart ma fem̄e avons engendré les enfans quy sensuivent, savoir—

Ma femme accoucha d'un fils a $4\frac{1}{3}$ heures du matin le 19 Octr lan 1667 ; son nom fut jean Sauselle son parain fut mon pere et moy, et sa marine fut Marie Sigart soeur de ma femme quy le presenter en place de Marie Hays[1] femme de mon beau pere, comme luy escrivit ; il fut batisé le 23 Octr a l'eglise de flessingue par Dumolin.

Mon enfant jean Sauselle p^r nee sy dessus est decedé de ce monde le 25e Aoust l'an 1668 agée de 10 mois.

Ma fem̄e accoucha d'un fils pour la seconde fois a $11\frac{1}{2}$ heures du soir le 30e jan^r 1669 ; son nom fut jean, batisé le 3 Fev^r 1669 dans l'eglise a flessingue, son parain estoit Danl Gatou et marine anne Pyl fem̄e de Otto de la porte, anne pil vandermede wan ameyde [*sic*].

This godmother's name has been given us before, in the note on her death,[2] and seems to have been Anne Pyl Van der Amede. The position of godparent was probably one of some honour, and the following note seems to show that Jean Sauchelle contrived to please both his own and his wife's relations by conduct which was, perhaps, scarcely straightforward :—

Memoire, que Gatou et la fem̄e de l'oncle otto ne sont quen place de mon beau pere Sigart et de Mad^e Larnes quy sont les vray parain de nostre jan com̄e je leur ay ecrit le 1 Febrier 1669, dont Gatou ny ma tante ne le scavent.

Ma feme accoucha pour la 3^e fois d'une fille a $12\frac{1}{4}$ d'heure de la presmidy le 30^e Decr 1670 ; son nom fut Marie ; son parain fut Otto delaporte et Riche Jans[3] sa marine. Memoire, du 31 xb^{re} jay ecrit a francois Sigart oncle et a Marie delacroix feme de C. Hays pour parain et marine, on luy a donne son nom aussy Marie.

Ma feme accoucha pour la quatrieme fois d'une fille a $4\frac{1}{2}$ heures de la presmidy come jetois a Mildel. le 4 may 1673 ; son nom fut

---

[1] Isaac Sigart had remarried after the death of Susanne Delacroix, his first wife.
[2] See page 85.   [3] Wife of Jean's brother, Gabriel.

Caterine, son parain fut Noé Sauselle mon cousin, et sa marine Suzanne delaporte ma cousine.

Mort de nostre petite fille Caterine Sauselle, est decedé a 10 heures du soir le 21 du mois d'Aoust l'an 1673 dans la ville de furnne dans un cabaré sur le marché apellé la rose Noble, le 22 courant je l'ay fait mettre en un coffre que je fis sitot faire, et la fit porter a Dunquerque par une feme apellé Anna, et la laissé la a Ma feme pour la faire enterer a Dunkerque le 22 ditto par les moyens du cousin Jacq⁸ Rollin, et party si tot de Dunquerque ou j'avois esté inconnito pour chez moi, pour flessingue, a cause de la guerre. J'avois conduit ma feme pour Calais avec Marie et Caterine, ou jeu cest perte en chemin sy prompte, ayant party de flessingue par le navire St Marie apartenant a jean hervieu le vendredy 18 Aoust par Ostende a 7 heures du matin, et arrivé en bonne sante la, 2 a 3 heures de midy le dit jour, et party le 21 Aoust d'Ostende par nieuport en carosse et de la pour furne ou la pauvre enfant est decede.

Memoire, que ma feme Sara Sigart a esté a Calais depuis que some marié les [18] Aoust 1673 est party d'icy, et je l'ay conduit jusqua dunquerque quoy que la guerre, elle a resté a Calais quelque mois chez son pere, et elle est arrivé icy a flesingue le 11 Jan^r 1674 ayant esté chercher jusqua Nieuport, je dis jay esté au devant come il se voit, pour de copie ou je lui ecrivois.

It was during this visit of Sara Sauchelle to her father in Calais that he died, as we are told:—

Mort de mon beau pere Isaac Sigart a Calais, je dis a guisnes, ou il tomba mort for subit le 23 Octr 1673 et fut aporté a Calais, ma femme estoit a Calais alors pour voir ses amis, et enterré le 24 Oct^r.[1]

Ma feme accoucha pour la 5e fois d'une fille a 9¾ d'heure du matin le 1e de Novr 1674; son nom fut Catrina nome, son parain Corniles govers beau fils de l'oncle Otto, et Marine ma soeur jenne Sauselle. Le lundy 12 9bre est morte a 4½ de la presmidy la dite Catherina.

Ma feme accoucha pour la 6e fois d'un garcon a 4 heures de midy le Dimanche 15 de Mars 1676; son nom est nome Robert, parain est Robt Hays et marine Marie Sigart ma belle soeur, come

[1] Cf. Guines Registers, p. 76.

je leur ay ecrit, en place ont esté le S^r francois Beurse et ma sœur Elizabeth Sauselle jay dit quelle est Marine ; batise le 22 Mars 1676.

Mon fils Robert sy desus est decedé de cette Valée de misere le 18e Septr 1676 a 10½ heure du matin ; 18 Sept a mem^{re}.

Ma feme accoucha pour la septieme fois d'un fils a 4½ heure du soir le 24 de jan^r 1678, et fut batisé le Dimanche 30e D^o ; son nom fut Isaac, represente par le cousin Maximil^n Wanbech et Elizabeth Sauselle, en place de ma cousine apellé Susanne Van teylingen, feme de jean Sauselle, et de Isaac Sigart mon beaufrere a Calais come je leur ay mandé et come il ont ecrit apert leur lettre.

So ends the record of the Sauchelles which Jean the younger has left us. From his hands the record passed to his sister Elizabeth, and her additions to her brother's work must now become our guide. First she tells us of her brother himself.

Mon cher frere Jean Sauselle est deceder de cette vallée de misere a Flesingue le 9e de Novr 1678 a 4 heures et demy du soir par un mercredy, a eu grande connoissance jusqua la fin et a eu une morte douce, il a parle encore une demy quart d'heur devans que mourir et moins. Je l'avons fait enterer dans le tombeau de mon grand pere la porte aupres de mon pere et de ma mere, il est deceder environ etant agee 39 an : il a laisse 3 enfans a savoir, Jean, Marie et Isaac tous fort jeune.

Marie is, of course, Marie Minet, who was nine years old at this date. She, too, has told us of her father's death, placing it a year later than her aunt does. It is from her also that we hear of the death of her mother, which took place at Dover, whither, as we have seen,[1] she had accompanied her daughter on her marriage :—

Mon pere jean Sauselle est decedé du monde et a esté enterré dans l'eglise francoise a flessingue le 30 juin 1679.

Le 28e de Mars 1699 a 5 heures du matin Dieu a retiré ma chere mere de ce monde et la mit en sa gloire. Elle a esté enterré dans le simitier de la paroisse S. Mary pres le frere et sœur de mon mary et un de mes enfans premier ne come en lautre part.

Ma chere mere etoit le janvier 1646 née le dernier jour du mois, son parain Charles delacroix et marine Antoinette desormeaux pour memoire a la posterité de mes enfans.

[1] See p. 60.

94   THE HUGUENOT FAMILY OF MINET

The death of one more sister is recorded by Elizabeth—that of Jenne, the youngest of the family, who had married Zacharie Grandidier, and who appears as godmother to Daniel, son of Isaac and Marie Minet, in 1699.[1]

Ma chere soeur est decede au Seigneur le 3ᵉ d'Aoust a 5 heures du matin 1711 elle a vecu et elle est morte en bonne Chrestienne, je dis ma soeur jenne Sauchelle femme de mon beau frere Zacharie Grandidier.

In the same year comes the record of her own husband's death.

Mon cher mary Pierre le Gay est decede au Seigneur le 19ᵉ de Mars 1711 a 10½ du soir d'une mort subite, Dieu nous fasse la grace de nous mettre tous en son Paradis. Cestoit un homme bien craignant Dieu de son vivant.

After this year (1711) there is no further record made by Elizabeth, who continued to reside at Berlin, where she married again—a David Guerard, 'periwig-maker'—and where she had charge of her nephew, James Minet, who went out to her in 1712 as a boy of fourteen.[2] She died in 1723, leaving Marie Minet, her niece, her heiress, to whom came, no doubt, the 'longish parchment cover book', in which is one last entry in the niece's writing:—

Madᵉ Le Gay ou Eliz. Sauselle, cette chere tante est décedé a Berlin, ma laissé son heritiere universelle, l'éternel l'aura recue en mercy, mon fils James Minet a fait enterrer honᵇˡᵉᵐᵗ elle étoit femme de Pʳᵉ Le Gay cy dessus.

[1] Registers of the French Church at Dover, p. 14.   [2] See p. 103.

CHAPTER VII

ISAAC MINET'S CHILDREN

*If with his Father's goods he doth possesse
His Goodness, all the world must then confesse
That that Sonnes Honor doth it selfe display
To be the Fathers equall every way.*—JOHN TAYLOR.

OF his six children, all born in Dover, Isaac has left very full accounts, which, with such information as it has been possible to gather from other sources, will form the matter of the present chapter.

Isaac, the eldest, born in 1694, had for godfather Thomas Minet of Canterbury, and for godmother, Madame Sauchelle, his grandmother; the child, however, lived only for eight months.

John, the second son, his father speaks of as follows:—

I, Isaac Minet at 32 years of age, the 16th of December 1691 maryed Mary Sauchelle daughter of Mr J^n Sauchelle of flessingue in Zealand, and of Sarah Sigart his wife, daughter of Mr Isaac Sigart of Calais. We were maryed at London by Mr David Campredon in ye french church of artillery ground Spitlefield and we came to Dover where I was establisht before in ye house of my brother Stephen; since wch time, by God's blessing we have lived in good credit and reputation, and have gott five sons now living, viz

John Minet borne ye 24 Sep^t 1695,[1] his godfather my brother Ambroise, godmother Mis Elizabeth Sauchelle, wife of Mr Peter Legay, she now living at Berlin.[2] Baptized 30 Sep^t. S^d John Minet is a studient now at the University of Cambridge about 4 years (1717).[3] He was curatt one year to Mr Dawling at ocum near Dover.

The 18th of August 1720 my eldest son John Minet, being

---

[1] Registers of the French Church at Dover, p. 13.
[2] She was Marie Minet's aunt.
[3] He took his B.A. degree in this year (1717), and his M.A. degree in 1721. He was a member of what was then called Catherine Hall, now St. Catherine's College.

aged about 25 years, gave me fifteen pounds to keep for him, it being the first money he hath earned for six months, from ab^t January last y^t he hath preached as curat for Mr Dolling at Ockum, Ewell, and Capell.[1] I prayse God for it, and pray his blessing may be continued on my s^d son . . . 15. 0. 0.
& he payd me since for ½ year more 15. 0. 0.
                                                                                    ─────────
                                                                                    30. 0. 0.

I have made good the 30l. above mentioned to my s^d son John Minet in his acct. I. M.

The 29th June he went to be curatt to Doct^r Wise at Canterbury; he bords with s^d Doct^r and hath 15l. p^r annum besides his bord.

He rec^d prists order from archbishop Wake in his chapell at Lambeth, I present, ye Sunday 20 May 1722, being Trinity Sunday. He was curatt to doctor Wise at Canterbury six months to Xmas 1722.[2] Y^e 14 xber 1722 I rec^d advice from Mr J^n Browne of Canterbury y^t counsell^r Willm Turner had that day given my s^d son the living of Eythorn near Waldershare, for wch living I am chiefly obliged to Sr Robert furness who first proposed it to me, and constantly recomended him to ye parishioners, especially to maj^r Rich^d harvey; I am next obliged to Mr Papilon ye son, and to his father, and very much to S^r philip york, solicit^r generall, to Mr Dale presbiter^n minist. at Canterbury by the recomandation of Mr Billingsby, to collonel Marsh, Mr Lavaure, Doct^r Wilkins, Mr Durant, Mr Macqueen for his certificat, Doct^r Cross for d^o, Captn James Lambe for his good will.

172⅔. After Xmas 1722 my s^d son went to London in order to have his institution etc^{ra}, he came home to dover ye 15 January, and the 17 D^o he was inducted in ye possession of ye Rectorage of Eythorn by Doct Thom. wise then of Canterbury in the presence of Mr David Campredon[3] minist. of Siberts wooll[4] alias Shepherds well Mr Stockwood precept^r of yong Mr furness, Edward maxted church warden of Eythorn, Doct^r Pemble chirurgeon

---

[1] Alkham, Ewell, and Capel-le-Ferne, villages near Dover. John Dauling was Vicar of Alkham, 1694-1727 (Capell was a chapel going with Alkham), and Vicar of Ewell, 1695-1726. Hasted adds that he was also Rector of Ringwould. See Hasted, *Hist. of Kent*, viii. 141, 146; ix. 436.

[2] In the *Registers of St. Alphage, Canterbury* (edited by J. M. Cowper), p. 244, he is mentioned as curate, Thomas Wise being the rector.

[3] See p. 56, note.   [4] Sibertswold, six miles from Dover.

ISAAC MINET'S CHILDREN

of s^d place, Mr Thom. Rooth of Dover, myself and others, I pray god it may be for the edification of ye people and for his own confort.

The charge of his being admitted to that living is as under :—

Payd Mr Counsell^r Turner who gave him ye presentation, for ye stamp etcr.		4. 2. 0 *
Given to his three manservants 1. 11. 6		
to 6 or 7 womenservants 2. 2. 0		
		3. 13. 6 *
To charge of ye fiat at Lambeth and 5 servants . . 2. 15. 0		
To ye institution at doc͞t Commons and to ye clerk . 5. 2. 6		
To the first fruits at ye s^d office 15. 7. 9		
June ye 27 : to the tenthes p^d at Canterbury . . 1. 11. 3		
and for procuration 7. 10		
		23. 15. 4 *
To charge of a journey to London and expence		4. 10. 0 *
To ringing of bells at Canterb^y and Eythorn		15. 6 *
24th Janary : To Mr Richd Edborough for having preacht at Eythorn since ye death of Mr Cason from ye 30th September to ye 13 of January inst. being 17 Sundays . .		15. 14. 6 *
For ye relaxat and instrum^t of induci͞n at Canterb^y . . .		1. 7. 0
Feb. 1723 : for a horse bought by Mr Belner [13. 13], and for a sadle and bridle etcr		15. 15. 0 †
		69. 12. 9
June 28 : To Saml. willmott for Mr Edborough to the 24 June inst. for being curatt		3. 3. 0 *
		72. 15. 9
172⅔ Payd to Mr Jⁿ Cason at Eythorn for one quarter of ye kings tax 2. 5. 0		
and for ½ yeare window D^o to Michelmas last . 15. 0		
		3. 0. 0 *
Payd also for several goods as chairs tables etc^{ra} bought of Mr Cason as under I say further		10. 16. 0 *
May ye 3rd : payd to Saml. Willmoth for ½ year kings tax .		3. 0. 0 *
and for half a year window tax to Lady day . . .		15. 0 *
for 3 Loads St. foin		1. 15. 0 *
In part of wch rece^d for delapidation of s^d Mr John Cason 13. 0. 0		
March 16th : p̄d to daniel Minet for 2 pieces serge . . .		3. 16. 0 †
for a piece lindsey Woolsey also green		1. 10. 0 †
for 12 dozⁿ galloon		12. 0 †
for charges and freight, I say caryage		7. 6 †
		6. 5. 6
for more serge from Canterbury .		13. 6 †
for making of the bed to star		
for 92 lb. of feathers from Calais . . . 3. 3. 0		
for a quilt, I say a tick etcr. . . . 2. 0. 0		
for making y^e bedd		

N.B. all these articles are passed in his book of accts kept by me. N.B. the articles markt thus * are past in his acct curr^t in book of his afairs and those markt † in d° book in acc^t of what I give him, so this acc^t is of no use.

MEMORANDUM y^t y^e 5th of Feby 172$\frac{2}{3}$ my son made an agreem^t wth Mr Samuel Wilmoth dated y^e 2nd inst. by wch he is to give him 120*l*. for y^e glebe land and great and small tithes belonging to the living of Eythorn, to be payd at 4 severall payments, viz. 30*l*. at midsomer next, 30*l*. y^e 5th of 9ber, 30*l*. the 5 feb. and 30*l*. the midsomer day 1724; and y^e s^d wilmott is to quitt y^e house 3 mõ after warning and to be allowed for y^e same after y^e rate of 3*l*. pr annum.

MEMORANDUM y^t the 24th Janu^y 172$\frac{2}{3}$ my son Minet did agree wth Mr Richd Headborough to officiat and preach for him at Eythorn once every sunday for wch he is to pay him after y^e rate of twenty pounds a year without any obligation of one side or y^e other for any limitation of time.

The 14 of Sept 1724 my son Jn Minet Rector of Eythorn maryed Mis Alice Hughes daughter of Mis Elizabeth yong, wife in second maryage of Wm Veel esq^r of Capell and comptrol^r of y^e customs of Kent, her grandmother madam Alice yong widow of Captⁿ Wm. yong.

The 20th Octob 1725 his wife was deliverd of a boy who was baptized by y^e father in Eithorn Church and was named hughs, Mr Wm. Veel and I godfathers, mad. yong godmother. 24 8tob 1725

The Sunday 4th of feb 172$\frac{7}{8}$ my son Jn Minet's wife was deliverd of a daughter abt 3 afternoon, wch was baptized by her father in Eythorn Church afternoon, my son Isaac godfather madam Veel and my wife godmothers. Shee was named mary.

The 3d June 1744 my son John Minet's[1] wife was at ab^t midnight deliverd of a son who was named [Henry].

---

[1] John Minet had in all twelve children; the following is a complete list of them:—

1. Hughes, b. 20 Oct. 1725; d. 4 Feb. 1728. 2. Mary, b. 4 Feb. 1728; d. 21 Oct. 1794. 3. Hughes, b. 30 June, 1731; d. 23 Dec. 1813. 4. Alice, b. 9 June, 1732; d. 1 July, 1733. 5. Isaac, b. 26 Aug. 1734; d. 28 Oct. 1776. 6. Alice, b. 29 July, 1736; d. Jan. 1738. 7. Elizabeth, b. 12 July, 1737; d. Jan. 1738. 8. Henrietta, bap. 10 Oct. 1738; d. 20 Feb. 1800. 9. James, bap. 16 Oct. 1739. 10. Alice, bap. 1 May, 1742. 11. Henry, b. 3 June, 1744; d. before 1765. 12. William. The baptisms of all these children, except that of William,

Marie Minet also gives us short notes concerning all her children, which, though they afford no new facts, are curious as showing that she preferred writing in French down to the end of her life. Her account of her son John's children is incomplete, as it does not extend beyond 1734:—

Mon fils John Minet s'est marié le 14ᵉ Septr 1724 a la fille unique de Mad^e Hughes, de present femme de Wm. Veel Esqre. et nommé Alicia Hughes, par la grace de Dieu il leur ont esté né les enfans qui suivent. 1 garcon né 20 Octobre 1725 quy a vecu 3 an le Seigneur la retiré a luy, cet enfant mourut le 4ᵉ Febry 1728 il etoit nommé Hughes.

Il luy fut né une fille quy fut nommé marie, elle fut batisé par son pere 4 ou 5 jours apres. Je fut sa mareine et mon fils Isaac Minet Parin. Dieu la benie, amen.

Ils ont un fils quy leur fut né le 30ᵉ Juin 1731 [Hughes].

Ils ont une fille nomme Alicia née le 9 Juliet 1732, est morte le 1ᵉ de Juliet 1733 par un Dimanche Dieu la retiré a luy par un ange, agé d'environ 1? mois.

Le 26 D Aoust 1734 la femme de mon fils est achouché d'un fils dont son pere et Mad^e Young ont esté parin et mareine et nommé Isaac. Dieu le benie par sa grace Amen.

There is but little to be added to this account of John Minet. Appointed rector of Eythorne in 1722, he added to this, in 1743, the living of Lower Hardres, near Canterbury, and the chaplaincy of Dover Castle,[1] and for fifty years, till his death in 1771, he lived a quiet and studious life. Alone of Isaac's descendants, he has told us nothing of himself, and, beyond one autograph, there is not a line of his writing remaining. He had a considerable library, as we are told by his son Hughes, whose notes, written in many of the books, give us almost

occur in the Eythorne Registers; but the burials of the six who died young, and, one would suppose, at Eythorne, are not entered there. With regard to the six who did not die in infancy, Mary, Hughes, and Henrietta we shall meet with later on. Henry went out of his mind, and died before 1765. William was alive in 1767, when a legacy left to him by his uncle William's will was paid him by his brother Hughes, but he apparently was also out of his mind, to judge from the expressions Hughes employs with regard to him. Isaac died at Hoxton.

[1] The salary of the chaplain of Dover Castle, or rather of the Cinque Ports, was 36*l*. 10*s*. Though John Minet died in 1771, he appears in the Army Lists as holding the appointment as late as 1787!

the only indication of the nature of his father's literary interests; these notes will be referred to later, when we come to speak of the son. One or two references to him are found in letters from Peter Fector, at Dover, to William Minet, in London, and these bear out the view of his character, as a scholar and student, which Hughes' notes suggest. Peter Fector speaks of him on more than one occasion as advising him in the choice of books; we find, for instance, this in a letter of November 2, 1740: 'You desired your brother Mr. John Minet to advise and assist me in the choice of books, and to put me in the way, which he has done, and is ready to assist me in everything he can'; and again, in 1743, he says: 'He is always ready to assist me with books or anything else that tends to my improvement.'

In 1720 John Minet was, as we have seen, curate to Mr. Dauling, one of whose cures was at Capel-le-Ferne; and it was here that he became acquainted with Alice Hughes, whose mother, Elizabeth, had inherited the two farms of Capel-sole and Capel-church from her father, William Young, who had bought the property in 1691 from Oliver Wright.[1]

William Young was a captain in the East India Company's service, and commanded the 'Degrave' in 1701 on her voyage to Madras, where he died of fever in that year, leaving his son William, who had been second mate, to succeed him in the command. The 'Degrave' was wrecked on the homeward voyage on the coast of Madagascar, and William Young, the son, was shortly afterwards killed by the natives. These facts would hardly be worth recording were it not that one of the few survivors of the crew of the 'Degrave' was Robert Drury, who wrote an interesting account of a fifteen years' captivity on the island.

Very great doubts have from time to time been thrown on the genuineness of this narrative, which it is not my province to discuss here; they will be found fully dealt with in a recent edition of Drury's narrative, ably edited by Captain Oliver.[2] The fact that there was a ship called the 'Degrave,' and the existence of Captain Young and his son, William Young, who are frequently mentioned in the earlier portion of Drury's story, receive ample confirmation from two copies[3] of the work now in my possession, and formerly belonging to Hughes

[1] Hasted's *Kent*, ed. 1799, viii. 144. See also Ireland's *Hist. of Kent*, ed. 1829, ii. 159.
[2] *Madagascar; or, Robert Drury's Journal during Fifteen Years' Captivity on that Island.* Edited by Capt. P. Oliver. London, 1890.
[3] Second edition, London, 1731, and a later edition of 1807.

Minet, great-grandson, on his mother's side, of Captain Young. In these Hughes has made the following notes in his own handwriting:—

> This, so far as my frequent conversations on this subject would, and could admit of (with my dear mother) I say all or many of them, corroborated and further confirmed (as to the loss of the 'Degrave' and the death of the Captain and his son particularly) in my mind the truth of Drury's narrative.

Again, in a marginal note to p. 60 (ed. 1807) he says:—

> This, and many other passages relating to Captain Young the father, and afterwards his son, who became Captain, accords with what I have heard from my mother, who was granddaughter to Captain Young the father, and whose wife, my mother's grandmother, I well remember. She died at Eythorne, aged 96, at my father's house. This book is particularly interesting to me, whose maternal great-grandfather Cap. Young the father was, and who am now reading these narratives above a century after they happened, and at 80 years of age.
>
> H. MINET.[1]

Capel-sole farm passed, probably under William Young's will, to his daughter Elizabeth, who, by her first marriage with Henry Hughes, of Deptford, became the mother of Alice Hughes, who married John Minet in 1724. Alice Hughes inherited Capel-sole from her mother, and on her death it passed to her son, Hughes Minet. Capel-church passed to Young Veel, son of Elizabeth Hughes by her second marriage, and after his death was sold, in 1753, by decree of the Court of Chancery, to William Minet, from whom it passed to Hughes Minet, in whom the two properties were again united. They remained in the possession of the family until 1874, when, on the death of Hughes Minet's grandson, Charles William, they were sold.[2]

---

[1] Further evidence as to the 'Degrave' and Captain William Young will be found in Colonel Yule's *Diary of William Hedges*, Hakluyt Soc., London, 1888. In vol. ii. p. ccx. we find the following note in a letter dated Nov. 16, 1600 [? 1700]: 'Your Honours chaplaine put on board the Degrave, and approved by the Bishop of London run away herefrom and left the ship. Wee understand he is a very lewd, druncken, swearing person, drencht in all manner of debaucheries.' In vol. ii. p. ccxxv. Captain Young is named as going to Bombay, with others, to receive charge of that island from the King's officers. And again, in vol. iii. p. xli. a letter from John Pitt is dated 'From on board the De Grave, Capt. Wm: Young commander in Porta Nova Road, July 26. 99.'

[2] For the Hughes pedigree, see table *L*, and W. Beetham's *Baronetage of England*, vol. iii. p. 403 (Ipswich), 1801. The baptism of Young Veel will be found in the Registers of St. Mary, Dover, August 10, 1708.

John Minet died at Eythorne, November 13, 1771, and was buried in the church; a tablet on the north wall of the chancel records his name.[1]

Of Isaac, the third son, his father tells us:—

Isaac Minet borne y⁰ 11th of Octob 1696,[2] he was baptized same day; godfather Mr Peter fannet for Mr Isaac Sigart, father, of Calais; godmother my sister Elizabeth Gillis, he is brought up at home in my buissinesse. The 5th July 1722 he went to Ostende by way of Calais, to a sale of East India goods and thence to amsterdam to see y⁰ countrey. In Augt 1723 he went to berlin by way of Calais. He was maryed at Eithorn by his brother Jⁿ Minet the 6 August 1726 to Mⁱˢ frances Knight, daughter of Capᵗ Thomas Knight of Dover. He had two sons, yᵉ first lived abᵗ [*blank*] monthes, the last about 15 monthes dyed Aug 1730.

My son Isaac Minet was born the 11th of October 1696 was taken sick of a feaver yᵉ 27 Sept 1731 wᶜʰ lasted very viollent till the 11 October 1731 when at ten of yᵉ clock at night god tooke him out of this world, into life eternal.

Hee was buryed yᵉ 14th octob. in yᵉ church of St Mary in a grave where was buryed [*blank*] and his wife in yᵉ yeare [*blank*]; and the stone being very large and roome on it for 3 or 4 inscriptions, I did with yᵉ consent of yᵉ churchwarden wood had sᵈ stone polisht and yᵉ formʳ inscriptions of brasse and statuts new putt on, and the inscription as under cutt on yᵉ stone, wᶜʰ wᵗʰ yᵉ first moving cost *l.* [*blank*]

' Here is intered Mr Isaac Minet Junʳ who was borne yᵉ 11 October 1696 and dyed the 11 October 1731, hee had by frances his wife two sons Isaac Knight and Isaac who lay here also.'[3]

While his mother adds to her brief record a few words of tender resignation:—

1726 le 6 D'Aoust mon fils Isaac Minet s'est marié avec la fille de Capᵉ Night, je prie Dieu de les benir ensemble.

---

[1] See p. 218 for the inscription.   [2] Registers of the French Church at Dover, p. 13.

[3] The baptisms of these two children will be found in the Registers of St. Mary, Dover, May 15, 1727, and November 4, 1728. Both were named Isaac Knight. The death of the second will be found in the same Registers; he was buried August 19, 1731.

Ils ont eu deux jolies enfans que l'Eternell a pris a luy, l'un agé de six mois et l'autre a l'age de 2 ans.

Mon cher fils Isaac Minet cy dessus et mort a 11 heures du soir apres une maladie de 13 jours, il avoit ce jours 35 ans, estant son jour de naissance 11ᵉ Octobre 1731.

L'Eternel nostre Dieu l'aura receu a mercy pour le placer parmis ses elus et chers bien aimé, amen. Dieu nous console, cella etant tres affligeant de voir mourir ses enfans, bon Dieu nous assisté par sa grace, Amen.

The Isaac Sigart of Calais who appears as godfather was, no doubt, the one who is mentioned more than once in the narrative of the escape.[1]

Isaac Minet was the only son who remained at Dover in his father's business; and that its success was largely due to his ability appears from what his brother William says in his account of the state of the house after his father's death,[2] and also from one of Peter Fector's letters.[3]

Isaac's third son, James, spent the whole of his life in business in Berlin. His father tells us of him :—

James Minet my 3rd son was borne y^e 15th March 169$\frac{7}{8}$,[4] godfather Mr James Hays, y^e son of James of Calais; godmother my sister mary then wif of Peter le maitre, a chirurgeon at Canterbury.

He went for berlin in prussia the [13] october 1712, in order to be near y^e añt of my wife, whose name is Elizabeth Sauselle, widdow of Mr Peter Le Gay, who by her will made my wife her heir, and Mr Jackary grandidier[5] and I execut^{rs} of her testamen^t. It happen^d that before he gott to Berlin our s^d ant was maryed to one Mr Guerard, a perewigg maker who had many children, but by maryage they made no commonalty of estate, so y^t the inheritance will not be much diminished ; he hath bene there without coming home till now, 1722.

1724, Sep^t. My s^d son came to dover by ye way of holland and so to London, he was at his brother John Minet's wading[6] and stayd at dover till y^e [14] 9ber, when he returned to berlin by way of Calais

---

[1] See pages 26, 36, 89.   [2] See p. 139.   [3] See p. 129.
[4] Registers of the French Church at Dover, p. 13.
[5] Husband of her sister, Jeanne Sauchelle.   [6] September 14, 1724.

and holland, in order to settle in comp ẇ Mr Elias Huot, we gave him yᵉ house at berlin worth abᵗ 1000*l*. sterl, 2 suitts of clothes, 100 Rixdʳ, 13*l*. for his journey, severall medalls and 2 pieces of gold worth abᵗ 5*l*.

9ber 1724 I gave my son James a gold watch and two silver dᵒ

cost together .	.	.	.	*l*.33. 13. 0
on whᶜʰ he left	.	.	.	. 10. 10. 0
				23. 3. 0

he went for Calais yᵉ 14th 9ber 1724; his añt Rooth gave him a 5 guinea piece.

My son James Minet, my sᵈ son James, whom I would have had come to England to bee neare mee and his mother and brothers and to wᶜʰ purpos I writt him did by his letter of [*blank*] 1731 advise yᵗ hee was ingaged by an agreement to bee in company wᵗʰ mr. Huot of berlin in Prussia for 2 yeares and a half, where I pray God bless him.

About yᵉ monthe of May 1713 ¹ my deare wife was resolved to undertake to goe to berlin in prusia by way of holland to see her ante Mⁱˢ Elizabeth Sauchelle widow of Mr Pʳ Le Gay, in order to perswade her to come to England, but yᵉ resolution was altered and wee sent our son James Minet who is now coming home May 1739.

On fryday the 25th Septembr. 1741 my son James Minet arrived at Dover abt. six after noone from Berlin, hee having taken his pasage at Rotterdam for London the wind having drove yᵉ shipp to yᵉ North foreland hee landed at margate where hee took a chaise and came here.

To this his mother adds the following :—

1713. Mon tres cher fils Jacques Minet est party pour Berlin 13ᵉ Octobre pour la premiere fois ou il a esté 12 ans, puis sa tante este morte et il nous est venu voir et a resté 6 semaines ou 2 mois.

14 Novembre 1724 a 9½ heures du matin mon fils James est reparty pour Berlin pour sy etablir en societé avec Mr Huot, L'eternel l'assiste de son St Esprit en tout bien avec la bonne santé ; il a amené son frere Wm. Minet avec luy pour le laisser en Hollande pour apprendre la langue Hollandoise, 1724.

¹ ? 1712. See p. 103.

Le 11 Avril 1733 mon cher fils James Minet est party de Douvre apres avoir esté icy 5 a 6 mois, il estoit venue pour demeurer avec nous a Douvre, mais il a mieux aimé sans retourner, Dieu le preserve et me console.

It would seem from this that he went to Berlin in 1712, when he was only fifteen years of age, and was under the care of his mother's aunt. Madame Le Gay had just lost her husband, and it was hoped that she would come to England; as she refused to do this, James was sent out to her, and on arriving found her already remarried to David Guerard. The youth remained there for twelve years, returning home in 1724; two months later he returned to Berlin, where, with capital advanced by his father, he established himself in business with a Mr. Huot. He was again in England in 1733 and 1741. On his father's death, in 1745, he received as a legacy under his will the 1,000*l*. which had been advanced to him in 1724, together with the business premises and other houses in Dover.[1]

It is probable that he returned to England at this time, though the fact cannot be established; but he certainly was over again in 1767, when he acted as executor to his brother William, who had died in January. His nephew, Hughes, who was one of his co-executors, complains that his uncle 'putt the executors to great difficulty by delaying his jorney to England so long.' He died seven years later in Berlin, and was buried, as he wished, in the vaults of the Church of the Neustadt, in Berlin, where his name appears in the registers. 'L'Eglise de la Ville Neuve' is otherwise known as the Dorotheenstädtische Kirche, and was one of those allotted to the Huguenots who settled in Berlin. The church was rebuilt in 1858, but the French Church had ceased to use it in 1841.[2] It will be noticed that his will[3] is witnessed by the 'conseillers et greffier de la chambre royale de justice superieure francaise,' which is evidence of the autonomy of the French colony in Berlin, which lasted until 1811. The Hausvogteiplatz, where he lived, still exists, though much changed, and is between the Jägerstrasse and the Domhofsplatz.

What business James carried on there is nothing to show, but probably it was connected with banking; he seems, however, to have been a fairly well-known person in Berlin society, as in a collection of

---

[1] See Isaac Minet's will, p. 211.
[2] *Geschichte der Dorotheenstädtischen Kirche*, von R. Stechow. Berlin, 1887.
[3] Page 213.

memoirs, personal and political, written by Dieudonné Thiébault, he occupies three pages.[1] The character given of him is not a very favourable one, and would seem to be somewhat of a caricature ; nor, as we know, are the facts strictly accurate ; seeing, however, how little we know about him, the passage is worth quoting in full :—

Je n'ai plus à parler ici que d'un Anglois, M. Minette, propriétaire des paquebots de Douvres, qui lui valoient près de vingt mille livres sterlings par an. Cet homme, laissant une partie de ses revenus à ses neveux, qui, sur les lieux, faisoient valoir le fonds, vivoit depuis très-longtemps à Berlin, où il s'étoit fixé autant par caprice que par circonstances. C'étoit un Anglois original, de la grosse espèce : il avoit trois belles maisons à Berlin, et, dans chacune, un appartement qu'il se réservoit. Il alloit selon sa fantaisie déjeûner dans l'une, dîner dans la seconde, et coucher dans la troisième. Quelques vieilles connoissances lui faisoient la cour ; et ce vieux battelier, dur, grossier, et insolent comme les gens de son état qui ont fait fortune, avoit besoin qu'on lui fît la cour. Il y avoit sur-tout un vieux militaire, major de la place, qui, n'ayant pas de fortune, étoit fort assidu à venir dîner avec lui. Après le dîner, M. Minette vouloit jouer aux échecs, où il mettoit bien plus d'amour-propre que d'intelligence. Quand le pauvre major avoit la complaisance de perdre, il étoit traité d'âme basse et vile qui vouloit plaire ; et quand il gagnoit il étoit accablé de sottises comme mauvais joueur et rigoriste. Après avoir rencontré deux ou trois fois ce riche malotru, toujours simple dans son costume, et plus que familier dans son ton, je demandai à M. Sulzer ce qu'il en pensoit. ' C'est,' me répondit-il, ' le plus malheureux des hommes. Il est excessivement riche, et n'a que de la morgue, de l'insolence, de la grossièreté et des caprices où l'on ne trouve pas l'ombre du sens commun. Un seul mot peint son malheur ; c'est qu'il n'a aucun plaisir à faire du bien, lui qui pourroit en tant faire. Il est blasé sur tout : il ne lui reste plus d'autre activité que celle qui lui vient de son extravagante originalité, et de la vanité la plus sotte qu'il y ait au monde.'

Ainsi recordé sur son compte, ce ne fut qu'avec la plus froide

---

[1] *Mes Souvenirs de vingt ans de séjour à Berlin ; ou Frédéric le Grand, sa famille, sa cour, son gouvernement, son académie, ses écoles, et ses amis littérateurs et philosophes*, par Dieudonné Thiébault, de l'Académie Royale de Berlin, de la Société libre des Sciences et des Arts de Paris, &c. Paris, An xix. (1804). For the passage relating to James Minet, see vol. iii. p. 309.

indifférence que je le regardai ; il le sentit : et comme il avoit remarqué qu'on me témoignoit quelque considération chez le chevalier Mitchel,[1] chez la comtesse Scorcewska, et ailleurs, il voulut me faire quelques avances. Il me rencontra un jour avec M. de Castillon, le père : il nous aborda ; et, après les complimens ordinaires, il gronda mon collègue sur ce qu'il y avoit long-temps qu'il ne l'avoit vu ; il lui demanda quel jour il lui feroit le plaisir de venir dîner avec lui ; et ensuite se retournant de mon côté : ' Monsieur,' me dit-il, ' vous n'avez pas encore dîné chez moi ; il faut y venir, le jour qu'il vous plaira.'—' M. Minette,' lui repondis-je, ' je vous suis bien obligé ; mais je ne puis pas avoir cet honneur-là.'—' Et pourquoi donc, puisque je vous laisse maître du jour ? '—' C'est que je suis engagé.' Cette réplique de ma part produisit l'effet que je voulois ; elle le déconcerta, l'humilia, et me délivra de ses poursuites.

Parmi les maisons qui appartenoient à M. Minette, il faut compter d'abord l'un des plus beaux hôtels de Berlin, placé sous les arbres, derrière la bibliothèque publique, et presqu'en face du palais du prince Henri. M. de Guines avoit loué cet hôtel, qui ensuite fut occupé par le ministre de Gœrne [sic]. M. Minette, fier d'avoir le ministre de France pour locataire, crut avoir acquis le droit de se conduire avec lui comme pair et compagnon. Un jour qu'il le vit à la promenade avec plusieurs dames de la cour, il vint sans façon l'accoster et se placer familièrement à côté de lui ; puis, il se mit à faire l'énumération de tous les François distingués qu'il avoit souvent reçus chez lui à Douvres. ' Mesdames,' dit M. de Guines, en riant, ' ce que M. Minette vous dit là est très-vrai : à moins d'avoir des ailes, on ne va point de Calais en Angleterre sans passer chez lui, car le paquebot lui appartient ; il y est né, c'est comme sa maison.' Ce fut ainsi qu'il renvoya cet importun et l'écarta pour toujours.'

Hughes Minet, whose opinion of his uncle we shall have occasion to refer to later, writes in the margin as follows :—

This account is no doubt exaggerated, but its cirtain, from my own experience, that in part the character of this uncle of mine is not devoid of truth, for a strange mortal he was.

Of Isaac Minet's five surviving sons, four followed in their father's footsteps, devoting themselves to business ; and to Daniel, of whom

---

[1] English Ambassador at Berlin.

we have next to speak, was due the foundation of the London house. How this came about is fully described in the notes his father has left :—

Daniel my 4th son was borne the 18 November 1699;[1] godfather my brother Daniel Minet of flessingue, godmother Mis Jane Sauselle, wife of Mr Jackary Grandidier at Berlin. He went to paris and lived wth Mr John Cottin ab^t 19 months where he improved himself very much, he went from dover 20 March 171$\frac{7}{8}$ and was there to y^e October 1719, and when I designed him to come home, he introduced himself in Sr J^n Lambert's service who was then at paris, and was with him there till the month of March 1720, and in Aprill following he went to Sr J^n Lambert at London, where he workt till March 1721 that ye South Sea fell and ruined infinit number of persons of all rancks, I say ye S. S. bubbles, where he also lost all he had gott at paris and some of my money, and of grief he fell sick and was dangerously ill, but it pleased god to send him his health again, and he being recovered, was advised by Mr Tobias Bowles to make aplication for the comission of buying the tobaco for ye fermers of france, to wch end he went to paris, and solicited himself the duke d'aumont, mareshall Tallard and ye cardinall du bois, but could obtain nothing, but one mons^r delasalle being sent over by Mr Paris de monmartel and Mr J^n Cottin, the last recomanded my s^d son to s^d delasalle, who being come to dover ye 4 Sept 1721 took my s^d son to London with him who log^d wth him and assisted him to buy 3000 hogh̄ of tobaco, and to shipp them for france, and s^d Mr. delasalle being gone over for paris my s^d son hath bene since inployed by him to buy ye tobaco for s^d company, and I was at London in May 1722 when he recēd an order to buy 5000 hogh̄d of Tobaco, wch he hath done to ye full satisfact of his inployers; so y^t by ye grace of god he will continue, and make his establishm^t at London as a merch^t, having allready very good credit on the exchā. and s^d Mr Cottin having promised him his comīss wch in time may be very considerable.

My son daniel Minet did mary at London at ye chapell of Somersett house the 17 xber 1723 m^is Anna Maria Atkyns, eldest daughter of Mr Robert Atkyns merch^t in austin fryers London, and of Mis Anne Bonnell, his lady; he had wth her abt 2000*l.* and a

---

[1] Registers of the French Church at Dover, p. 14.

years bord and lodging in Mr Atkyns' house I gave him 1000*l.* in maryage.

The 12th Sept 1724 his wife was deliverd of a daughter who was named Anna Mary, I and my wife were godfather and godmother.

The 14 Septemb 1725, 4 morning, his wife was deliverd of a son who hath bene named Edward, Mr Edwd Atkyns, and Mr Kinsey atkyns being godfathers.

my son daniel Minet of London died y^e 12 may 1730 aged 31 years, he was in very good credit as a merchant, he left one son named daniel ab^t 8 months old, and his widow worth ab^t 3000*l.* besides her portion of 2000*l.* in y^e S Sea annuityes and agreed to remain in y^e same house wth my son Wm and to be $\frac{1}{3}$ interested in y^e wine trade, y^e $\frac{2}{3}$ being on my acct managed by my s^d son.

His mother adds but little to the above information, but again we notice how tender and womanly is her way of giving it :—

Mon fils Daniel Minet cest marié le 17e xbre 1723 age de 24 ans avec une jeune fille nommé Anna Maria Atkins de Londres agé de 18 ans de bonne famille, Dieu les benisse. Amen.

Mon tres cher fils Daniel Minet cy dessus est decedé le 12e May 1730 a 3$\frac{1}{2}$ heures du matin, L'Eternel nostre Dieu la retiré a luy ; il estoit tres resigné et soumis a la volonté du tout puissant, il estoit un tres bon homme, toute ma consolation. Il a laissé un fils agé de 7 mois nomé Daniel que je prie le bon Dieu de benir et le croitre en sa grace. Le pere avoit 30 ans et demy quand il est mort, il na esté que 5 a 6 jours malade, il a esté enterré dans sa paroisse a Londres.[1]

Jay eu ce cher enfant a Douvre 3 mois et sa nourice avec luy il alloit seul quand il a party dicy, il avoit 3 an le 22 Octobre 1732. L'enfant D. Minet né le 22e Octobre 1729.

Of Daniel the younger very little is known. In the year following her husband's death his mother retired into the country, probably to Hertfordshire. At the age of thirteen he was left an orphan, and evidently William Minet, his uncle, practically adopted him. He does not seem ever to have been connected with the business, which, no doubt, had he desired, he could have entered. His tastes must have

---

[1] St. Dionys Backchurch. Letters of administration were granted to his widow on May 28, 1730.

been rather of a literary and scientific kind, for on May 7, 1759, he was entered as a student-at-law at the Inner Temple, and in later life became both a Fellow of the Royal Society and of the Society of Antiquaries.[1] He was never called to the Bar—perhaps because of his appointment to the post of Surveyor of Customs, which he obtained through his uncle's influence with Lord Chancellor Hardwicke.[2] He is buried at Bengeo, where on the north wall of the church a monument to his memory still exists.[3] A fine portrait of him, said to be by Gainsborough, is in my possession.

The business which Daniel the elder had established was continued on his death, in 1730, by his brother William, who carried it on until his own death, in 1767. That he was well fitted by his training for the post, as also for the responsibilities of the Dover business, which fell largely on him in 1745, appears from what his father tells us of him:—

> William Minet my 5th and last son was borne the 8th Decembre 1703 and baptized ye 11th by Mr Campredown;[4] his godfathers old Mr Isaac Lamb notary and Captn Charles Gibson, who then had the transport of prison^{rs} of warr from dover to Calais, wch was a very good employ, being p^d 10 livers for every french prison^r and 10 shill. for each English prison^r and 5d p^r man for Proviss^n p^r day. He had some Tincture of Latin, at 17 years he went to Dieppe

---

[1] Through the courtesy of the Society of Antiquaries and of the Royal Society I am able to give the following extracts from their minutes, which show the qualifications on which Daniel Minet was admitted as a member of these two bodies:—Minutes of the Society of Antiquaries of Thursday, March, 5, 1767: 'Testimonials were presented recommending Daniel Minet of the Inner Temple, Esqre, a gentleman well versed in the History and Antiquities of this kingdom to be elected a member of this Society, of which honour he is desirous; and upon the personal knowledge of the subscribers is recommended as likely to become a valuable and useful member. (Signed) Charles, L^d B^p of Carlisle, J. Ayloffe, Greg^{ry} Sharp, F. Morell, T. Astle, A. C. Ducarel.' The election followed on April 9, but, so far as the records of the Society show, he never took any active part in its proceedings. The *Memoirs of Fellows of the Society*, a manuscript by Mark Noble, now in the library of the Society, speaks of him as dying in 1790, at his house in Grosvenor Street. The Minute of the Royal Society referring to him is as follows: March 19, 1767.—' Daniel Minet, of the Inner Temple, Esqre, a gentleman greatly conversant in various branches of litterature, being very desirous of the honour of election into the Royal Society, we the undersigned recommend him on our personal knowledge as worthy that honour, and if chosen, likely to prove a usefull member thereof. (Signed) Cha. Carlisle, Jer. Milles, Jos. Ayloffe, Greg. Sharp, Tho. Astle, And. C. Ducarel. Ballotted for and elected June 18, 1767; admitted November 26, 1767.' It will be noticed that the names signing the two proposals are almost identical. The Bishop of Carlisle was President of the Society of Antiquaries in 1765, and was succeeded by Jer. Milles in 1768.

[2] See a letter from William Minet to the Duke of Newcastle, p. 116.

[3] See p. 220 for the inscription, which is also given in Clutterbuck's *Hist. of Hertfordshire*, ii. 29.

[4] Registers of the French Church at Dover, p. 14.

where he was 1 year and 4 months wth Mr John Charmell he came from Diepe the [*blank*].

My son William yᵉ yongest of yᵉ five went to Mr Jⁿ Charmels house, Merchᵗ at Dieppe, 22nd July 1720 and borded with him to yᵉ 21 Octob 1721; is 5 quarters at yᵉ rate of 500 Livers or 16: 13: 4 a yeare made 625 Livers . . . *l.*20. 16. 8
and he spent for his other expenses, clothes,
    linnen, etc. learning 513 Livers . . 17. 2. 0
                                                       37. 18. 8

9ber 14th 1724 my sᵈ son Wm Minet for Amsterdam in company of his brother James, in order to learn yᵉ language, I gave him for his jorney etc. *l.* 10 sterling and I gave him for a token [*blank*] He since is wᵗʰ Messʳˢ Stephens and franklyn merchˢ at Rotterdam, where I pay 500 guilders pʳ annum for his bord, he was placed there by Captⁿ Thomas Pillans.

My sᵈ son Wm Minet come from holland the [*blank*] Septembr 1726 and was at home and keept my books from sᵈ time to yᵉ 10th of May 1730 when I receᵈ news of my son daniel Minet being very ill, he went to London and my sᵈ son daniel dying the 12th Dᵒ I went to London yᵉ 13th and after I had settled acct with yᵉ widdow I was advised by severall friends to continue yᵉ french wine trade in wᶜʰ my sᵈ son daniel was fixt and versd, and I left my sᵈ son Wm in yᵉ house wth yᵉ widdow who desired to keep ⅓ interest in yᵉ sᵈ wine trade, her husband having ½ in yᵉ same, on condition that the rent and charges shall be payd by half between them, and they lived together in very good inteligence till yᵉ first June when yᵉ widdow desired to quitt the trade and house and retired in yᵉ contry wᵗʰ her son, but still in such good friendship and love that she lodges wᵗʰ him when in town, and her son is at Scool, 1737.

My son Wm Minet being then Merchᵗ at London, writt me yᵉ 9th of xber 1737 that he had the good fortune of a Lottery ticket No 56525 coming up two thousand pounds yᵉ 8 dᵒ of wᶜʰ he had given half to his nepveu Daniel Minet so that he hath *l.*1000 for himself and *l.*1000 for his nepveu, god be praysed.

Of Isaac's five sons, it was William, the youngest, who in the next generation succeeded to his father's position as head of the family, and one is glad, therefore, to be able to add to the slight sketch of his early life given us by his father. The materials for this have been left us by William himself, and consist of a number of exercise-books covering the period 1720-1728. The earlier books, written during his stay in France with Mr. Charmels, consist mainly of grammatical exercises and translations in French, Italian, and Spanish, and show a thorough knowledge of the two former languages; others deal with arithmetic and book-keeping, the exercises in which are all worked out in French. On his removal to Holland, Dutch becomes the chief object of his study, and his knowledge of this soon equalled his knowledge of French. The study of book-keeping he also continued in Holland, and some of the exercises in this become of more interest, taking the form, as they do, of a record of his own personal expenses, dealt with, as though they were a merchant's affairs, with the minutest machinery of *brouillon*, cash-book, journal, and ledger. Evidently the love of business method, so strong in his father, and which we shall find again in the next generation in Hughes, was equally characteristic of William. Let us, at the risk of revealing his private concerns, make a few extracts from these accounts.

The first entry in the Journal runs as follows:—

> In the Name of God: Amen.
>
> Journal containing a general & perticular state of my afaires, begun 1 July 1725.
>
> *Rotterdam July 1.*
>
> Account of sundrys belonging to me here in Holland only.
>
> D^r.   To Stock.
>
> f. 576 : 2 : 0. for I say, for estimation of sundrys, moderately valued as p inventory amounting to $l.$65 : 18 : 11. Sterl. exch^e att 36 p l. sterl. as und.

By Inventory of wearing aparel, old & new	.	$l.$21:14:7
By d^o of Linnen	. . . . .	4:6:4
By d^o of Books	. . . . .	2:15:6
By d^o of papers, wroten books, maps, etc^{rs}	.	0:3:2
By d^o of gold, silver, & cop^r uncurr^t	.	12:4:2
By d^o of rings	. . . . .	
By d^o of kniknacks	. . . . .	12:3:2
		53:6:11 ƒ576:2:2

I say $l.$53:6:11 & not as above.

The next entry shows him 'D^r to Is. Minet Senr for $l.$10 : 10 : 0.

I receiv^d from Dover, I say parting from thence'—probably the 10*l*. mentioned in his father's account. The entry of the expenses of his journey tells us that he reached Messrs. Stephens and Franklyn's, in Rotterdam, on June 12, 1725, after having visited 'Newendam, Saaedam, Amsterdam, Tergou, and Schiedam.' Later comes an entry charging Isaac Minet, junr., 1*l*. 3*s*. 2*d*. for thirty-six bottles 'flasked spaw water,' to which, with methodical minuteness, is added 7*d*. for 'small charges paid for its being carried abord.' Barem's 'Arithmetic,' La Fontaine's 'Fables,' an English Common Prayer Book, and a French Psalm-book 'with claspes,' do not seem dear at seven-and-sixpence. But the accounts are not entirely concerned with mere petty personal matters, as we find among them entries of bills drawn on him by his brother Daniel, in London, for amounts of 150*l*., from which one must infer that he was already engaging in actual business as his brother's agent. The next year he adds to the 'sundrys belonging to me, a fine ivory snuff box bought by my order and for my use as per letter of Benoist,' at a cost of twelve shillings and tenpence, and further adds to what, judging by his first account, must have been a somewhat small stock of linen, ' 2 ells of cambric for furnishing 6 shirts as per my order of 6th inst. those sent before not fit, and to be disposed of.' In the same year he makes a journey to France, half the cost of which is charged to Messrs. Stephens and Franklyn, who are further debited with one-half of a small loss incurred on changing gold at 'the mint at Arras and Amiens.'

William's cousin Mary, daughter of Thomas Minet of Canterbury, had married Jeremy Fector, and lived at Rotterdam, where William must have seen much of them, and where, for the first time, he made the acquaintance of their son Peter, now a child of three, and afterwards to become his partner. One or two entries in his accounts relate to these Fectors: under the head of 'necessary expences' is a sum 'paid Jer. Fector for sundry work of cloathes for me, and other things as ψ acc^t at large in brouillon,' and another item refers to a loan made to Fector, and records the receipt of 145 florins and a bill for 200 florins payable on demand, in satisfaction of a debt of 345 florins. Half the bill was paid later, but there is no trace of the balance.

At the age of twenty-three William returned home (1726) fully qualified to take his place in his father's house of business, while he still continued, as his exercise-books show, to improve his knowledge of foreign languages and of book-keeping, many of the examples being now worked out in Dutch. One of the books only affords evidence of an interest in matters outside mere business. It contains copies of poems from various sources, some being paraphrases of Psalms; this book is dated as completed on August 27, 1728.

During this Dover period he had the example and help of his elder brother, Isaac, as well as his father's training, and on the death of his brother Daniel in London (1730), though he was only twenty-seven years of age, he was considered fit to be entrusted with the sole management of the house in London. Evidently his commercial education had been thorough and sound, and this, added to his natural abilities and strong character, fully fitted him for the responsibilities he was now called upon to undertake. During the first fifteen years of his London life he had, no doubt, his father's experience and advice to rely on, though it must be remembered that the means of communication between London and Dover were far from being what they are to-day. The continued growth and prosperity of the business in London and in Dover during the twenty-two years it was under William's guidance, are the best evidence of his capabilities in this direction.

It was not, however, business ability alone that William inherited from his father: we have remarked elsewhere on the straightforward uprightness, the strong common-sense, and the infinite kindliness of Isaac's character, and all these qualities recur in an equally strong degree in the son. We have seen how Isaac, a younger son, became in his generation the practical head of the family, and gathered round him its less fortunate members; so William, also a younger son, filled in his generation the same position. The executorship accounts, which his nephew Hughes has preserved to us in the minutest detail, are full of evidence of help given to various members of the family during his lifetime, while his will adds further proof of his generosity in the same direction. A deep feeling for the traditions and continuity of the family shines out in all we know of him—a feeling carried into his will, in which he expresses his strong desire that James should return to England, and take his place at the head of the family and of the business.

Unmarried himself, he adopted his nephew Hughes, who came to live with him at the age of fourteen; he made him a partner, interested himself deeply in his marriage, and on his death left him one-half of his fortune. Daniel, his other nephew, left an orphan at the age of fourteen, became another object of his care; it was to William he owed the post which he held of Surveyor of Customs, and, equally with Hughes, he shared in his uncle's fortune.

Of his conduct towards Peter Fector, with whom the relationship was more distant, we shall hear in the following chapter.

Nor was it only in such ways that we find William recognising and fulfilling his duties as head of the family. The accounts above referred to show him recognising the ties of kinship in a direction which specially interests the historian of this French-born family. James Minet, the brother of Ambroise, had, it will be remembered, remained in France at the Revocation, and in a former chapter we traced this branch of the family down to 1737, when they still lived at Frencq; the following entries show that William must have kept up some connexion with the French branch as late as 1766, the year before his death:—

To Francis Dupont of Boulogne for paid by deceased's direction to Elizabeth Gordon a poor young woman in a convent there .	6.	6.	0
To William Colliot of Boulogne for charity he gave by direction of deceased to Mr J. M. Darras, de Cormont, and other poor people at Boulogne	3.	14.	9
To John Francis Colliot of Boulogne for paid in 1766 to Peter Minet who called himself a poor relation of the family living near Estaples	2.	2.	0
For paid Mary Quandalle another poor relation at the same place	3.	3.	0
To Mr Peter Fector for money given to another poor relation in France.	1.	1.	0

Ambroise Minet had come from Cormont, and Cormont, Frencq, and Etaples are all near each other. Unfortunately, beyond these entries, there is no further record of the 'poor relations,' and 1766 must remain as the date of the final break of all connexion with the family in France, which thus survived the change of country just eighty years.

Much of our knowledge of William's character comes to us from the remarks of his nephew Hughes, which in the two following chapters will be somewhat fully quoted. Considering what Hughes owed to his uncle, the tone of these criticisms seems somewhat surprising, and one can only explain it on the assumption that Hughes never fully understood, or was in sympathy with, the character he was criticising. William was evidently a very reserved man, but little given to confide his thoughts to others. Hughes, whose more emotional nature was apt to express itself somewhat freely upon occasions, never realised or understood this, and so, beyond a certain point, his judgment of his uncle's character cannot be relied on. This reserve was the one point in which William's character fell short of his father's, and one can but fancy that, had he found a wife to be to him what Marie Sauchelle had been to his father, the true kindliness of his nature might have found in him the same genial expression.

He lived in Fenchurch Street, next 'the Golden Ball,' whence a letter, written November 17, 1735, to Sir H. Sloane, is dated,[1] and his name appears in the London Directory as of the same street, where he continued to reside until his death. From 1747 to 1759 he was a director of the London Assurance Corporation. One further letter, which I have found in the British Museum,[2] may, perhaps, be quoted, as it relates partly to his nephew Daniel :—

His Grace the Duke of Newcastle

May it please your Grace

I cannot hinder the strong inclination I have to tell your grace the great pleasure I had to see you re-established in H.M's favour and to see the good old cause put under the care of the best subjects his Majesty ever had.[3] Your grace has been but seldom importuned by me but I am not insensible of the favors received thro' the hands of my most good friend the late earl of Hardwicke who obtained by your grace's means the place of one of the surveyor's of H.M's customs for my nephew Daniel Minet, and he still enjoys the same.[4]

Permit me in my own name and in that of all my family in Dover to congratulate your grace, to whom may God give health and length of days to continue as you always have been most eminently serviceable to our gracious king and to this most blessed country of religion and liberty. The wish of the son of a French refugee cannot be doubted being sincere, as your grace well knows our steady attachment to H.M. family and government for near fifty years.

Recommending myself to the favor and esteem of the D. of

---

[1] Brit. Mus. *Letters to Sir H. Sloane*, 2,222, fos. 137, 139. The letter is of no interest, merely forwarding an enclosure from one Brand Henry Schilden, of Hannover. On March 5, 1739, there is a second letter, asking for a reply to the enclosure in the first.

[2] *Newcastle Papers*, vol. 284, 32,959, fo. 50.

[3] The Duke of Newcastle was Privy Seal under the Marquis of Rockingham, who took office July 13, 1765.

[4] Lord Chancellor Hardwicke came originally from Dover. See page 66.

Newcastle I remain with the most profound respect, may it please your grace,
> your graces most obedient,
>> and most devoted humble servant,
>>> Wm MINET.

Dover, 15th Aug. 1765.

William died on January 18, 1767, at his house in Fenchurch Street, and is buried with his father in St. Mary's, Dover.[1]

---

[1] See page 214, where extracts from his will are given, and page 218 for the inscription on his tomb.

CHAPTER VIII

THE BUSINESS

> Of those things whereof they have abundance, they carrie forth into other countries great plenty. By this meanes of traffique or marchandise, they bring into their owne countrey not onely great plentie of gold and silver, but also all such things as they lacke at home.—Sir THOMAS MORE.

WE have seen how the Dover house, founded by Stephen some time before 1686, was developed and carried on by Isaac until his death in 1745, and how the London house, founded in 1721 by Daniel, Isaac's son, was continued by his brother William; it now remains to trace the continued progress of the two houses, which, in the hands of William, became practically one on his father's death in 1745.

In doing this we shall have occasion to speak of Peter Fector, who entered the Dover house as clerk in 1739, and whose connexion with the business covers a period of seventy-five years. With regard to the earlier portion of this time we derive considerable information from a series of letters written to William Minet, some by Jeremy Fector, of Rotterdam (1740–42), and some by Peter Fector, his son (1740–46).

These letters are curious in themselves, and additionally interesting from the light they throw on the nature of the business, as well as on the characters of those engaged in it.

The first introduction of Peter Fector was, as has been already said, another instance of the kindly help Isaac was always ready to extend to the members of his family. Mary, the daughter of his brother Thomas, had, as we have seen, married Jeremy Fector, of Rotterdam, and their eldest son, Peter, coming over in 1739, at the age of sixteen, on a visit to his great-uncle, an offer was made him of a clerkship in the business. This offer was eagerly accepted by his parents, and they wrote the following letter to William Minet, who, owing, perhaps, to his father's advanced age, undertook to shape out this new arrangement for him. Jeremy Fector was originally from Mulhausen, and his German origin, and even his queer accent, betray themselves in the curiously-spelt French of his letters. In transcribing the letters I have ventured to suggest explanations of the more obscure words, though not always, I am afraid, with success.

To Mr William Minet, Merchant in Fenchurch Street, London.

Rotterdam Le 31 Mey 1740.

Monsieur Wiliam Minet.

Monsieur,—Nous avons bien recu l'honneur de vottre Letter d 13 Cour^t par lequelle nous avuens apris aveque bocoup d Joÿe que vous sait[1] determiné d prantre dans vottre comptoire Nottre fils pieter. J'ay ne sauré exprimme la satisfaction ca nous donne de voir qu'il restera tens de si bonne mens,[2] il est encor Jeune, J'aÿ crente fort quil dombas dan les men d quelquin qui auree pas pri garde a sa contuitte, mes apaisant[3] nous somme foor satisfait estants perswaide que vous lui donera que de bon cunsel, ce est pour cela nous les lessons[4] tout antier en vottre convernement[5] vous aure la bonté de Lui fair Donneur L'instruction est L'Edication que vous Jugé Nesesaere quil Doit avoir pour lui Randre capable de Vous Estre udil en vos afaire en Lengm[6] destre Em Estat de Cannier[7] sa viee honetemant. A Lescar d ses habits Jaÿ Croy pas quil an a becoin encor Car jaÿ lui a fait 2 habits comblet, in Surtout, est in Cappat & Robe de Chambre, est asse d lenges[8] pour 2 a 3 ans avant son depar, mes nonopstans cela si vous juge approve de lui fair farre in habit u audre chasse vous bouve estre asure jay sera tout Jours been Contand, est vous prome d vous far bon tout ce que vou dboursse pour lui, estan bien perswoite que vous faire point de freet[9] inudil pour lui. Je Croy quil seirat bien contant daprantre cete bonne nouvelle il ma Ecret diverse lettre pontan quil est a dover, il me marque tout Jour que M^r vottre perre avet pocop dEstim pour lui est lui promete quil faira tout posiple pour lui bien Blasser,[10] ce que nous voions en Efait, est nous savons pas Comman Repontre[11] a um si Grante bonte que de prier Dieu de compler de sa plus sente Penitictoon vous, votre Cher

---

[1] Etes.   [2] Dans de si bonnes mains.   [3] Mais à présent.
[4] Le laissons.   [5] Gouvernement.
[6] Afin (?) d'être en état de gagner. The word 'Lengm' completely baffles me.
[7] Gagner.   [8] Et assez de linge.   [9] Frais inutiles.
[10] Placer.   [11] Répondre à une.

perre, est votre familis, Ce Sont Nos Voex Sincer, Restem aveque gran respecks,

> Monsieur, vos tres humble Servitur
> est[1] Servant, JEREMI FECTOR
> est[1] M. M. FECTOR.

P.S. Jay salue Monsieur Du Boys de vottre part il ietoit bien esse d aprandre que vous save le desen de le prandre en votre Comtoir, il espair que vous aure pa de regret d vottre bonne Intantion est quil est bien assure que vous auree pocop de Servis d Lui Ce que Jaÿ soit[2] ossi d tout mon Couer—Ja donne la Letter En clos a la post pour Amsterdam—Ma famme & moy vous prient d voir la bonte de saluer Nostre frere & lui assure de nos amitie son fils Thoma se port for bien.

Ce est Jaÿ[3] Monsieur Cossart que Jai pans[4] de plasser Notter pieter mes Jaÿ soyte[5] bocup mie quil seroit aveque vous, Jaÿ lui dit qul restera a Londre.

That Peter Fector was equally grateful for the opening afforded him appears from the following letter, which he writes to William Minet, and in which he refers to his father's letter of thanks. The F. Colbran he speaks of was probably the father of R. Colbran, a clerk in the house, of whom, both from Peter Fector and from William Minet, we shall hear more later on. Mary, or Molly, Detrier was the daughter of Elizabeth, Isaac's sister, whom he had brought over in the boat in 1686 as an infant :—

To Mr Wm. Minet, Merchant in Fenchurch Street, London.

Dover yᵉ 31 May 1740.

Honᵈ Sir,—I Recᵈ the Favour of yours of 29th inst. wherein I see you have received a Letter from my Father, and that he is very well pleased that you have resolved to take me in yʳ Compting house of wᶜʰ I really do not doubt, and he and I have the utmost reasons to return you our hearty thanks for the good thoughts concerning me and hope by the Grace of God, that I'll prove to be an honest and Diligent Servant and always try to do my Endeavour and submit to yʳ good Directions.

[1] Et.   [2] Je souhaite.   [3] C'est chez.
[4] Pensé.   [5] Souhaite.

Secondly I'll follow your good advice concerning my prononciation and writing a fair hand, and I'll apply myself those few moments I have to spare, also I am very sensible y^t it can but be to my advantage.

Your dear Father my Beloved Uncle seemed really to be a little at a mending hand, I pray God restore him his full Recovery for the good of many.

Mr R. Colebrand is very much obliged for the Trouble taken about his prints and will be satisfied with whatever you'll please to do about them.

My cozen Detrier gives her kind love to you, so as I with this am doing, and subscribe myself entirely under your good Directions and am with great obligation,

    Good sir Your most humble & obe^d Servant,

               PETER FECTOR.

Pray Sir give my Service to Mr Daniel.

The next letter shows us Peter Fector already well-established in the business. When we consider that he was only seventeen years of age, and had been but little more than six months in the counting-house, the self-satisfied tone of the letters may seem at first a little startling ; to judge, however, by the success of the writer in after-life, his confidence in himself was fully justified. We may well understand the quarrel with R. Colbran, who, as an older man, with longer experience in the business, would, if he was treated by Peter in the style in which this letter is written, have been more than human if he had not shown some feeling at what he must have considered the impertinence of a young beginner. The letter is valuable, as giving us a pleasant glimpse of Isaac's domestic life :—

     To Mr Wm. Minet.

          Dover ye 2nd November 1740.

Worthy Sir,—I rec^d your most Agreeable Letter of the 1st Inst. and have read the contents with due attention. I observe what you mention about my Stile and bad writing ; the latter is oftentimes occasioned for want of time ; I make myself more and more capable of the Dover Buissiness and take notice of whatever occurs ; and hope to make myself entire master of it in time, which you may depend upon. I do not abuse the Goodness of your Father, on the

Contrary I use all possible means to make myself capable of becoming a good Servant. I have, as you observe, the finest opportunity of making myself acceptable amongst Gent^n by reason of a great many's coming to ye Compting house; of which I take Notice in order to fullfill y^r good Directions. I write, Cypher and read good English and French authors when I have no Bussiness to hinder me, a Quick Genius is the best of all which I hope to obtain in time. I do not doubt but what you may have 5 a 600*l*. with an apprentice well educated and have 7 years Service Gratis; for which Reason I own that it greatly deserves my Attention; I will not loose a moment that remain without applying it to good use. it is true you wrote me the 7th August last; since which time I have performed your Directions; I see you desired your Brother Mr John Minet to advise & assist me in the choice of Books and to put me in the way, which he has done & is ready to assist me in every thing he can. I am persuaded y^t what you write is to Discourage me from Idleness, and to encourage me and stir me up to have a better notion of life and make myself capable of attaining to it, I know that y^r Good Father is a Gent^n that perhaps does not redress some small faults, which by other persons I might be taken notice of for; I therefore redress them in myself, for I know that I should be the Looser if I did not; I had a letter from my Father yesterday who wrote me they were all well and gave their Respects to you, they are very well pleased with my being here. I do not keep any bad Company never go to any Taverns or Ale houses, but spend my time at home as follows: after rising I go down to the peer heads and Elsewhere to Enquire what ships are come in and gone out, and then I come home to Breakfast, after that I am in the compting house till Dinner time unless some out-of-doors Bussiness prevents it. After Dinner I go again in the Compting house, till such time it pleases your good Father to go in; which is most times at 4 or 5 a Clock, and then we begin to play at Draughts till Eight: after Supper I play again at Wisk with your good Father and Cozen Molly—till 10 or 11; this being a true account of my passing my time, I think proper to let you know it. There is no Fencing master here, else I should take a Delight in learning some of those Arts 'tis true a man is but little esteemed if he has none of these Qualities; it is partly my fault that I have learned none of them at Holland, no help for what is past though now I repent it, I'll enquire for a good musician but I believe there's none here—you may depend that w^t news happens I'll inform you of. R. C. and I agree pretty well, though we had once a sort of a quarrell, in open streets which all the Town knows, and I don't doubt but you know it also, so that I think it needless to repeat it. But y^r Father my Master, adjudged the matter and found he was to blame; he ordered us to live friendly and quietly together, which we at present do, I observe he does not over and above like me now, also I am in some things a little to sharp for him (entre nous) it is very necessary somebody should be here to look after every trifling matter, 'tis certain your good Father cannot attend buissiness as usual; for which reason I shall do my best to transact the buissiness to satisfaction. I am young and experience makes men perfect; and I hope by the Grace of God I may do well, all in good time Sir; Cozen Detrier gives her service. I told her you ordered the butter up to Lond. and so to Dover; she thanks you for your care. I do copy dayly such page as this out of Dr Clark's Catechism which is an excellent Book and gives me a true Notion of Religion. I should be very sorry Good Sir that you should not favour me any more with your good advise, for indeed young people cannot have too much of it; it is now the 27th this Letter has been neglected some days, by reason of being bussy ab^t the Rice Ship. I am certain y^t what you wrote is out of a true regard to me, and I shall all my Lives time be bound to pray for you for it; I am (after begging Excuse for this long Epistle) with great obligation,

        Worthy Sir,
            Your most humble and obedient Servt
                    PETER FECTOR.

Peter Fector's letters were evidently written in answer to instruction and advice that he received from William; that he expressed himself thankful for this we have seen from his own letter, though how far he really felt so may be open to question. He would seem to have imagined himself, and indeed to have been, fully competent to take care of himself in every way. That his father was sincerely grateful for the advantages enjoyed by his son appears from a second letter to William :—

To Mr Wiliam Minet, at London.

Rotterdam le 23 feb. 1741.

Monsieur & cher Cousin,—Jay pouve pas menpecher par cette ocation de vous d vous saluer en vous remercien de tout la bonte que vous demainie taut Jaure [1] anvir mon fils Pietre a dover, Jay suvent d sa nouvelles est il me mark toujours que il pet Jammes [2] asse Reconoitre Lecar [3] que monsieur vottre perre & vous aves pour Loui; il me tit que vous Lhonoree quelque foi de Luy Ecrirre de Letters d bon Instruction pour Luy Recommender de bien amployé son tans, est d tacher d le perfectioner en tout ce qui est neserre,[4] don Jay peut assec [5] vous de monier [6] mon Reconnoicanse pour votre bonte, Est jespair qu'il Repontera a votter bon desen par sa diligance & bon Comporteman & opeisance, Ce est que Jay lui Recommant toujour deprier Dieu pour Vottre Conservation & celle d vatre pere Ce que nous faison ossi en vous Saiton [7] tot sorte de penitiction & continiation din bonne sante—Jay svis aveque im profont Respect,

Monsieur,
Votre tres humble Serviteur,
JEREMI FECTOR.

Ma femme vous salue, est vous asur d sa Grante Recoinosance d vottre bonte est vous pri d le Contenuer enver son fils Pieter.

Peter seems to have got into trouble with William by going off to Holland without leave, and treats his guardian's remonstrances somewhat cavalierly in the following letter:—

Mr Wm. Minet.

Dover the 14th March 1740-41.

Worthy Sir,—I was very sorry I had not the time to acquaint you of my going to Holland, also the order for Shipping the Goods saved out of the Fane Brig[n] lost near this Harbour came only on Friday being the 13th Feby last, when I begun to write you a Letter to ask your Leave to go, but it being late I could not save that post, and on Saterday being the 14th, the Expedition was Loaded and ready to sail so that I imagined it would be of no Signification

---

[1] Témoignez toujours. [2] Qu'il ne peut jamais. [3] L'égard.
[4] Nécessaire. [5] Dont je ne peux assez. [6] Temoigner.
[7] Souhaitant.

to write, been [sic] I knew they intended to sail the same Evening or on Sunday as they did, so that I hope you'll Excuse me. It is true I should in Duty have wrote you when I came back from Holland, but having been pretty bussy I omitted it. All Friends in Holland gave their Respects to you, they were all well. Mr. DuBois Desired me that when I writt to London to Give his Humble Service to you. I have no Letter unanswered from you, so that if you sent me one it must have miscarried, for it never came to my hands, wch I am sory for. If you please to write me, wch way and when you sent it I'll enquire for it. I have nothing further to add, but that I remain with the greatest Respect,

   Worthy Sir,
    Your most humble and obedient Servant,
             PETER FECTOR.

Pray (Sir) give my service to Mr Daniel, I hope he is better.

Once again Jeremy Fector expresses his thanks for his son's position and prospects; we learn, too, that Peter had in some way specially distinguished himself, and had, we may infer, been advanced in the firm :—

   Mon^r G. Minet.
           Rotterdam le 13 Juliet 1741.

Monsieur,—Mon^r Duc Nous a Comminique ce que vous nous aves fait L'honoer de nous marquer de notre Fils pieter tougant son sejour Jay vous, est nous voyons fort bien La Resson ; nous vous somme est serron toujour tres oplige d bonne Intention que vous aves de Les avancer est nous sommes tres contant quil rest Jay Mon^r vottre pere notre honoret Oncle est nous Soydons[1] que il comport toujour d'un Manniere que Mon^r vottre pere et vous soyee contant d Luy, vous saves que nous vous Lavons donne tout antier an votre disposition, est nous somme perswoite que vous & Mon^r voter pere orron soyn d loui anfen dans tans u odre il poure de vinir[2] un honet homme ce pour cela nous somme tres contant de quele manniers que vous pleare d agier avequ louj, est ce souvent[3] un Grande satisfaction por nous de voir quil poura estre de servis en votre cherre family, est pour Luy Rantre plus capple nous

---
[1] Souhaitons.
[2] Aurez soin de lui, afin que dans temps ou autre il puisse devenir.
[3] Et cela est souvent.

vous prions de bon Coeur dauor la bonte de Luy donner tans en tans d vottre bonne Consel est saage presept, esperant quil manquera pas de les opserwer & de see contnier.[1] Ca nous sercit les Pluys grent plesir dumonde d aprantre. Nous avons ossi apri que notre fils pieter a Este enploje dans un afaire doneque vous aves Rantu[2] un Grand Servis a vottre voisin est qu'il a u £.20 S^t pour sa part—set en verite un bonne Crativication—il toit vous Remersier Comme nous lui Recommantes de montre la Cratitude par ea bon Compertement—Jay pas outre choses a Ecrere que de vous dirre sancerrement que nous sommes tres mortifie aprantre que vous settes atack dun si rude duleuer—nous prions Dieu pour vottre sulagemet & Retablicement de perfecte Sante & qui weul vous complar d sa plus S^t benetiction. Ce son les soyte de sees qui ont Lhonoer de ce nomer,

      Monsieur,
    Vottre tres humbl Serviter & Servante
        J : & M : FECTOR.

The next letter was evidently written in answer to some more good advice, and marks an advance in business abilities, and, may we add, in consciousness of them. In it we first hear of Miss Molly Minet, then aged fourteen, who was afterwards to become Mrs. Peter Fector :—

    Mr Wm. Minet.

          Dover the 29th April 1742.

Sir,—I have received your kind Favour of the 23rd Inst. and observe its contents. I hope Sir you have a better opinion of me than to think that I would open any Secrets out of the Family to Samson[3] or any others. It is true I keep a little more Company with him than with the other Capt^{ns} because he is much about my age: but that does not make that I should let him in any family particulars: However Sir I am very much obliged to you for giving me a Caution. Young People cannot have to much of good Advice. You may depend Sir that I do and will use my best Endeavours to exert myself so as to be Master of the Buisseness of the House at Dover as well in the Calculation of Dutys and Clearing of Ships,

---

[1] S'y contenir.   [2] Rendu.
[3] Captain of one of the packet-ships belonging to the house, with whom Peter Fector had sailed on his journey to Holland in the previous year.

as becoming acquainted with the French Language, and getting the better of foreign Expressions &c.

I should think myself blameable to the highest Degree if in the two years past I have been with your Hon^d Father my worthy Master I had not applied myself to the Buisseness so as to be capable thereof in Case anything unforeseen should happen. I Do assure you Sir (without having a vain Conceit of myself) I think I am full as capable of this buissiness as Mr Colebran, in all respects and I dare venture to say, that if it should so happen that he should get a place, that it would cause me no manner of Uneasiness; on the Contrary I believe the Buisseness would be managed better; whereas at present one trusts to the other and by that means some small triffles are forgot. Since Mr Jas. Minet's departure from hence, I have constantly been in the Counting house, casting up Dutys and perusing several acc^{ts} of Ships clear'd for Newyork, on which I have made several Observations and I can enter and do all y^t is necessary in clearing such a Ship as well as Mr Colebran. I am sensible it had been a great advantage to me to have been with you some time, but that not having fallen out to be my Lot shall apply myself in the Station I am in and I hope so as to give Satisfaction. I shall always use my best endeavours to oblige and assist my Worthy Master whom I pray God to Preserve. I have sounded Samson once to drive some small trade with me, but did not give ear to it, he is like the rest of them, get and scrape up what they can for themselves. Whenever Dr Lynch comes, shall shew him what Civility I can. The Rev^d Mr Minet came here last Night with Miss Molly Minet from Canterbury, having been at the Visitation; he sends his Love to your Brother, and heartily wishes him a good Voyage and a soon and safe Return. Please also to present my best Respects to him and desire him if he goes home by way of Rotterdam, to present my dutyful Respects to my Father and Mother &c. So conclude and remain very Respectfully

Sir,
Your most obedient humble Servt
PETER FECTOR.

Sir,—My Master is pretty well, he sends his Love to all the Family he has received Mr Jas. Minet's Letter, in a protection for Capt Ball for which you are Creditted 10sh. 6d. in petty acc^t. Here is no news worth Notice.

In the next letter we part with Jeremy Fector for good. He and his wife Mary remained abroad, while Peter, his son, became completely English; his other son, Thomas, returned, we may suppose, 'par la premier chalupe,' and died in 1751, leaving an only daughter, who settled at Utrecht (see Table *D*).

Mon^r Guil^m Minet.

Rotterdam 2 Sep. 1742.

Jay voulu pas manquer par sete ocation d vous Remercier pour tout la Bonte que vous demonye toujour Enver mon fils pietre, jay prie Dieu de vous Reconpencer en vous complan[1] avec ses sents Benitiction et pour conserver vous est tout vos proch dans un perfait sante et prosperite pocop dannes.

Mon fils Thomas vous dirar lEtat de notre Sante, jespere qu'il oret un bon passage. Jay Lui ordonne de Revinir par La premier Chalupe qui part apre son arivee car jay[2] Gren tanplus quil Rest, Tant plus danger il aure a passer La mer. Je finis en vous assuren de mes tres hulble Respect est en vous prient de me croir de tout mon Ceur,

Monsieur,
Vottre tres hmbl Servutter,
JERE: FECTOR.

Ma fame vous salue et ce recomant a votre bons grases, el est son fils P^r.

The next two letters show signs of continued difficulties with R. Colbran; and, while the writer is still grateful for the interest taken in him, we seem to see signs of a growing independence, and some evidence of chafing under the good advice that was, it would seem, administered in large quantities, and not always in the most judicious way. Peter Fector's surprise at the New York ships clearing their cargoes for Madeira would not have been so great had he known that, under the Navigation Acts, goods imported into the Colonies from Europe were liable to duties, and, while Madeira was not much out of the way in a journey to New York, it had the great advantage of not being considered as part of Europe. If he had inquired, he would probably have found that the cargoes were not unloaded when they

---

[1] Comblant. [2] Je crains tant plus.

reached Madeira. It is this circumstance which accounts for the large amount of really good Madeira wine to be found in the United States at the present day [1]:—

To Mr William Minet, London.

Dover the 5th April 1743.

Sir,—I Received your kind Letter of the 25th to 31st past and return you my sincere thanks for all your good wishes in my behalf, which I shall always endeavour by my behaviour to deserve from you. I greatly esteem your kind advices which carry such a weight with 'em, that I am at a loss to find words to express my grateful acknowledgements for the same. I take 'em as a mark of your affection and friendship to me: Surely I can't study to much to obey and give you all the Satisfaction I am able. I do all I can to improve myself in the English and French Languages, in which I flatter myself I mend daily. I observe the Admoninition you give me as to playing and diverting your good Father: I do assure you Sir, it is a pleasure to me because it is so to him, I have and will always consult his ease and satisfaction: he is to be sure one of the best of Man in the World, and I think it is a very great Blessing that I am fallen into so good a Family, for which I can't be too thankful to God Almighty.

As to the buissness of this House, I think myself fully qualified to transact anything that may offer, as well as Mr R. C. having during these 3 years daily instructed myself therein, and I do assure you, Sir, should anything better offer for said R. C. I should not be at a loss, but do everything with ease and so as to give Satisfaction to your good Father and the Family. I have of late wrote a pretty many Letters, which your Father did all approve without ordering any alterations. If please God I live 'till the 26th May next, I shall be 20 years old, a good age to work; I should be glad to see the buissness of this House flourish as it did in your late B^r Isaac's time: there is nothing I hate more than Idleness.

I had a Letter last week from my Father and Mother who assure you of their Respects, and at the same time I had one from my B^r who thanks you for all y^r Civilitys shewn him when in London. I was sorry Mrs Suzon Halbert[2] could not stay at

---

[1] For a full explanation of this *cf.* Adam Smith, *Wealth of Nations*, ii. 256. (Lond. 1799.)
[2] The writer's aunt. See Table *D*.

Rotterdam; my Mother loved her as much as if she had been her own Child, but she is of an odd temper and could not agree with my Brother. I see Mrs Otto is going to travell with a Lady, I wish her well, Pray assure my Unkle Mr Thomas Minet of my Dutyfull Respects. Your B^r Minet's[1] youngest Daughter Miss Henrietta was taken very ill of a fever the 29th past and had died in all likelyhood in less than 24 hours, if by the good Providence of God, Dr Lynch had not been just at hand to administer Relief, she was bled twice, purg'd and blistered all in one day, and they little expected her to Live. I have not heard since, so hope she is better. The Hamper of Oporto has been sent to Him, he is always very ready to assist me with books, or any thing else that tends to my Improvement, and on the other hand, I do all I can to oblige him. I was heartily sorry to hear of your Indisposition, I hope the worst is past and I pray God to grant you soon a full Recovery. Cozen Detrier sends her Love to you. I have nothing further to add at present, save my best wishes for your health and happiness and craving the Continuance of your Friendship, which concludes me to be with the truest Devotion and Respect,
     Sir,
  Your most dev^d and obedient humble Servt,
          PETER FECTOR.

Mr Wm. Minet.
        Dover the 15th October 1743.

  Sir,—I duly received your kind favour of the 20th July last, and do most sincerely thank you for the good advice you are pleased to give me, which without doubt merit my greatest Attention. I do all what is in my power to improve and make myself Master of the buissness of this House and studying other usefull Imployments. You are pleased to say that you are sorry I have so much time on my hands unemployed, to few Examples of Industry, and to many Temptations of spending time and that you not only believe it, but you are certain of it. You will give me leave to say in answer to this, that I think I employ my time as much to the purpose as any body in Dover, which my writings will always show, besides I read good English and French Authors. I verily believe some false Representations have been made you

---

[1] The Rev. John Minet, of Eythorne.

about me, else I am well persuaded you would not reprimand me as you do in most Letters to your good Father, and to Justifie my conduct I think it incumbent on me to assure you that I never spend my time in Taverns, I go to the Coffee house but once a week and that is Sundays just to read the News and my Master is the best Judge whether I spend any time otherways, he knows that I play six hours with him every day, and that I employ the rest of the day in the Counting house. I shun Company as much as possible. It is true I went once with Mr White and a party to Lyden Spout[1] if I had been enclined to pleasure, Mr White would have been glad of my Company for a good deal of that, but never went with them on any other party, tho' during their stay here they went several times to Deale Folkston &c^a but always made an excuse that I could not be spared. I am of age to know what is for my good, therefore do my utmost to qualifie myself for buissness and to converse with the World. If at any time you think me guilty of a neglect or fault, I should take it extreamely kind, if you would please to reprimand me by a private Letter, for on your admonitions in your Letters to your Father about my taking too much pleasure &c^a Myn Cameraat has told some people that I am out of your favour and that you reprimand me dayly, which I can't say but has vexed me very much, the more so, because I don't think I deserve it. I am very sensible that all you alledge is for my own good and to discourage me from Idleness and that it is purely out of a good Inclination towards me. I take it as such, and shall always preserve a due Sense of all your favours.

I am sorry to see by the Letter of Mr Danl Crommelin of Amsterdam wrote you, that he feared Dover would lose the clearing of the Newyork Ships, by reason of its being done with more Dispatch and the Charges less by 25 p. cent, at Newcastle, I don't conceive how it can possibly be, unless they don't land the Goods, My Master has lately had several Letters from Newyork giving him many thanks for the Dispatch of their Ships and the good usage they have met here, all Commanders that have been here since my time have been extreamely well pleased with the port

---

[1] In Hougham parish, close to Folkestone. 'Near the bottom of the cliffs are three holes, called Lydden Spouts, through which the subterraneous waters empty themselves continuously on the beach; and the belief of the country is that the waters of the Nailborne, at Drelingore in Alkham, at least four miles distant, communicate subterraneously with these spouts' (Hasted, ix. 452).

and usage, all our Officers are very civil and always willing to do any good natured thing, without exposing themselves, most of the ships that cleared here of late years reported above half their Cargo for the Madeiras, tho' it is not designed to be landed there, mais en cachet a Newyork, our officers are not unsensible of it, but they don't seem to mind it. I always flattered myself the Ships were used as well here, as I thought they could be anywhere, and no more can be done than one's utmost: Newcastle is out of the way, unless Ships go North about, which they have done since the War with Spain, to prevent their falling into the Hands of 'em. Poor Captn Knowler lays dangerously ill, there is no hopes of his Recovery, I hear Captn Ridley is to have his Packet. Captn Pybus has a fine time of it, my Master paid him 16*l* 5. o. this day for freight of 10 horses and 5 Servants for the Duke of Marlborough, which came over in two packets with the Males, and therefore wo'nt pay the Capt^{ns} one farthing of it, which I think is hard and unjust, considering the Trouble they have with 'em and the ware and Tare of their tackling &c^a. he would not so much as excuse the Servants but insisted on having a Crown a head, Il est fort arabe, beaucoup plus que le dernier M^r H^{ble} [?]. I give you Joy of the Living you have obtained from the Lord Ch^r for y^r Brother,[1] I pray God he may live to enjoy it a great many years. Please to assure my Unkle[2] of my Dutyful Respects and Love and Service to his Family and all other Friends. My Master holds it brave and hearty God be praised. Your having been afflicted so long a time with the Pains of the Gout has given me the greatest Concern, I most heartily pray God to grant you a speedy deliverance from 'em. I have nothing further to add at present, Except assuring you that I shall always have the strictest Regard to your kind advices, knowing them to be good and of great Service to me and therefore the oftener you favour me with them, the greater my obligation shall be to you. I am with the most affectionate Esteem,

Sir,

Your most obliged and obedient humble servant,

PETER FECTOR.

The last letter of the series is written in a very different spirit, and

---

[1] This was the living of Lower Hardres.   [2] Thomas Minet, of Tower Hill.

shows us Fector, young as he was, and with only four and a half years' business experience, trading on his own account and venturing no small sum, while he writes to William in a spirit of perfect equality. It would seem as though the 20*l.*, which only three years before had been the foundation of his capital, had increased rapidly and considerably, so that we are not surprised to find him six years later on spoken of as owning one-third of the Dover house. He speaks of his credit, both in Dover and in Holland, being worth 1,000*l.*, and the reference to the 'Eagle' would seem to show that the fortune on which the credit was founded sprang from what would in these days be considered not too creditable a source :—

Mr William Minet.

Dover, 5. September 1744.

Sir,—I had the honour to write you the 25th past since which I have received your esteemed favours of same date and 27 d°. I observe that you do not care to be concerned in the wines I bought in C° with Mr Samson all what you are pleased to say on that article is very true, but as the case stands I must beg of you to ridd us of said Wines as soon as may be and to the most advantage : all I go upon is that our Wines are good and hope they'll come to a good market. I have entered into this affair and must get clear of it as well as I can. I have paid my Master 200*l.* on account of my half concern in said wines. I am surprised at Mr Samson's Neglect in not paying you 600*l.* or 500*l.* at least as he promised me he would the moment he came to Town—I wrote him to the purpose about it. It is not reasonable that my Master should be exposed, altho' the wines are insured ; however if any unforeseen accident should happen, I am always to be found, and would part with everything in the World before any one should suffer by me. Your Father expressed some Uneasiness at our not paying the Money, and really so much that I could not have expected more from the greatest Stranger, I thank God my Credit is good and had I occasion for 1000 Pounds I could get it at Dover, and even if that was to fail, I could at any time draw for so much or as much more on Holland, with assurance of my Bills being punctually paid—I am far from blaming your Father's Precaution ; but as the wines are insured I think he does not run any great hazard, and besides I hope to get enough out of the Eagle's Prizes to answer for the Wines or more : even if this had not been the case, I always flattered myself that if anything offered whereby I might get a penny and in cases where your Father did not care to enter that I might depend on getting some Money from him, but I have never had occasion for it before this time and his being uneasy about it has caused me a great deal of vexation. I told him that if he insisted upon it, I could get a Friend to spare me the Money. This happening on my first setting out in the World has greatly discouraged me and am resolved never to Enter into anything of that Sort to be obliged to Friends. I have been very low spirited ever since, but am sensible that this is nothing to the various Disappointments that happen in this Life, so must make myself easy and put my Trust in God who is the only Comforter in all cases. I have lived with my Master four years and a half, and I am sure nobody can say but what I have discharged the Duty of a faithful Servant, and the Interest of the house has always stuck so close to me that if I was to be a Partaker I could do no more. You may imagine that I take a great deal of pleasure, but people here know the contrary, for I take as little pleasure as anybody and really I don't find time for it—I can assure you that the Business of this house has been rather more since the War, then before. Scarce one packet arrives but brings half a dozen Letters at least with accounts for sundry small sums of Money to be distributed among the prisoners, I go 2 and 3 times a week in the prison where I have 3 hours work, because people abroad desire Receits for what is paid, the Commission on these Articles is small, being but 6d. in the Pound, but the Number of Sums make it answer pretty well, you are sensible that regular accounts are to be kept in these matters and as much as if they were of 10 times the consequence, I take care to answer all such Letters by Return of the Packetts, and the people on the other side are well satisfied. You may depend that neither the Privateer nor any buissness in the World will make me neglect that of the House. The Eagle Privateer's Cruize was out the 31st past, so have no more concern in her. Captⁿ Bazely has a new one a building, he offered me a part, but I thank him, because in my Situation it is not so becoming. I am very glad to be thus far clear of that troublesome Buissness, and shall not be fond of entering into that Branch again. You'll be so good Sir as to Excuse the Liberty I take in opening myself so freely to you, but you have given me so much prove of your Friendship by repeatedly giving me good Advice, that I should think myself blameable to the highest degree if I did not and I dare say you'll give me all the Satisfaction you can. This serves for Advice that Captⁿ George Stringer in the Hopewell Sloop sailed out of this Harbour for London this morning where I hope he'll arrive safe, he has on board according to the inclosed Bill of Lading 29 pipes Mamzee and 7 pipes Vidonia Canary Wines of which I send you Invoice here annexed the first cost besides some Charges here is 992*l.*—I beg that when they are come to your hands you'll be so kind as to do the needfull about disposing of the same for the most to our advantage, in short do as if the Wines were your own, and whatever you do therein shall be kindly approved, and when an End is made of said Wines you'll transmit me the account of Sale and neat proceeds. There is also on board of Stringer, a pipe belonging to my Master, marked on the Bung P B F and on the head I M 160. the number of the Lot for which he has not signed Receits—nor for 6 pipes and 2 hhds. of Mr Elcock marked F E L and 2 pipes and 2 hhds. of Mr Magnus's markt M so that Stringer has on board in all 45 pipes and 4 hhds—as to the Charges on Mr Elcocks and Mr Magnus's Wines I have nothing to do with, Mr Birch the Cooper has paid all and will send them acc^t. You'll observe the freight is 5 sh. p^r pipe only which you'll be so good as to pay and charge to account. I have had a Letter from Mr Thomas Minet, he says he'll assist all he can in selling the Wines. Pray give my Duty to him when you see him and love to his Family. I'll never undertake such another Concern without consulting you first. I beg pardon for troubling you with such a long Epistle and am with the sincerest Sentiments of Gratitude for all your favours most respectfully,

       Sir,
     Your most obedient humble Servt,
          PETER FECTOR.

 Cozen Detrier has sent on board of Stringers, two Crocks one with Samphire and the other with Wallnuts which she desires you to accept with her Service.

We have no more of these letters preserved, though, no doubt, there must have been many more between this date and 1751, when we first know definitely that Fector was a partner. On Isaac Minet's death, in 1745, William was a good deal at Dover and left Peter Fector in charge of the Dover business, with full and detailed instructions, which, unfortunately, have not survived; they would, probably, have been characteristic and amusing. At this time also Colbran, the clerk, was dismissed by William, and not without good cause, if what he tells us of him in the note to be given later on was true.

Having established himself so firmly in the business, Peter next wished to ally himself with the family, and proposed to Mary, daughter of John Minet, of Eythorne. We have seen the interest that John had taken in the young man's education; and Eythorne being only six miles from Dover, no doubt Mary had often been over to see her grandfather, while, doubtless, Fector himself had often ridden over to Eythorne.

He must, to judge by the following letter, have proposed in 1746, Mary being then eighteen years old; but evidently the proposal was not well received by either the lady or her family :—

Mr Thomas Minet.
Dover 21 January 174$\frac{7}{8}$.

I desire no more than a just competency to live Genteely and bring up a family should I ever have any, and though I don't just at this time think of changing my Life yet I have it in distant View and hope between this and a year or two I shall meet some Lady where a Regard may be mutual, but never shall think of any woman again unless I have some assurances that if I make my addresses they shall be acceptable. I have dear Sir undergone and put up with many things in the last affair that I should never have done had I not imagined that uniting myself to a family I have such a deserving an Esteem for and cultivating an alliance in the Eye of everybody equally agreeable would have met the desired success, but that affair is quite at an End and I hope for my Good. There is no forcing Inclinations nor would it appear prudent to be so much in Love as to desire it. I am really sorry the affair did not take place for all the family's sake, but as I have acted with the strictest honour I must be Commended and not blamed If I have Justice done me.

I am &c^a,
PETER FECTOR.

It is difficult to understand why this letter should have been written to Thomas Minet, instead of William, with whom all the previous correspondence had been held; and it might be inferred from this fact that the proposal had been to marry one of Thomas's two daughters, if it were not that on the letter is a note by Mary's brother, Hughes. 'The original of this was sent (open) under cover to Mr Wm Minet for him to seal and send or deliver to said Thomas Minet who lived on Tower Hill. It was sent most assuredly for the purpose of mortyfying Mr W. M. it relates to his courtship of his niece, (my sister) which lasted 6 or 7 years.'

Why William Minet should be 'mortified' by the perusal of this letter is not at all clear. Remembering that the endorsement was made long afterwards, when the relations between Hughes Minet and Peter Fector had become somewhat strained, and bearing in mind the tone of William's account of the marriage, written when it actually took place, six years later, and the relation in which William stood to Peter, one is almost tempted to doubt the statement, and to suggest that Peter thought it only right to acquaint one who stood to him almost in the position of guardian with his views at that moment.

The letter is interesting in itself for two reasons: first, as an illustration of the unromantic and businesslike character of its writer; nor will the touch of self-satisfaction, which we have noticed in his other letters, pass unnoticed. Secondly, Peter Fector's writing to his uncle Thomas shows that he was in friendly relations with his mother's family, while it also proves the connexion still existing between the Canterbury and Dover Minets.

Fector's perseverance and success were as marked in love as in business, and in 1751 he carried out his purpose. However much some of the family may have opposed the match, it would seem that, notwithstanding Hughes' remark, William approved of it, and the following account of the marriage, and of the honeymoon, shows him as taking a pleasant and kindly interest in the young couple:—

On Saturday 13 July 1751 my neice mary, daughter of John Minet and Alice Hughes his wife, was married to Mr Peter Fector of Dover merch^t, my cozen Mary Fector, wife of Jeremy Fector, of Rotterdam her son ;[1] Mr Derouselle[2] gave her in mariage, he and Mrs Minet present. They were married at the Cathedral Christ Church Canterbury and in a chariot proceeded directly for London

---

[1] 'Registers of Canterbury Cathedral' (*Harleian Soc. pub., Registers*, ii. 92).
[2] See Table *F*.

via Maidstone, and came on sunday evening to towne and were lodged 16 days from 14 July to 29 ditto at the house of Mr William Bonham Backen in allein court near Leadenhall Street[1] at my desire, these were with me 4 or 6 times. They continued in London 16 days during w^h time they went to the sundry places in and about London to see w^t was worth while, my neice never having been in London before. I made 'em a present of *l.* [*blank*] to buy 'em a jewel or plate, they bought their cloths, house goods, and were much taken up. I had 'em at diner and super sundry times, sent 'em wines, engaged to pay lodgings, lent 'em my post chaise to see Putney, Richmond, hampton court, Windsor and places adjacent, honslow, stains, Brentford, Chelsea, Kingsington. They saw also with Miss Molly Minet (his) or D Minet[2] their cozen (hers) Greenwich, tower, river-keys, St Pauls, Westminst^r new bridge, Abbey, and returned back to Dover ye 29 July, and got 1 Augt, and dined in their way to Dover at Mr and Mrs Derousell[3] who civily treated 'em. God grant this mariage wch I W. M. who write this had originally in view even before my d^r fathers death and which for 4 or 5 years or more has been off and on, and likely once or 2^{ce} to be quite on, I pray it may be of comfort use benefit and credit to all the partys, and a comfort to my B^r John Minet. S^d Mr Peter Fector I believe is worth about *l.* [*blank*] which is chiefly his $\frac{1}{3}$ of the stock and capital of the house at Dover the $\frac{2}{3}$ of which is my property and belongs to me; the billan of which books is sent up to me every year and ought to be dated 30 June; it am^{ts} this present year by Gods blessing to *l.* [*blank*].

This my fathers house w^h I call our paternal house of commerce having subsisted with reputation honour and credit and been a nursery from whence my father got his honest livelyhood after his being banished and persecuted from his native home Calais, I thought it a deed incumbent on me at his death, 1745, 8 April, 5 afternoon, to take the house name and buissness under my care and protection and with my name cash credit interest skill and assistance, keep it up and maintain it in business which I did with great care labour pains writtings watchings early and late, altho sufficiently loaded with my wine trade,

---

[1] A small court on the north side of Leadenhall Street, close behind St. Andrew Undershaft; see plan in Stow's *Survey*, book ii. p. 55 (Lond. 1720).

[2] See Tables *A* and *B*.   [3] See Table *F*.

THE BUSINESS

buissness, and other London house concerns as well, comercial in all comissions, in exchanges, stocks, French and Portugall wines administrations executorships, arbitrations, tending the London Assurance Company as a Director, so y^t properly the suport of this Dover house was w^t time I should have employd for my recreation, but the desire I had of its being kept up for ye hon^r and credit of the name as well as my own person, I spared no pains time toyl and labour friends or writtings, to revive its former name; for in 1730 June, say 12 May, my B^r Daniel Minet in London died, and in 8ber 1731 my B^r Isaac Minet jun^r died; 7 years before the house florished and was in greater buissness and credit than ever before because of our having drawne the New York Philadelphia Rhode Iland and Carolina ships to clear at Dover, land their goods, reship 'em for Holland and hamboro which was at good profit credit and satisfaction to my d^r father and his house and thereby drew great number of ships from 25 to 39 to 41 the year my poor B^r Isaac Minet dyed much regreted and lamented by Dover in particular where he was so well beloved, y^t there is no doubt but by the natural interest of the house and that peculliar to himself, by his pains in bringing such a beneficial branch of commerce to the towne wch had been 35 years ago peculier to the place but driven away to Cowes and other places, to the great detriment of the towne, and now brought back wch caused vast sums to be spent in ye towne by the sailors receiving all or part of their wages, made a trade and money to circulate am^o the Custom officers besides ye bountys, I say dutys, fees and to ye surveyors, searchers, landwaiters, alehouses, brewers, bakers, butchers, slopshops, chandler shops, and many sort of tradesmen, and dealings with sundry species of shopkeepers who sold as well as took of their goods, also helpt the farmers poultrers gardners etc, all wch little by little dwindled away and was lost as well by my B$\overline{rs}$ death as my fathers age and incapacity; but also in a good measure by Rooth Colebrand my fathers comptoir clarke whose infidelity incomplaisance indifference to y^e house and sordid attachment to his own private interest disgusted several comanders, and not knowing how to satisfy the officers, and ignorant of the method to please 'em, not only disgusted several but occassioned complaints y^t since m^r I. M. jun. death Dover was worse y^n any other place to clear at, so they returned to Cowes in peace, to newcastle and orkneys in ye late war, it has been very rare and seldom any have cleard except 1 or 2 in 1749, 2 or 3 in 1750 and 1751.[1]

This Rooth Colebrand disgusted several people friends of the h° who used to complain to me, but as during my late fathers life I could not mouve him without inconveniencys knowne to myself, I waited till after 8 april 1745 to discharge him totally from our service, he wanted to ride rusty but I kept him under by dint of firm resolution, cost w^t it would and consequence ever so great, not to suffer him to do or say anything to the prejudice of my father family or house y^t I obliged him to submit to settle and work at books and accounts and finally to be discharged from our house. Some people soon after thought better of him of which Mr Vincent Underdowne was one and helpt him to be ye comptrolers clark at ye custom h° where he has been till ye time of my writing this Augt 1751. He married Mr John Johnson ye pilot's daug^t; he used to go fidling with his father from alehouse to alehouse 1718 to 20 when he disliking it, chose to go to sea and was equiped to go with a fishing boat and as I was going to Dieppe,[2] B^r Isaac courting Mrs Widow D——, I advised my father to take him to copy, run of errands and so forth, clean shoes knives and light and sweep counting house wch he did so well y^t he sweept the farthing draw, he carried of bottles of wine innumerable, and my dear father being often indolent and careless frequently left the key in his blew chest or cash drunk [? trunk] wch this R. C. frequently robbed of gold and silver peices, my father not being able to perceive his loss for want of a regular cash [account] wch was neglected by R. C. who found his acc^t, he also defrauded considerably in his marketing bills and housekeeping and this for 7 or 9 years before P. F. was admitted into the house in 17[39] so y^t God only knows the prejudice y^t Villain has done ye house ; as I told him before and after my fathers death if he was to pay me 1000 guineas I did not belive y^t he would make amends for w^t he had defrauded ye house of, and as to his treachery in opening a letter from the Canarys by the Juffrow Caterina, Capt Hans Benn for Dunkirke, he cald cap. Baseley com^r of the Little Eagle privateer who went on board and seized her and ye matter, case, of y^t affair is still depending in Doctors Com-

---

[1] The profits of the house for these years bear out this statement. They fell from 1000*l.* in 1745 to 483*l.* in 1752.

[2] 1720.

mons and not ended 1751 August; I told him had I been downe at y⁵ time of yᵗ false treacherous act of infidelity of betraying y⁵ secret of y⁵ family and contoir I would have cut his throat and no jury in England would have found me guilty for riding y⁵ world of so great a villain; yᵗ if he presumed to delay time and not bring up the books ballance etc, I would run y⁵ 2 foot ruler downe his throat so made him tamely do all yᵗ was needful, till with y⁵ general consent and applause of y⁵ people of Dover and sundry in London I discharged him out of the house, for the doing all which it need not be doubted but it cost me a great deal of warmth heat passion patience and resolution, and had great need at yᵗ doleful time seeing my dear father languish and suffer cruely near 2 months before his end, however by Gods grace and assistance I got the better of it and after my fathers death I instituted Mr Pʳ Fector who had lived 5 years with my father to be my agent and attourney at Dover and on the 1st May 1745 I departed for London and left instructions in writting how Mr Fector should proceed.

From this it appears that after his father's death, in 1745, William, having his own business in London to attend to, had left the management of affairs at Dover in the hands of Peter Fector, who must have become a partner some time between 1745 and 1751, as on his marriage in the latter year he is spoken of as owning one-third of the stock. The first articles of partnership were not, however, drawn up till 1759, upon the occasion of Hughes Minet's approaching marriage.

Hughes Minet was a son of John, the rector of Eythorne, at which place he was born in 1731. He was educated at Canterbury, and received his business training in London, under his uncle William. He went to Dover in 1752, when his uncle gave him a share in the business on his attaining his majority. His position as a partner, as well as Peter Fector's, is definitely recognised by the articles of partnership of the Dover business of 1759, which are expressed to be made between 'William Minet of London and Peter Fector and Hughes Minet of Dover, Merchants and partners in the house of business carried on at Dover, under the name of William Minet and Company,' and by which the business is divided, one-half to William, one-third to Fector, and one-sixth to Hughes. The deed is not, perhaps, drawn in strictly legal language, but still is very careful and detailed, even to providing for William's accommodation when he should come to Dover :—

It is agreed that Mr William Minet shall have the best appartments reserved for himself, or for any Friend or Friends he may either bring with him or send down, in which they shall be received as being at his own House in the most friendly manner, and he the more insists on this as being the principal Founder and chief concerned in the Business of the Partnership since the already mentioned year 1745, the Epoch of Mr Isaac Minet's Death by which (and after the Declension of Mr James Minet of Berlin and his desiring Mr William Minet to continue the same) the natural Right of it devolved on him. The blue Room therefore on the first Floor (as being the best appartment) is to be kept at and for the sole use and behoof of the said Mr William Minet and his friends, except that he agrees that Mrs Fector may Receive her visits there after her Lyings-in ; and make use of it on some very few and particular occasions of Consequence where the offer of it cannot be avoided ; and therefore, lest it should often happen, it is agreed that another Room on the first Floor shall and may be furnished if absolutely needful, more than it now is, that among other services it may receive some persons to whom it may be proper to make an offer of a Chamber, though not necessary to use the best Room ; which, if often repeated would be contrary to Mr William Minet's Intentions in the furnishing it, which was on these very conditions and no others, done at his own Expense, and for the cost of which he has been debited, as p^r Inventory and accounts does appear, and to which Mr Fector, on these conditions did agree.

It is clear that Hughes had but a poor opinion of his uncle's abilities as a draughtsman, for he makes the following note on his copy of the articles :—

The annexed confused and nonsensical articles of partnership were by me copied from a still greater mass of nonsense, written by my self-sufficient and unwise uncle, Wm Minet, who instead of employing a man of the law to draw up articles in proper and legal form, thought he could write them as well as a professional man. If he had been endued with common sense he would have had them so drawn, and made as binding and obligatory as possible. This was also an ex post facto piece of business for there ought to have been proper articles long before when P. F. would have conformed to reason the more readily; at least there ought to have been such in 1752 when I was admitted as partner, whereas even these ridiculous ones were delayed (and they were the first) until 1759. I well remember I was ashamed of them at the time.

As a matter of fact, this criticism is without foundation, and was only prompted by the differences which arose between the surviving partners after William's death.

From 1752 till 1761 Hughes Minet and Peter Fector worked together at Dover, and William carried on his own business in London. In 1761, Hughes removed thither on his marriage with Mary Loubier, while the Dover partnership was re-arranged by a memorandum bearing date October 20, 1761, which recites that :—

> Whereas Mr Hughes Minet did dwell at Dover as an acting partner there before his marriage in January 1761, but now does and is to dwell in London, and is become a partner with his uncle Mr William Minet; and in consideration of a greater share of time and labour that will fall on Mr Peter Fector residing at Dover, it is agreed that Mr William Minet shall give and allow Mr Peter Fector over and above the one third part which he now enjoys one sixth part of his the said Mr William Minet's one half.

Peter Fector was to reside in the house at Dover, and to be allowed 180*l.* a year towards the housekeeping expenses, upon the condition that William Minet was to retain 'the full use, liberty and property of the room called the Blue room for his own use whenever he goes to Dover, when the said Mr Peter Fector engages to receive him and his friend (if any) whenever he has a mind to go and spend a few days or months there, either as a family visitor or about the inspection of the business'; Mr Peter Fector also engaged, 'that in the like manner Mr Hughes Minet our partner shall be also received at the said house in a friendly and amicable manner as relations, friends and partners should be received.'

We have seen how Hughes criticised the earlier partnership articles, and this variation of them does not escape his characteristic annotations ; but again, in reading these, we must bear in mind that they were written under the influence of the estrangement which unfortunately grew up between himself and Fector. He writes thus in the margin :—

> This incoherent Mem° was wholly Mr W. M's production who was too self sufficient to think that he stood in need of help or advice : neither did he ever ask mine or that of anybody else.

And, again, lower down we read :—

> This concession of W. M. to P. F. was in a manner forced from s^d W. M. by P. F's threats and violence of behaviour upon my marriage ; which nobody at present, however well they may think they know him can have any idea of. He was nearly stung to madness at my sudden apparent prosperity in life, for the pecuniary advantage of my marriage was by my uncle's vanity too much magnified for truth and for policy (as I woefully found in the end) Fector's behaviour also to me under all this was the most brutal that can be imagined. Neither had I any resources since my uncle himself was forced to bear with this man's usage and threats of setting up a house by himself.

Whether there was any truth in Hughes' explanation of his uncle's motives in increasing Fector's share, or whether it was a voluntary act, done out of pure kindness, cannot be determined ; the insertion of the following clause in this memorandum is, however, evidence to some extent of William's desire to guard against dangers, some signs of which may already have betrayed themselves :—

> Mr Peter Fector, who by Mr Hughes Minet's marriage and dwelling in London, becomes a Trustee in a higher degree for the share and property, profits and well doing of the house, does solemnly promise on the faith and word of honour of a gentleman that he will in all things act with all the justice and fidelity possible, and will consult the interest and welfare of the same, and wholly employ his mind for the well-doing and prosperity of the whole and promote the interest of the house. As it is morally impossible for the partners of the house at Dover to divide, without incredible difficulties, trouble, discord and vexations there are the more reasons for us to be united and Mr W. Minet declares that it is on the conditions and hopes of avoiding any disagreements that he enters into an additional agreement, and on the firm promise of each one's trying all they can to live happily and contented.

At this point, again, another of Hughes' characteristic annotations occurs, but one so tinged with the bitterness of his later feelings towards his partner, that even at this interval of time it seems better not to reproduce it.

The capital of the Dover house was, it appears by this memorandum, 20,000*l.*, and the profits are spoken of as being likely to amount to 1,000*l.*; on which Hughes says in the margin:—

> This plainly shews what the idea was of the then probable profits of the Dover house. And although indeed at this time, 1761 and 1770, the said profits were on an average more than this sum,[1] yet this long continued and impressed idea on my mind in a great measure was the standard I went by when I made the paltry bargain with P. F. in 1770, for my relinquishment and separation from him.

Hughes Minet and Peter Fector must both have been able men; but Fector was clearly the abler business-man of the two, and it was, perhaps, the half-unconscious recognition of this superiority that was the cause of Hughes' bitterness towards him. All through their long lives it becomes more and more clear that Hughes regarded the business as one founded by the Minets, and Fector as an intruder, who owed his position in it to their goodness; but while he is resenting this intrusion, we cannot help feeling that what he really feels so bitterly, is Fector's superior capacity, which Fector, on his part, was not backward in asserting. While blaming Hughes for the ill-feeling he exhibited, we must not forget that Fector, able as he was, was also ambitious and self-confident—as, indeed, appears in the correspondence we have quoted from above—and was at all times inclined to push his own interests in ways that must have been peculiarly galling.

Looking at the facts after the lapse of more than a hundred years, it would seem that Hughes had little to complain of. The son of a country clergyman, had it not been for his uncle William's practical adoption of him, his prospects in life would have been but slight. His uncle put him into the Dover business, and gave him a share of the London business as well, and though it is possibly true, as Hughes states positively, that William's hand was forced in the 'concessions' he made to Fector, yet we have no other evidence of it, and, indeed,

---

[1] They were, actually, 1,767*l.* and 2,197*l.* for these two years.

his conduct to Fector throughout, even to the mention made of him in his will, is very strong evidence the other way.

Whatever 'concessions' may have been made to Fector, they were as nothing compared to what was done for Hughes. At the end of the memorandum from which we have been quoting occurs another note in Hughes' hand which illustrates this well. He writes:—

> By the above agreement thenceforward Mr Wm Minet's $\frac{1}{2}$ was reduced to $\frac{5}{12}$, Mr Fector's $\frac{1}{3}$ was increased to $\frac{5}{12}$, and my $\frac{1}{6}$ was supposed to be continued $\frac{1}{6}$. But the above division was only nominal and passed off as so divided to P. Fector, for in reality by the concession which my uncle also made to me of $\frac{1}{12}$ out of his share, his said remaining interest in the Dover profits was $\frac{4}{12}$ or $\frac{1}{3}$ only, Peter Fector's $\frac{5}{12}$, and mine $\frac{3}{12}$ or $\frac{1}{4}$. The said concession of $\frac{1}{12}$ my uncle made to me was by a separate memorandum which he gave me, and of this P. Fector had no knowledge neither is anything said about it in the above mem° to him. My uncle agreed with Mr Loubier [Hughes Minet's wife's uncle] that I should have $\frac{1}{3}$ of the profits of both houses, but from my marriage to the day of his death [Jan. 1767] I never had more than $\frac{1}{4}$ of the profits of the Dover house although indeed I had $\frac{1}{3}$ of those of his house in London. This was a sort of deception, but I never told Loubier of it, and patiently submitted. Indeed he advanced the whole capital of the London House 10,000*l.* himself, without charging me any interest upon my share, or making me advance it. This was, I thought by way of compensation, neither could it be advisable for him to appear to hold a less share in the Dover house than P. Fector did. This concession, and upon such an occasion— for my marriage did not injure P. F. but the contrary, relieved him from my presence at Dover—was assuredly the cause in a great measure of my having been compelled to do the like (as happened) afterwards; and it compleatly shows the ascendancy whc. he had, even over my uncle.

Though Hughes lived in London after his marriage in 1761, he cannot altogether have given up his residence at Dover; for, becoming a freeman by purchase in 1755, in 1765 he served the office of mayor. William died in 1767, and the feeling between the surviving partners, which respect for him had till now kept in some control, became more evident. They met at Rochester, February 21, 1767, and drew up a new agreement, of which Hughes says :—

It is to be observed that not only this but also all other hasty agreements entered into between us were written by P. Fector himself; as must be apparent (to those who know his character) from the turn he gives to each sentence, and the minutiæ of every condition making in his own favour.

The main points of the agreement are :—
1. That the firm shall be known as Minet & Fector (it had hitherto been Wm. Minet & Company).
2. The capital to be 12,000*l.*, owned equally, and the profits equally divided.
3. Peter Fector to be allowed 250*l.* for housekeeping expenses at Dover so long as Hughes Minet does not reside there.

A separate memorandum was signed the same day, by which Hughes agreed for every year that he should not reside at Dover to allow Fector 25 per cent. of his half-share of the profits. On this we have Hughes' usual marginal note, in which he says :—

This was brought about by P. F's grumbling and complaints of hardships, mixed with distant menacing hints, and resentment at Mr W. Minet's usage by his will, and it was evident that without I had signed this, he would not have agreed to the proceeding.

This note is followed by a calculation of what the effect of the agreements would be, on the basis of an assumed profit of 5,150*l.*, of which it is shown that, after making the allowances for housekeeping and rent provided for in the deed, Fector would take 3,350*l.*, while only 1,800*l.* would be left to Hughes, which, considering that the two were equally interested in the capital, does appear, in the absence of further information, an inequitable division. The calculation concludes with a somewhat weak-minded protest :—

Lett my children have done with all connection whatever hereafter with this man and his family rather than ever submit to be imposed upon in this manner. Oh, Mr Wm Minet, I had rather you had protected me as you promised to do from the rapine of this man, than have left me any part of your residue.

It is obvious that no partnership in which such an antagonism of feeling existed could long endure, and we are not, therefore, surprised to find it dissolved by a deed of October 18, 1770, in the margin of which we find, as usual, Hughes' explanations:—

> I entered into this unwise agreement under a great distress of mind as well as of body, owing to the death of my wife and of my uncle, and of her uncle and Aunt, all within a short space of time and also above all, whilst I was in this state more owing to the oppression and ill usage which I met with from this very Peter Fector. But above all I feared that my sons, had I died, would have been ill used, I having not a soul to appoint for their protection in quality of Executor or Guardian.
>
> If I had not made some sort of agreement with P. F. I should have perished, for my health was very bad and my sons would (in their infancy) have been deprived of a father. But I had better have quitted the connection with him without any consideration whatever than under such conditions to have taken the comparatively inconsiderable sum of money that I did. I was however compelled to be in haste to get rid of him.

By the agreement itself Hughes disposes of all his interest in the Dover business for 25,000*l.*, payable by five yearly instalments of 5,000*l.*, and agrees to take 1,200*l.* as his share of the profits for the current year.[1]

Whether the terms were fair or not, one cannot now say. Hughes himself, in later years, asserted very vehemently that they were not. Be this as it may, however, we can only consider that no one had a better opportunity of knowing the value of what he was surrendering than Hughes himself, and if he agreed to take less than a fair value, he should have blamed himself, and not his partner. The deed does contain two points which seem to show that Fector was certainly not unmindful of his own interests. Hughes, who, it must be remembered, was continuing his business in London, was to transact gratuitously all the agency business for the Dover house for five years, or to allow Fector a sum of 600*l.* a year in case he did not; while he further bound himself to hand over to Fector, for no consideration, the house at

---

[1] Under the agreement, and as the profits actually were this year, Hughes would only have received 787*l.* 18*s.* 2*d.*, so that in this respect he did not come so badly off. During the next thirteen years, until 1783, when he resumed his partnership with Fector, his share of the profits under the old agreement would have amounted to an average of 2,672*l.* 15*s.* per annum, which, as the event showed, was what he was disposing of for 25,000*l.*

Dover which had been left by William to his brother James, of Berlin, in case it should come to him on James' death. But this latter clause, as the event was, never took effect.

Looking at the circumstances of Fector's first connexion with the business, and considering the effects of the agreements of 1759, 1761, and 1767, we can only account for the increased share he gained under each on the theory that his business abilities were such as to render his continued connexion with the firm worth the high price he put on it. It must be remembered also that William Minet, and, later, Hughes, had the London business to attend to, and so could not devote the necessary time and attention to Dover. Nor is it likely, from what we know of Fector, that he was not fully conscious of his own abilities, or backward in claiming the value at which he estimated them.

The partnership was now at an end, and with it the connexion of the family with the Dover business, which had lasted eighty-four years. Hughes, however, continued the London branch, probably in his uncle's house in Fenchurch Street, and there acted as agent for Fector till 1775, when (his wife's death being, as he tells us, the moving cause) he ceased himself to take any active part in it. It was perhaps at this time that Fenchurch Street was given up, and the business transferred to Austin Friars, where it was managed by Lewis Miol. Mr. Miol was a Huguenot, and would seem to have been in business in Austin Friars previously. What the arrangements may have been we do not know, but till 1783 Miol carried on the Minet business, and acted as agent for the Dover firm. In 1783, Hughes' three sons were growing up, and he was anxious, he tells us, to find them occupation, while, possibly, he himself was not unwilling to resume a more active life; in any case, in this year Miol retired and Hughes resumed the direction of affairs. Nor was he content with this: overtures were made to Fector for a resumption of the Dover partnership also, and this was carried into effect by a deed signed at Ashford, February 15, 1783, which was to remain in force for twenty-six years (till 1809). By this deed the two houses were practically amalgamated, and the capital (18,000*l.*) was, with the profits, to be divided, two-thirds to Fector and one-third to Hughes; provision was also made for the introduction of the sons of each partner as they should come of age. The only other matter of interest in the arrangement relates to the house at Dover, which on James Minet's death had come to Isaac Minet, Hughes' youngest son, who was still an infant;

of this Hughes agreed that his son, so soon as he came of age, should grant a lease to Peter Fector.

This arrangement lasted six years, and apparently the two partners got on better, for in 1789, on Hughes' two younger sons, John Lewis and Isaac, and Fector's two sons, John Minet and James Peter, coming of age, a fresh deed was agreed to, by which they were all constituted partners, while the capital was increased to 20,000*l.*

From 1787 to 1814 the partnership continued, but gradually the old differences reappeared, and on the death of Hughes Minet (1813) and of Peter Fector (1814), the two old members of the firm, the partnership was finally and for ever put an end to. Peter Fector's life had been a long one: he entered the house as Isaac Minet's clerk in 1739, and died in 1814, leaving Isaac's namesake and great-grandson, a man of forty-seven, one of the surviving partners. His wife, Mary, who had died in 1794, was buried at Eythorne, the place of her birth, and her husband was laid by her side. They were attached to the place, not only by Mary's early associations, but also from the fact that they had bought land in the neighbourhood.[1]

The Dover business from this date remained entirely in the hands of the Fectors, and its later history can be shortly disposed of. Peter Fector left one son, John Minet Fector, surviving him.[2] He carried on the business till his death in 1821, after which date it was continued for the benefit of his son, John Minet Fector, a minor, who only came of age in 1833. He did not remain in it long, but in 1842 disposed of it to the National Provincial Bank, thus finally closing the Fector connexion with a business which, founded by Stephen Minet in 1686, had remained in the families of Minet and Fector for a period of 156 years.[3]

It remains to trace briefly the fortunes of the London business, carried on by the Minets alone from 1814. Hughes Minet died in 1813, and left two sons, John Lewis and Isaac, who continued at 21, Austin Friars. On the dissolution of their partnership with John Minet Fector in 1814, they took as partner John Stride, who had been a clerk to Lewis Miol previous to 1783. In 1821 the firm made an attempt

[1] See p. 219 for the inscription on their tomb.
[2] John Minet Fector will be found frequently mentioned in a *History of Dover* by W. Batcheller (Dover, 1828), where, among other details, is an amusing account of a banquet he gave to 2,300 persons, on October 27, 1820, to celebrate the return of his family from abroad.
[3] John Minet Fector the younger was elected Member for Maidstone March, 28, 1838, and the election being declared void, he was again returned on June 15, 1838. The other Member was B. Disraeli, in whose *Letters* he is twice referred to (ed. Lond. 1887, pp. 141, 143).

PIER HOUSE, DOVER

to re-establish itself at Dover, presumably in opposition to the Fectors, and a bank, called The Old Bank, was opened under the management of Lewis Stride ; but by arrangement with the Fectors this was closed in 1825. In 1828 the Minets retired altogether from the business, which was henceforward carried on by the Strides alone until 1842, when the house founded in Fenchurch Street by Daniel Minet in 1721 ceased to exist. It may be noted as a curious coincidence, that the business at Dover and that in London ceased to exist in the same year.

The old house at Dover, known as Pier House, in which the original Isaac Minet had lived, passed, as we have seen, on his death in 1745, to his son James, of Berlin, who in 1749 rebuilt it in conjunction with his brother William, on the agreement that whichever brother survived was to possess the whole of it, an arrangement described and commented on by Hughes in a note endorsed on the probate of his grandfather Isaac's will :—

> The houses etc^{ra} belonging to Mr Isaac Minet (my grandfather) at Dover are by this his will left to his son James Minet, but as he never came over from Berlin to take possession or carry on the business, the same were occupied by William Minet his B^r (or Peter Fector his agent). This last enduced his B^r James to consent to the family H^o of business being pulled down, and they agreed to go halves in building that which now exists, making the preposterous agreement that the survivor should be the proprietor of the whole : about which however no documents, except letters ever existed. Wm Minet acted evidently upon the principle of becoming possessor by surviving his brother (because as he, his B^r was the oldest, so that he must die first) as may be seen by that farrago of nonsense in his will. All which went for nothing as Mr James Minet survived him some few years.
>
> This remark is made by me, Hughes Minet, 14 April 1804.

James left Pier House to his godson, Isaac, Hughes Minet's third son, then only seven years old. Upon the renewal of the partnership between Hughes and Peter Fector in 1783, it was arranged that on Isaac's coming of age, which would be in 1788, he should grant a lease of the house to the Fectors for forty-two years, from 1783. This was done, and the lease then granted only expired in 1825. Pier House, on Isaac's death in 1839, passed to his eldest son, Charles

William, and was finally sold and pulled down in 1872, in the course of improvements carried out by the London, Chatham and Dover Railway. It stood between the Harbour Station and the Dock Basin, on ground now partly covered by a spirit-warehouse.

No. 21, Austin Friars, the house in which the London business was carried on from 1783 to 1838, was not without interest as an example of one of the older merchants' houses of the City of London, and when pulled down in 1888 attracted considerable attention. A few notes as to its history, derived chiefly from old deeds in my possession, may not be without interest.

The house appears to be marked in Ogilby's map of 1677, and belonged in 1694 to R. Young, S. Barrington, and E. Young, who mortgaged it in that year to one R. Stamper. In 1705 it passed from the Youngs into the possession of Herman Olmius, son of Johannes Ludovicus Olmius, of Arlon, in the Duchy of Luxemburg. Herman Olmius died in 1718, and by his will the house passed to the three children of his daughter Margaret, wife of Adrian Lernoult, the result of this being that towards the end of the century the ownership of the house was divided into six shares. In 1778 Lewis Miol took a lease of the house for twenty-five years, and it was here, no doubt, that he carried on the business which he had taken over from Hughes Minet. When Hughes returned to business in 1783, he took an assignment of the lease from Miol, and it must be from this year that the connexion of the Minet family with Austin Friars dates. Hughes Minet surrendered the lease under which he held the premises in 1790, and having succeeded in purchasing one-sixth of the house, took a fresh lease of the remaining five-sixths for thirty-five years. This lease expired in 1825, when John Lewis Minet, who under his father's will had succeeded to the freehold of one-sixth, took two new leases, of two-sixths and one-half respectively, for thirty-one years. These two leases were both granted by various descendants of Margaret Lernoult.[1]

The new arrangement had only continued three years when J. L. Minet and his brother retired from business, and were succeeded by Lewis Stride, who, however, remained in 21, Austin Friars, but a short time. The house continued to be owned by Isaac Minet, who succeeded to his brother's interest, until 1838, when he assigned the lease

---

[1] Some account of the Olmius family will be found in vol. ix. of the *English Illustrated Magazine*, at page 239. It is a curious coincidence that the father of this Adrian Lernoult was an old friend of Isaac Minet's in Calais, and is twice referred to in his Narrative (pp. 26, 36). He was also connected with the Sigarts; (see page 89, note).

of five-sixths, which had still eighteen years to run, and conveyed the one-sixth of the freehold to J. Thomas. Isaac himself had, since 1803, been interested as tenant, and since 1811 as freeholder, in 13, Austin Friars, where he resided, and it was, doubtless, this fact which caused him to part with No. 21. The former house still remains in the possession of the family, and was rebuilt in 1877 by James L. Minet.

CHAPTER IX

HUGHES MINET

A little wearish old man, very melancholy by nature; averse from company in his latter times and much given to solitariness; a famous philosopher.—R. BURTON.

HAVING in the last chapter diverged from the direct history of the family in order to complete the account of the business, we may now return to the more personal narrative, and in this chapter deal with the fourth generation, in the person of Hughes Minet. Of John Minet, who represents the third generation, very little is known, perhaps because he was never connected with the business. What his father, Isaac Minet, has told us of his earlier years we have read in a former chapter, and his son Hughes, we shall find, makes one or two references to him; but beyond a single autograph on a deed, not a scrap of his own writing remains.

In speaking of Hughes Minet, the difficulty arises rather from a redundance than from a lack of materials. From his early youth—there is evidence of it in his sixteenth year—down to the very last year of his life, it was his habit to express his opinions of men and of things on almost every book, paper, or document that came into his possession. These notes still exist on the margins of his books and on the fly-leaves at their beginning and end, on the backs of engravings, maps, and plans, and all over such portions of deeds as are not occupied by the engrossment. They are invariably written in very black ink, and in a firm, upright, round hand, and are not infrequently enforced with heavy points of exclamation and thick black or red lines, in the ruling of which Hughes was a thorough master. However thick the lines or black the ink, the whole work is always neat and methodical. Nor was he always content with this mode of expressing himself: he would constantly copy out, with the utmost labour and neatness, the whole correspondence on any subject that might have been occupying him, adding characteristic annotations in the margin of his copy. This he would bind in rough brown paper, the whole strongly sewn with red tape, the ends of which would be secured to the cover by a large red seal. Should the matter under consideration require the help of a tabular statement—and much of this kind of correspondence refers to matters of business or accounts—a large sheet of paper of the exact size and shape required would be prepared by fastening together several smaller sheets with wafers, on which, tabulated and methodised by the most magnificent red and black lines, the figures would be set out, and the calculations carried to the utmost fraction, with a clearness that would make their teaching plain to the meanest intellect.

The perseverance, thoroughness, neatness, and, above all, the method exhibited by Hughes in thus recording his opinions of men and things, throw much light upon his character; if we add to these the opinions so recorded, we are able, to a great extent, to picture to ourselves the whole man. Therefore, while supplying in the following sketch of his life the main dates and events, we shall, as far as possible, let him speak for himself.

His father's fourth child, he was born on June 30, 1731, at Eythorne, in Kent. One would like much to know what his early home-training may have been; but up to his sixteenth year we know nothing. From that time onwards we have the help of a number of books which his father gave him, and in which, in later years, Hughes made his usual annotations; the titles of these, with the comments contained in them, will be our best guide to the influence exercised and the training bestowed by the father on the son. First among them must be placed a small manuscript book, entirely in Hughes' handwriting, the title-page of which runs as follows: ' Instruction morale d'un père à son fils, copied by H. Minet 1747'; at the end of the book is the following note:—

> These three little paper books were written by me Hughes Minet from a printed original belonging to my dear father the Revd John Minet (who was rector of Eythorne about 45 years) and at the desire of my dear father, I being then about 16½ years of age; the contents of the same he recommended me to consider as recommendations from himself to me, as if emanating originally from himself. Eythorne Feb. 1747.

The date 1747 must refer to the time the copy was made, as it is evident that this note was added about 1766. Pages 50 to 80 of the book have been torn out, and about 1811 Hughes makes this further note :—

Who could have torn these leaves out I know not. Oh! the reflections that the reperusal of these three small books of my own copying (as far as from these mutilated pages it was possible) bring to my mind, now as I am by God's blessing arrived to almost fourscore years of age !!!

H. Minet.

Another book is entitled 'The Wisdom of God,' and must have been a birthday-present from his father ; it contains this note :—

The gift of my honoured father Mr John Minet to me Hughes Minet June 30th 1749, ætatis 18.

The 'Memoirs of Several Ladies' (Lond. 1755) was also, he tells us, a gift from the same source :—

This book was given me by my dear father the Revd John Minet of Eythorne. It is a most excentric performance, in which a great deal both sublime and nonsensical may be met with, but nothing bad.

The following year we find another work mentioned, entitled 'A Demonstration of the Being and Attributes of God' (Lond. 1728), in which is a much longer note :—

This book is a present from my honoured father the Revd Mr John Minet at Eythorne the 1st day of Jany 1756. Persons of science need no such demonstrations as this and the rest of the kind by the Boyles, the Rays, and the Derhams, and even the Bentleys, all of which this of Clarke exceeds in extravagance. The existence of an intelligent being, the first cause of all things is sufficiently apparent in all the works of nature ; the only merit these writings can have is that they needlessly put us in mind of the existence of that God who is the first cause of all things, for in truth they do no more, and they do even *that* very indecently and unbecomingly on many occasions.

In the second part of the same work, under the name of the author, the Rev. Samuel Clarke, is written 'A high Church priest,' and between the first and second parts occurs the following note :—

'The arguments contained in the foregoing demonstration are long since exploded, consequently the following discourse is of much more importance to read frequently, the other may be read once'; the above no doubt I was told by my dear father when he gave me this book and such must have been the orthodox opinion then (nearly 60 years ago). But as I have as great a right (now in my 83rd year) as any one, let him be who he will, had, or has, to think for me I presume to say that I am of an opinion quite contrary to theirs as to the merits of this book. I confess that neither of these discourses please me. I think that the doctrines are founded upon a false metaphysical conception of the Deity, and that the arguments are in many respects inconclusive and presumptive, and in some instances even blasphemous.

Two more books are noted as having been given him by his father: in 1758, 'Reflexions Morales de l'empereur Marc Antonin'; in 1759, 'Commentaires d'Hiérocles sur les vers dorez de Pythagore.' There are also notes in two other works, which may be quoted as adding slightly to our meagre knowledge of John Minet:—

This was one of my dear fathers hamper, (refuse) books. He however full well knew the merit of it, but, poor man, he had not room for his library and for those books which as a good scholar he had oftenest call to turn to and read. He was rector of Eythorne in Kent 40 years and upwards, and no man could, and with reason, be more beloved by his parishioners than he was.

This was one of the many books which my dear father for want of sufficient room in his book closet, consigned to the garret, from which I rescued it as being in many respects curious and remarkable.

There are many other 'hamper' books, and among them we may note 'Anecdotes de Florence, ou histoire secrète de la maison de Médicis,' and 'Heures perdues et divertissantes du Chevalier de * * *'; while further gifts from his father are '"Histoire de Louis XI.," par Varillas,' 'Elite des bons mots,' and 'La manière de bien penser dans les ouvrages d'esprit.' John Minet's education had been altogether in England, but he had evidently, to judge from his library, kept up a close acquaintance with French, in which language his son was equally at home; indeed, for seven successive generations a fairly familiar knowledge of that language has been maintained.

Save once, when he speaks of her descent,[1] Hughes never mentions his mother, though he was thirty-seven years old when she died, and we are unable to trace what influence she may have had on the formation of his character. He was at school at Canterbury, and when there attended the French service in the Cathedral crypt; this must have been before he was thirteen, as in 1744 he went to live in London, with his uncle William. This he himself tells us in a note endorsed, characteristically enough, on the back of a Grant of Arms he obtained from the Heralds' College in 1799, in which, after saying that he had himself intended applying for this grant earlier, he adds: 'It was also what my uncle William Minet talked of doing ever since I can remember, viz[t] ever since my first coming to his house in Fenchurch Street London in the year 1744 when I was 13 years of age.' From this age William practically adopted him, and it must have been during the eight years, 1744–52, that he received in his uncle's office the business training which qualified him to take charge, with Peter Fector, of the Dover business at the age of twenty-one. Before going to Dover, however, his uncle sent him abroad, as we learn from a note written on the back of an engraving of Louis XV., where he says:—

> I bought this print at Paris when I was there in the autumn of 1752. It is a striking likeness. I particularly noticed him at the hunt at Fontainebleau to which I was introduced by M[r] de Butler to whom I was recomended by my uncle [*i.e.* William Minet of Fenchurch Street] who knew him. It was his province to hold the stirrup whilst the king mounted, I consequently stood quite close to him, and for a considerable space of time during the formalities. The King did me the honor of speaking to me, I being handsomely dressed in green and gold, the livery of the hunt, without which no body could be there. He asked me how my grandfather at Dover[2] (dead long before) did who had sent him so many fine English horses, how I liked France, etc[m]. He appeared affable, and his debaucheries had not ruined his countenance at least.[3]

On his return from France he was at once made a partner in the Dover business, his uncle giving him an interest of one-sixth, valued at 1,166*l.* 13*s.* 4*d.*, Fector having two-sixths, and William the remaining half.

---

[1] See page 101.   [2] Isaac Minet, who died April 8, 1745.
[3] Louis XV., born in 1710, came to the throne in 1715.

We have seen in the last chapter that the first articles of partnership were not drawn up till 1759, at which date the capital of the house had grown to 12,873*l*. 8*s*. 7*d*., making Hughes's one-sixth worth 2,145*l*. 11*s*. 5*d*.; so that William's adoption of his nephew had given him at an early age a position in life which his subsequent generosity still further improved.[1]

We know nothing further of him till 1755, when, on March 14, the Dover Corporation minutes show us that 'Hughes Minet, gentleman, was admitted a freeman by purchase.' His connexion with the business has been traced in the last chapter, where the opinions expressed on the various articles of partnership (all copied by himself in a book, and neatly indexed) may be referred to.

Peter Fector had married Hughes' elder sister, Mary, in 1751, and was living in Pier house, formerly occupied by Isaac Minet, but which had been rebuilt in 1749; and Hughes lived with his sister and brother-in-law. Even in these early days the two young men did not get on well together, and it must have been a mutual relief when Hughes on his marriage, in 1761, removed to London.

William had behaved with the utmost generosity to his nephew. We have seen how, in 1752, on his admission as a partner, he was given one-sixth share of the Dover business; and now, on the occasion of his marriage, this one-sixth was raised to one-third, while a third share in the London business, together with a sum of 2,000*l*., was added to this by the marriage settlement.

Mary Loubier, who was to become Hughes' wife, was daughter and co-heiress of John Antony Loubier. The Loubiers had come originally from Nimes, and, did we but know it, the story of their coming out of France would no doubt match with that of the family whose Huguenot blood this marriage served to reinforce. Though, however, nothing is known of this, we have a glimpse of the sufferings of one member of the family who remained in France and continued steadfast in the Reformed Faith. Susanne Loubier was arrested at Montpelier in 1723, and, with several other ladies, imprisoned in the tower of Constance, at Aigues-Mortes, for many years. Of the story of this imprisonment we have a full account in the letters of Isabeau Menet, a fellow-sufferer with Susanne Loubier.[2] These letters, written

---

[1] In 1752 the profits of the Dover house were 483*l*. 10*s*. 5*d*., and in 1759—a very exceptional year—they amounted to 3,392*l*. 0*s*. 6*d*. Hughes Minet has left a tabulated statement of the exact profits in every year from 1745 to 1811.

[2] *Isabeau Menet, prisonnière à la Tour de Constance*, 1735-1750 : A. Lombard, Geneva, 1873.

to Jeanne Menet, Isabeau's sister, who had escaped to Geneva, where she had married M. Lombard, are full of references to the writer's fellow-prisoners, and more than once contain enclosures and messages from Susanne Loubier.[1] The Loubier descent will be found in Table M; but, unfortunately, I am unable to connect Susanne with the English Loubiers, though, from the fact that Jeanne Lombard was in the habit of forwarding letters to Ireland through the Loubiers in England, it is not impossible that some connexion existed.[2]

The English branch of the family came from Nîmes,[3] and John Louis Loubier, Mary's maternal grandfather, was naturalised in 1700. They were in business in London, and it was no doubt in this way that they became acquainted with William and Hughes Minet. Indeed, we find Henry Loubier, Mary's uncle, sitting with William Minet for seven years as a Director of the London Assurance Corporation.[4] Antony Loubier, Mary's father, had died sixteen years before her marriage, and she was under the care of her mother's brother, John Louis Loubier,[5] who lived at Clapham, and who on her marriage made up her fortune, which was 4,200*l*., to 5,000*l*. The marriage would seem to have been to some extent arranged by William Minet, who was evidently well acquainted with the Loubiers; and the terms of the settlement were also of his drafting. These provided, *inter alia*, that a certain share of the husband's property should be secured for the benefit of the children of the marriage on his death, an arrangement which Hughes in later life thought most unjust, and which he com-

privately printed. The family of Menet, one branch of which came to England, we shall meet with later; see p. 189.

[1] *Op. cit.* pp. 49, 80, 84, 86.

[2] In L. de Magny's *Nobiliaire Universel* (Paris, 1866) (*s.v.* De Teissier), the family is said to be 'issue de la famille du vénérable et illustre Cardinal de Loubens, grand-maître de l'ordre de Malte en 1552.' The Loubens were seigneurs of Verdalle, and a search under these names in the *Armorial Général* might throw some light on de Magny's statement. The Loubier arms are quartered by the Minets in right of Mary Loubier, and, though never registered in England, are found in the *Armorial Général* (MS. Bibl. Nat. Paris; Montpellier, Montauban, fo. 239) thus:—'Loubier, Généralité de Montpellier, Bureau de Nismes. Antoine Loubier, marchand drapier, porte *d'argent à un loup sortant d'un buisson.*' The Heraldry books have been led into error by this; *e.g.*, Papworth, in his *Ordinary*, *s.v.* 'ship—and in chief,' gives the Minet arms correctly, but adds, 'as borne by C. W. Minnett (*sic*), quartering O'Callaghan,' the Arms of that family being similar to those of the Loubiers.

[3] Their origin was not forgotten. Antony Loubier, uncle to John Louis, by his will, proved April 5, 1734, leaves 20*l*. to 'the direction of the Society of children of Nismes, erected in London.'

[4] 'Henry Loubier, director, July 4, 1735; retired 1753. William Minet, director, July 1747; retired July 1759' (Books of the London Assurance Corporation). Henry Loubier appears in the directory of 1749 as of King's Arms Yard, Coleman Street.

[5] John Louis Loubier and his wife both died in the same year (1767), and are buried in Clapham Church. The inscription on the tomb is given in Manning and Bray's *Hist. of Surrey*, vol. iii. p. 367, where, however, the name is spelt Lewis.

ments on very severely. In his characteristic manner he made, on September 19, 1811, when he was arranging for his own will, a copy of such portion of the settlement as he objected to, and followed it with a long note, from which the following extracts are taken :—

I copied the foregoing to show to Mr Glover that he might the better comprehend the reason of my incerting [*sic*] in my will that long paragraph concerning the matter which, by the opinion of Sir Samuel Romilly, I was advised therein to comprehend. Accordingly on this day, 19 Sep^t 1811 at our meeting at Bletchingly for the execution of my will I read this paper to him [*i.e.* the extract from the settlement]: upon which he remarked that in his life he never met with an instance of the kind, and so have said many other lawyers heretofore. And he naturally asked how it came about, and why my uncle (upon whom I told him I wholly depended) submitted to them. In answer to which I adduced the best reasons I could, which were that my wife's uncle John Lewis Loubier having submitted in his own case to very hard terms on his marriage with one of the four daughters of — Berchere an enormously rich jeweller, he took pattern by that. Besides which, he was a very good for nothing and immoral personage, as I found out to demonstration compleat afterwards, but on which topick I am not enclined to enlarge. Of this my uncle William was at my marriage wholly ignorant, although he had known Loubier 20 years, or more. And it was (as I told in like manner to Mr G.) owing to this last circumstance that advantage was taken : for never sure was there a man more ignorant of the world than this uncle of mine, nor more positive in his own opinions : so self-sufficient was he that he would never take advice nor even submit to ask it.

Much more follows to the same effect, with elaborate calculations as to the effect the clause would produce upon his son's shares, and the note concludes thus :—

And so ends this narrative on which I have too long dwelt ; but my sons (my executors) are not to wonder at it when they reflect on the disturbance of mind that I full well remember this usage which my uncle met with from an old friend caused to him ; and which reverberated upon me.

The tone of these remarks illustrates what, at any rate in the solitude of his later life, becomes a marked feature in Hughes's character, and one which gives us the key to understanding much of the bitterness which unfortunately accompanied the Fector controversy. He was inclined to dwell overmuch on the darker side of the picture, and to allow his estimate of men and things to be influenced by the spirit in which he regarded them. Whatever cause there may have been for such an attitude of mind, one can but regret it, as indicating a certain want of the qualities of self-reliance and self-respect which were so strong in his grandfather's character.

His marriage drew Hughes to London, and he lived near his uncle; where, exactly, he never mentions, but his three children, born between 1762 and 1767, are all registered at St. Andrew Undershaft, which stands at the corner of St. Mary Axe, near by Fenchurch Street. He must, however, have returned to Dover in 1765, as in that year he was mayor of the town. His uncle William died in 1767. In the following year Mary, his wife, died at Eltham, in Kent, at the age of thirty-one. She was buried at Capel-le-Ferne, a spot endeared to Hughes by his mother's connexion with it, and in which, through his uncle's will, he was himself a considerable owner of property. Accustomed as we are to find Hughes expressing his opinions freely on all matters connected with himself, we are surprised to find that he never anywhere refers to his bereavement. We know, however, that though still in the prime of life—he was not yet forty—he felt his loss so greatly that he made up his mind to retire from the Dover business, which he did, by arrangement with Peter Fector, in 1770, and some five years later he gave up any active share in the London business. It was, perhaps, with the money that he received from Fector on relinquishing his share of the Dover business that in this same year (1770) he purchased, from Sir Edward Knatchbull, land in the parishes of Camberwell and Lambeth, which still remains in the family.[1]

Though he tells us nothing of his wife's death, his remarks on the death of his uncle are many and characteristic. Hughes was the acting executor, and the abilities which he no longer had occasion to give to business were diverted to the preparation of a most curiously elaborate set of accounts, showing the value of the property dealt with, and the disposition of its uttermost farthing, the whole contained in a

[1] The name of Knatchbull has been preserved in the road which runs through the property, now become a part of London; while the Public Library, with Calais and Cormont Streets, recall the Minet connexion with the place. The well-known market-gardener, Myatt, at one time occupied the land, and his name survives in Myatt's Fields, now become a public park.

book home-made, home-ruled, and home-bound, and enriched with copious marginal annotations. The title runs as follows :—

An Inventory and account of all and singular the goods, chattels, and credits of William Minet, late of Fenchurch Street London, Esq[re] (who died on Sunday the 18th day of January 1767) and the particulars of the administration of the same by Hughes Minet nephew to, and together with John Dolignon, acting executors to his will and codicil; which Will is dated on the 14th day of October 1765, but the Codicil refers only to the date of the said will and is itself neither dated nor signed.

On page 2 begins the statement of account. First comes a detailed list of debts due by the deceased, followed by a list of the 'goods, assets, and effects due to the Testator,' first among which comes the item 'Household goods, furniture, plate, jewels etc[ra],' valued at 702*l.* 5*s.* 6*d.* From Hughes' account of the disposition of these we can understand how much of family interest that would probably have survived had it fallen into his hands, must have vanished; he says :—

As to this article of household goods furniture & plate etc[ra] the inventory of the same which was taken immediately after the deceased's death was del[d] to M[r] James Minet to whom they were all bequeathed and who sent to Berlin all such part as was valuable.

Then follows a list of all the payments made on account of legacies and expenses, the balance being the residue, which, under the provisions of the will, was to be equally shared between Hughes and Daniel Minet, his cousin. Many detailed accounts follow relating to various matters connected with the estate, and finally comes a long declaration made by Hughes that all the foregoing accounts are just and right to the best of his knowledge, to which declaration is appended the following note :—

N.B. M[r] Daniel Minet had this book in his possession (to whom I delivered it for the purpose of his examining the same) from the 8th of November 1785 to the 10th of April 1786 on which day he brought it me back and del[d] it to me at my house in Austin-friars expressing his having found the whole of it right and just.

H. M.

Such is the minuteness of detail with which the whole is worked out that Daniel, if he had the patience to go through it, could hardly have found it otherwise.[1]

In November, 1766, William Minet had agreed to purchase a farm at Hayes, in Middlesex, and as this property still remains in the family, it may be well to record what took place with regard to it upon his death. Bought after the execution of his will, the land, which had not been conveyed to him at the time of his death, was not dealt with in it, and so passed to his brother and heir-at-law, John of Eythorne, to whom the conveyance was actually made. It seems to have been admitted, however, that William had intended to leave this property to his brother James for life, and afterwards to his nephews, Daniel and Hughes, and an arrangement carrying out this intention was made by a deed of May 24, 1767. After James' death, in 1774, Hughes and Daniel having come into possession of the land, Hughes purchased Daniel's interest, and became the sole owner.

From 1770, when Hughes retired from the Fector partnership, to 1783, when he resumed business, we know practically nothing of him. A journey to Berlin can, however, be with certainty assigned to this period; the authority for this is a note on the back of a print representing the Empress of Russia, the Archduke of Austria, and the King of Prussia dividing between them a large map of Poland; the title of the print is, 'La situation de la Pologne, 1773,' and the note is as follows:—

> Strange as it may appear that in such an arbitrary government as that of the King of Prussia such a print as this should be suffered to be sold, however I bought this libellous one at a shop in Berlin when I was there on a visit to my uncle James Minet (a few months before his death) in the year 1774.

Of Hughes' return to business in 1783 mention has been made in an earlier chapter, and it must have been in this year that he came to live at 21 Austin Friars; before this he had been living at Fulham, where he had bought a house, and where he still continued to reside when not in Austin Friars. Of his life between 1783 and 1802 but little is known. During the earlier years of this period his sons' education was progressing, and in 1788 the two younger ones joined their father in the business; but until 1802 there is nothing to record. In that year Isaac, his youngest son, married Susannah, only daughter of Sir Charles Pole, Bart.; and in connexion with

---

[1] See Appendix III. for an abstract of William Minet's will.

this marriage we may quote a characteristic letter written by Hughes to his daughter-in-law just after the marriage. It is addressed to 'Mrs Minet, at the Revd Mr Sayer's, Eythorn, Kent, by Canterbury,' where the newly-married couple were spending their honeymoon, in the house lent them by the bridegroom's cousin, John Minet Sayer, who had performed the marriage ceremony. The letter is as follows :—

> However much prudence required me to conceal it, it was impossible, my dear young lady, that I could avoid feeling an affection for you for some years past. It is now, as I think, five or six of them ago, that my eye, always vigilant in the interest of my children, pierced thro the veil that concealed, perhaps from all others, the strong attachment which my dear son your husband had for you. I always loved my son, and I perceived very emminent good qualities in you. I thank you much for your affectionate letter. Although nearly worn out, I am as much alive as ever to all that relates [to] the happiness of my children, and it is of course a great comfort to me, that the youngest of my sons has been fortunate in the grand and primary concern of life to be allied to a person of your merit. I believe I can answer for your making him as good a wife as I am sure he will make you a good husband ; had I not been convinced of this last point, my consent, for as far as it goes, and it goes far with a dutyful child, should not have been given, had all other advantages been ever so alluring. I flatter myself your prudence and that of my son will supply in these last respects whatever may be deficient, and I, on my part, shall always be willing to contribute to your satisfaction to the extent of my power.
>
> I am glad you like my nephew Sayer's modest abode, and I hope every thing else has been comfortable and agreeable to you. He came to see me at this place last Saturday. I am here trying to get ready a small house for Mrs Hurdis and her children against her recovery for she was the other day brought to bed of a girl.[1] The workmen here are exceedingly dilatory so that I cannot compass the end that I have in view and a great deal will remain to be done when she shall be here ; which I am sorry for.

[1] Mrs. Hurdis was the wife of the Rev. James Hurdis, Professor of Poetry at Oxford. She married July 18, 1799, and had three children, James Henry, John Lewis, and Harriet (posthumous), the latter being the one referred to in this letter. Her husband died December 27, 1801. She subsequently married Mr. Storer Ready, an apothecary of Westerham, and was living at Abbeville, in France, in 1831.

Mr Sayer and my John Lewis left me on Monday morning, and my nephew was, as he said, to return to Eythorn this very day. When you see him thank him for his visit to me.

I know not if I shall have time to write to your dear husband at present, so pray give my kind love to him and thank him for his letter. I am concerned that the difficulties of the passage from Dover to France are so considerable. It was always a very troublesome business, however (formerly) profitable, but now it seems to be made by the French a point d'honneur, a national concern, and by individuals not to be redressed.

Mr Sayer told me that Mr J. Fector had been in town, but how my dear son could I see him being here? I have written to the Father.

I had the honor [sic] to write a few lines to Lady Pole this week. I have been told by Mrs Hurdis that she and Sir Charles called at Fulham. I was not there, and Mrs Hurdis in the straw which was unlucky; present my best respects to them when you write, and be assured that I am to yourself with great attachment, and with my love to my son,

My dear,
Your most affectionate friend and father,
H. MINET.

Westerham in Kent,
25 August 1802.
(In Mrs. Hurdis unfurnished and unfinished cottage).

On the fold of the above letter is indorsed a note to his son :—

Mon fils—J'oubli de vous dire que je recois une lettre de Mad^{me} Newman, laquelle vous regarde de toutes facons. Compliments sur compliments sur votre mariage etc, et tout ce qu'il y a à en dire : je lui ai repondu mais ne ferez vous pas bien de lui ecrire deux mots vous même ? je croirai qu'oui.

In 1804 John Lewis Minet, the second son, married Miss Elizabeth Morgan ; and in April of the same year, partly, perhaps, because his two sons were no longer to live with him, and partly, also, because he contemplated retiring from active participation in business, Hughes sold the house at Fulham [1] and removed to Westerham, in Kent, where,

---

[1] The advertisement of the sale will be found in the *Times* of March 21, 1804. The house is described as ' a compact and convenient detached villa, with new-built coach-house, stables and billiard-room, walled gardens, pleasure-ground, lawn, shrubbery, hothouse, and two meadows containing together ten acres.'

at least as early as 1802, he had bought land. It must have been about this time that he purchased, in the parish of Brasted, the estate of Hevers Wood, two miles from Westerham and five from Sevenoaks; but it is doubtful whether he ever lived here, or whether he continued to reside at Westerham. In several places on the house at Hevers are the initials H. M., with the date 1808, showing that he carried out considerable alterations in that year. The estate at Hevers passed to his son John Lewis, on the death of whose widow it came into the possession of James Lewis Minet, by whom it was sold.

It was during these last ten years of his life that most of the elaborate calculations and tables that he has left were worked out, and the voluminous notes in all his books, which mostly date from this period, show us what were the chief occupations of these latter years.

'I was always,' he says in a note dated 1812, 'addicted to calculation and cyphering, therefore in the many lonely days that I have of late years past in solitude (not being always able to read), I own that by making these my motive in part was curiosity and amusement.'

There is a tradition that he used to sit in his library—a plan of which he gives in the carefully-prepared catalogue of his books—with a green baize apron on, as a protection, we may imagine, against the ink of which he was so lavish. Let the sketch of him be completed, as it was begun, by some extracts from the notes which must have been made during this period, and which will throw some light upon the literary side of his character.

In Milton's 'Paradise Lost' he writes:—

This work is no doubt very learned and shows transcendent ability. But for the rest, and judging as I have a right to do by the share of reason, whatever that may be, that it has pleased God to give me, I think and I believe that it has done more hurt than it has done or is capable of doing good by the heretical and daring liberties which the author has taken with the Divine Being. I doubt which of the two is the most execrable and abominable, Milton's profaneness or his absurdity. Ignorance is better than learning if no different use is made of it than to display talents at the cost of morality, and propagation of familiarities with the adorable and incomprehensible Being whose name even, should never be mentioned without a pause.

The class of books most fully represented in his library, and most fully annotated by his pen, is that of voyages and travels. In his library he followed on the map with the greatest interest and accuracy the explorations of Cook, Vancouver, and other discoverers of the time, and his collection of their works was a large one. This taste must have been an early one, to judge from a note written in 1752 (the year in which he first went to Dover) in a copy of the 'Voyages de Tavernier :—

> I bought these two valuable volumns of Peter Fector for five shillings. I know not how he came by them, but believe they were saved out of some ship wrecked on the coast, or more likely stolen by some privateer : certain it is that Fector did not know the value of them.

His bookseller was T. Bocket, who used to send him down new books, and with whom Hughes was in the habit of exchanging opinions on these works. A sample of such a correspondence occurs on the fly-leaves of 'The Pursuits of Literature, a Satirical Poem, 1797,' where Hughes writes, 'Here is what my bookseller writes me':—

> What you say of the Critical Review is too true, they are a contemptible and wicked set; but I am afraid the author of the 'Pursuits' will not think them worth his notice. It is selling very fast indeed. I send you a complete edition with all additions neatly bound. Dr. Davies, Provost of Eton, called on me yesterday; I never saw any man in such raptures with a book. He deemed it the first production of the age, so much erudition he never met with. He offered me 10 guineas to tell him the author, and that he would give him 50 if he wanted it which he does not.

The mention of the 'Critical Review' enables us to notice one more characteristic of Hughes Minet. He was a most zealous reader of the reviews of the day, and the pages of his books are full of references to the 'Monthly,' 'Critical,' and 'Anti-Jacobin' Reviews, as well as to the 'British Critic'; not content with mere references, sometimes he would go so far as to copy out, on the margin of a passage, long extracts from the review, adding his agreement or disagreement with the criticism in language at times extremely forcible. We have had in his remarks on 'Paradise Lost' an instance of his manner of expressing his views of the authors he was reading, and another, equally forcible, is found in a copy of Sterne's 'Sentimental Journey':—

> Mr. Yorick, the assumed name of Laurence Sterne, an unworthy churchman who had the impudence to publish his sermons—even sermons! under this libertine name of Yorick. The fellow's wit is marred by his licentiousness. I knew him, and also Madam, his fool of a wife, and also Madam his daughter, as great a fool as her mother.

For 'éditions de luxe' he had but little sympathy, though one would have thought their wider margins would have given him more ample space for his annotations. ' Pars minima est ipsa puella sui' he writes in such an edition, as a note on the 'sea of margin and rivulet of letter press' [*sic*]; and yet he cared for his books, to judge from a note in 'The History of Cornelia':—

> This ill-used, *twentieth hand* book was procured with the greatest difficulty being out of print. Mr Minet knew the value of it from his having had one some years ago, which now he has not, and he supposes that somebody has borrowed, englicé, stolen it.

Political economy and philosophy were favourite studies with him, as Sinclair 'On the Revenue,' Adam Smith's 'Wealth of Nations,' and Bolingbroke's works show, all these books being covered with annotations too long to reproduce here. Nor should one forget to notice the number of French works he possessed, which, added to the fact that many of his notes are written in that language, show him to have had a fairly familiar knowledge of it.

It is matter of regret that Hughes, with his uncle William's example before him, and his papers in his possession, should not have undertaken to write some account of the family, a task for which his literary tastes would eminently have qualified him. But, so far as the evidence goes, he seems to have taken but slight interest in the history and traditions of his ancestors. In one direction only did he do anything to perpetuate them. In 1799 he applied for and obtained a grant of Arms from the College of Heralds, whereby the right of the family to use coat-armour in their adopted country was officially recognised. Though dated in 1799, this grant, Hughes tells us in a note characteristically endorsed on the official parchment, should be considered as far earlier:—

This patent of arms &c I intended applying for in the year 1767 & took some pains to this effect at the Heralds' office at that time : but through hurry of business and meeting with impediments I did not at that time carry my intention into execution.

It was also what my uncle William talked of doing ever since I can remember ; viz‘ ever since my first coming to his house in Fen-church Street in the year 1744 when I was 13 years of age, but thro one cause or another he never carried this his design into effect.

However for these reasons, this Patent ought virtually to be considered as of nearly 60 years existence anterior to the real date of it.

The original grant, a magnificent document, signed by Isaac Heard, Principal King of Arms, and Thomas Lock, Clarenceux King of Arms, states in a preamble that 'whereas Hughes Minet of Fulham and of Dover hath represented that his grandfather Isaac Minet migrated from France at the Revocation of the Edict of Nantes, and settled at Dover, and that the Armorial ensigns used by his family are, *or, three ermine spots* ; and for crest *a wing*, which have not been duly registered ; the said Hughes Minet hath requested a Warrant for confirming and exemplifying the same with such variation as may be necessary.' On this follows the grant of the following Arms : '*Argent, in base, a boat on the ocean, therein passengers and rowers, proper* (in memory of the passage of Isaac Minet, grandfather of the grantee, with his Mother and other refugees from Calais to Dover as above mentioned), *three ermine spots in fess, and on a chief or, an oak tree on a mount vert* ; and for crest, *on a wreath of the colours a wing, elevated, argent, charged with three barrulets gules.*'

The statement, made no doubt on Hughes' authority, that the Arms used by the family previous to this grant were *or, three spots ermine*, is confirmed by such instances as I have been able to collect. This bearing appears, for instance, on Isaac Minet's seal impressed on his original will (December 10, 1744), as also on that of his son James (September 20, 1773).[1] We find it again on monuments in St. Mary's Church, Dover (Isaac Minet, 1745) ; in Eythorne Church (John Minet, 1771) ; and in Bengeo Church (Daniel Minet, 1790). In the

---

[1] Neither of these seals show *or* as the field of the shield ; but on such a small scale one would hardly expect to find this shown ; and even if it were, time working on a weak impression would very probably obliterate it.

two latter cases, however, the failure on the part of the heraldic artist to perceive that the *three spots ermine* were a distinct charge, has led to his multiplying them, and so making the bearing simply *erminois*.[1] In all the instances cited, however, the Arms, which we may safely assume to have been *or, three spots ermine*, and not *erminois*, are quartered with *argent, three bars gules*.

Two questions seem now to present themselves, the answers to which, could they be found, would probably throw light on the earlier history of the family. What claim did Isaac Minet imagine himself to have to the Arms he used? and what was the origin of the blazon, *Argent, three bars gules*?

With regard to the first point, he clearly had no right, so far as the College of Arms in England is concerned, to use them; but one is inclined to think that he must have imagined himself to have some claim to them in virtue of his French origin. A search in French armorials has, however, proved fruitless. Rietstap, it is true, under 'Minault ou Minot d'Anjou et de Bretagne' gives these Arms—*d'argent à trois mouchetures d'hermine de sable*, which, though closely resembling those used by the Minets in England, are not identical with them, and leave unanswered the question whence the latter were derived.[2]

On the second point, some little light is thrown by a letter from Ralph Bigland, Richmond Herald, through whose good offices the grant was made in 1799. Writing to Hughes in the August of that year, when the new grant was under consideration, he says: 'I enclose a sketch of the arms proposed to be granted; the alterations, as you will observe, are made from the maternal alliances of your ancestors, as they appear

---

[1] In the Eythorne instance the Arms have obviously been repainted within recent years. If erminois be wrong, as I have no doubt it is, the error has been perpetuated; for Burke, in his *General Armory* (ed. Lond. 1884), *s.v.* 'Minnett,' repeats it, taking it, no doubt, from Clutterbuck's *History of Hertfordshire*, ii. 29, where the Bengeo shield is given as erminois. The Arms in either form are altogether unknown at the College of Heralds.

[2] M. Vaillant, to whose antiquarian knowledge the point was submitted, writes thus :—' La possession d'armoiries par des bourgeois, des laboureurs [yeomen], propriétaires de biens ruraux qu'ils étaient tenus de défendre militairement, de personnes dont la position sociale correspondait à celle des Minet et des de Haffrengue, était chose fréquente. La bourgeoisie et la propriété immobilière y étaient corrélatives à un service militaire. Donc rien ne s'oppose à *priori* à ce que les armoiries que vous me décrivez appartiennent bel et bien à vos ancêtres. Quant à prouver le droit, c'est plus difficile.' M. Vaillant's researches have, however, resulted in finding some Arms which are curiously similar :—' L'armorial des principales familles du Boulonnois, du pays reconquis, gouvernement d'Ardres, et comté de Ponthieu, Picardie, et quelques villes d'Artois par Antoine Scotté de Vélinghen (1704), donne pour la famille Boulonnaise, de Bavre, famille militaire connue principalement dans le pays reconquis, *écartelé aux 1 et 4 d'argent a 3 hermines, 2 en chief et 1 en pointe; aux 2 et 3 d'argent à 3 fasces de gueules*.' The only variation, it will be noticed, is in the field of the first and fourth quarterings, which is *argent* instead of *or*.

on the seal of your grandfather. Such alterations are usually made; but should any other alteration occur to you or your sons, I shall be happy to attend to your or their wishes on the subject.'

The alterations Bigland speaks of were, no doubt, introduced into a second sketch, the first having shown only the boat in base, and in chief the tree on its mount vert. In the new sketch, which was adopted in the final grant, all the charges of the old coat are introduced, the ermine spots being placed in fess, and the three bars gules transferred to the crest.

The seal spoken of was no doubt the one with which Isaac's will, now at Somerset House, was sealed; the Arms on this being quartered, the second and third quarterings should, in strict heraldry, be those of some maternal ancestor of Isaac's who was also an heiress. Our field of search in this direction is, however, limited, as we are only acquainted with one of Isaac's maternal ancestors, namely, his mother, Susanne de Haffrengue, and of her we know certainly that she was not an heiress. The *argent, three bars gules* cannot, therefore, be the Arms of her family. Whose they were must remain an unsolved problem.

The crest used had always been a wing erect, but whereas before 1799 it was sable, in the new grant it is blazoned argent. A curiously apposite passage in Fuller's dedication of the eighth book of his 'Church History' to Sir Henry Wroth, suggests an explanation of this change. ' To be a fugitive,' he says, ' is a sin and shame, but an honour to be a voluntary exile for a good cause. Hence it is that I have seen in your ancient house at Durance the crest of your Armes with the extraordinary addition of sable wings somewhat alluding to those of bats, to denote your ancestours dark and secret flight for his safety. However God brought him home on the silver wings of the dove.'[1] It may be that, with some such thought in his mind, Isaac held the wing sable to typify his dark and secret flight; while Hughes, in brighter days, when prosperity had firmly established the family in England, kept the wing for its old associations, but changed its sable to argent.

The new Arms granted to Hughes are, as to the boat, obvious; indeed, the grant itself explains this. Whence came the tree? In the absence of any other explanation, may we venture to attribute to Hughes yet one more touch of sentiment, and to suggest that he wished thereby to express the firmly-rooted fortune of the family, and

---

[1] Thomas Fuller, *Church History*, book viii. p. 29. London, 1655.

was adopting for himself the words of Jean Sauchelle: 'Courage! je voy encore fleurir les *Minets* comme le cèdre au Liban.'

The motto attached to the new grant is 'Quantum est in rebus inane,' one evidently chosen by Hughes himself, who was ever fond of speculating on the vanity of life.[1]

Enough has been said to give some idea of the literary side of Hughes Minet's character. Strongly marked as this was, it was ever subordinated to the love of method and business which distinguished him, and which shines out so conspicuously in the last two years of his life. I have before me a bundle of papers prepared in 1812, the year before his death, enclosed in a wrapper which, accentuated with the thickest black lines, is endorsed, 'Balances of my Ledger, or Inventories of my Estate and Effects.' This bundle contains a series of papers which may be classed as follows:—

1. Statement of the value of his estate and effects.

2. Statement of the charges and duties to be incurred in proving his will.

3. Statement of the fortunes of his three sons as they will be upon his death.

The final statement of the value of his property is endorsed as follows:—

> These Accounts of the value which I have put on my property to place it in different points of view, I made chiefly to amuse my mind during the very many disconsolate hours I must and do pass alone, when my chief consolation is the consideration of your (my dear sons) welfare and prosperity in life. They may perchance be of some small use to you my dear executors when I shall be dead and gone; at all events they will show you in what manner I myself computed the property which it has pleased God that I have it in my power to bequeath to you; which provided it did not impede your own industrious endeavours I wish was much more considerable. I am well aware, my dear sons, that all this is much too trifling for any body but yourselves to see, or to be told that I thus pass my time, but can the mind be continually upon the stretch? No.

---

[1] A panel with the Minet arms was acquired, not long since, in London, by Mr. F. A. Crisp, who very kindly presented it to the writer. An inscription on the back of it states that the arms are those granted by Ralph Bigland to Hughes Minet in 1799, and the writing is evidently of that date. The arms are correctly given, but curiously enough the motto is the far more appropriate one, 'Aidons-nous et Dieu nous aidera.'

One sheet contains, 'My reasons for these accompanying statements, and other observations,' and though drawn up with a neatness which leaves but little room for criticism, it is noted, 'at my leisure to write this over again neater.' After a statement of what the papers contain he adds :—

If I have made any difference in my bequests to my sons among other things it is to be considered that my two sons who are in business will require to be more substantially supported in respect to credit, than if they had not such credit to maintain with the commercial world: for every thing is known. And for the rest, respecting my son John Lewis, I know that in him my two sons, his brothers, will find an affectionate relation and their children a second father. The benignant suavity of his nature makes me cirtain of it, and as yet he has no children himself. Moreover from the judicious and manly character which he possesses I think him as able as willing to befriend them. Let this be said, and it is meant to be said, without prejudice to the feelings of my two other sons who stand high in my estimation also, as they deserve to do in the opinion of everybody. I will say nothing more on this subject save that I recommend to them and to the whole family the continuance of that greatest Blessing in Life, an affectionate attachment to each other.

Formal, as the style of the age was, yet these words breathe the spirit of strong affection which, throughout his life, marked Hughes' conduct to his children; nor are they without a suggestion of that common-sense which made all his dealings with them so sensible and successful. The paper I have been quoting from concludes with a note that must be given, as final evidence of the strong reverence for accuracy of fact and detail which must have come to him from his grandfather, Isaac, which was so marked in his uncle William, and which has survived even to later generations :—

To save needless trouble of searching as to the age I may have attained when I die, I mention that I was born at Eythorn on the 30th day of June 1731, old style.

It is sad to think that the last words of Hughes which remain to us show his closing life troubled by the old difficulties with the Fectors. Peter Fector was yet alive, but his faculties were clouded; his son, John Minet Fector, had for some time past been carrying on an angry correspondence with John Lewis Minet and his brother Isaac as to the terms of the partnership. Hughes alone was acquainted with the history of the connexion, and two letters of his on this subject, dated December 14 and 15, 1813, are the last record left to us of his long life. I have refrained from touching in any way on the details of these unhappy differences, and so must pass over the contents of the letters; suffice it to say that they are clear and businesslike, and show no trace of failing intellect. He gives his sons the information they require, and commends them to the advice of Mr. Thomas Dawes, his solicitor: 'He can read fast, and matters strike him as quick as lightning, from which he makes deductions remarkable for solid sense.'[1] The letter of December 15, 1813, eight days before his death, concludes with these words:—

> I can say no more, only that I embrace you both, in the hopes that we shall at last see more quiet times. I am going to bed, but in bed or up am constantly and affectionately,
>
> yours,
> H. MINET.

My love to Betsy,[2] and to Susan[2] when Isaac sees her, Charles[3] is very well as the postman brings word.

On Thursday, December 23, 1813, he died in his house at Westerham, and lies buried in the churchyard there. On the wall of the north aisle is the monument to his memory.[4]

---

[1] For some time, it would seem, a strong friendship had existed between the Minets and the Dawes, which has continued uninterruptedly, through four generations in each family, down to the present day.
[2] His daughters-in-law.   [3] His grandson.
[4] See page 220 for the inscription, and page 217 for an abstract of his will.

CHAPTER X

HUGHES MINET'S CHILDREN

We whose generations are ordained in this setting part of time.—SIR THOMAS BROWNE.

ACTIVE life began for our grandfathers much earlier than it does for us, and therefore we are not surprised to find William, Hughes Minet's eldest son, entering the Army before the completion of his thirteenth year. I have been unable to find the date of the lad's first appointment as ensign, but it must have been in that capacity that he sailed for America on board the 'William' on May 8, 1775. During the first few years of his service the young soldier kept a diary, which is reproduced as illustrating some of the military movements of the War of Independence:—

1775.	8th May.	Embarked at the Cove of Cork on board the 'William.'
	12th May.	Sailed.
	17th July.	Arrived at New Boston.
1776	17th March.	Embarked on board the 'Empress of Russia.'
	24th March 2nd April	Sailed, and arrived at Hallifax [*sic*].
	10th June.	Sailed from Hallifax in the 'Empress of Russia.'
	25th June.	Came to anchor at Sandy Hook with the 'Grayhound' frigate, and another transport.
	29th June.	The rest of the fleet arrived.
	1st July.	Weighed at 5 o'clock p.m. and anchored in Gravesend bay at 8 p.m. same evening.
	4th July.	Landed on Staten Island quartered at Summerson's ferry.

1776.	6th July.	Removed to Fountain's farm.
	1st Augt.	Gl Clintons army arrived; a little after, the Hessians.
	13th Augt.	Embarked, landed without opposition on Long Island.
	26th Augt.	Marched at 10 o'clock at night to attack the enemy; landed at York Island; 5th Brigade took possession of New York; part of the city burnt.[1]
1777.	15th May.	Encamped on the highths [sic] near the landing.
	13th June.	The army having assembled about Brunswick marched towards the enemy, but not being able to force them out of their strong position returned 19th, and 22nd retreated to Amboy.
	10th Dec.	Camp near Kingsbridge.

Unfortunately, the diary, which one could wish were fuller, even for the period it covers, breaks off abruptly here, and of the youthful ensign's further adventures in America nothing is known, except that by a commission dated October 7, 1778, he was appointed to the 10th Regiment of Foot, then commanded by Lieutenant-General Edward Sandford; the commission is signed by Sir H. Clinton, 'Commander in chief of all his Majesty's forces within the colonies laying on the Atlantic Ocean from Nova Scotia to West Florida.' He must have remained in America till 1784, when we find him 'lately arrived in England.'

From 1784 to 1785 William remained at home, spending his time between Fulham and Austin Friars, as appears from references to him in letters written by his brother Isaac, which I shall have occasion to quote shortly. His commission as captain bears date June 25, 1785,

---

[1] This entry notices four events under one date, the first of which, namely, the attack on the enemy's position on Long Island, alone belongs to August 26. The landing on York Island (more correctly Manhattan Island, on which the town of New York is built) took place on September 15, and was the beginning of the occupation of the city of New York, the American troops having withdrawn on that day to Kingsbridge. The fire occurred on September 20. I have been unable to identify Summerson's Ferry, or Fountain's Farm; they are not given in William Fadden's *North American Atlas* (Lond. 1777), which has detailed plans of most of the operations of the campaign; these are also fully described in Irving's *Life of Washington*. The 'highths' are almost certainly Jersey City heights, whither the Army moved after the taking of New York.

when he was appointed to the 4th (King's Own) Regiment of Foot. Where or when he joined his regiment does not appear, nor is anything known as to what service he may have seen with it. The regiment was in garrison at Quebec in 1794, and remained in Canada till September 24, 1796, when the officers, sergeants, and drummers embarked for England; the privates were transferred to the 60th Regiment, and remained on in Canada. The transport was captured by a French privateer when nearing England, and, the regimental colours having been sunk, the officers were taken as prisoners of war to France, where they remained for a year before they could be exchanged. William was probably among them, as he remained captain in this regiment till November 29, 1798, though his commission as major is dated March 1, 1794. On January 1, 1798, he became lieutenant-colonel, and his last commission, as major-general, is dated July 25, 1810. After leaving the King's Own, in 1798, he joined the 5th (Northumberland) Regiment of Foot, with which regiment he remained, as major, till September 25, 1803, and no doubt took part in the operations carried on against the French in North Holland, where, in 1799, the regiment formed part of the column commanded by Lieutenant-General Dundas. At the end of 1799 the regiment returned to England, and was quartered at Silver Hill Barracks till the following year, when it was ordered to Gibraltar, where it was stationed till the Peace of Amiens. On its return to England the first battalion went to Guernsey, while the second was disbanded at Winchester. William, however, had left the regiment before this happened, as from 1803 till 1812, when he finally retired, he was serving as lieutenant-colonel with the York Rangers.[1]

On his retirement from active service William went to live at Bovingdon, in Hertfordshire, in a house bought by his father, Hughes. This house, which was leased to him in 1812, was probably made over to him by his father in his lifetime, as no mention is made of it in the latter's will, and on William's death, in 1827, it was sold as his property. He died at Bovingdon, unmarried, and was buried at Westerham.[2]

Hughes' two younger sons next claim our attention. Four years after his elder brother had been started in his profession, John Lewis, the second son, was sent to a Mr. Gavanon, at Arnhem, in Holland,

---

[1] The particulars relating to the services of these regiments are mostly taken from R. Cannon's *Historical Records of the British Army*.
[2] For the inscription on his tomb there, see p. 220.

where he remained for four years (1779-83), being joined there by his younger brother, Isaac, in 1781. The training which the two boys received from Mr. Gavanon was evidently intended to fit them for business, and we may therefore infer that Hughes, when he sent them abroad, had formed the intention of resuming business which he carried out in 1783. John Lewis left Arnhem in 1783, at the age of seventeen, and went to Boulogne to a Mr. Audibert, with whom he remained till June, 1785, when, at the age of nineteen, he entered the Dover house.

Isaac remained on at Arnhem till October, 1784, and from the time of the two brothers' separation at Arnhem, in 1783, till August, 1785, there runs a series of letters written by Isaac to his brother. These letters give such a complete picture of the character of the two brothers, that I have been tempted to make somewhat large extracts from them. They tell their own story, except in one or two instances, where I have ventured to elucidate them with notes :—

To J. L. Minet, chez Mr Minet, Fulham, près de Londres.

Arnhem :
July 2, 1783.

I am sorry you had such a disagreeable voyage, but thank God you are now all safe in England. It grieves me much that Mrs Debons[1] is dead. Here is nothing happened worth writing about since your departure, only as I said when you was here that I shall learn Dutch of Wessels who I have spoken to, and am to begin in a few days, and then I shall congédier Sardier who is grown more stupid of late than ever. Lewis Gavanon is arrived here since these few days, and as the weather is exceeding warm we are a going this afternoon to hunt about the environs of Arnhem to find a place to bathe in. So much for Arnhem news, or Isaac's news, for it is nothing to do with Arnhem, it is all about me.

To the same, at Fulham.

Arnhem :
July 16, 1783.

Pray present my love to my cousin Peter Fector[2] if he is in London, & tell me when you think he will be married; I now never think of him but I think of our Dear Good Father, who is again

---

[1] His mother's sister, who had married a Mr. Debons, of Lausanne.
[2] James Peter Fector, son of Peter Fector, married November, 1783, to Frances Lane.

going to shut himself up in the smoke of London only for our sakes. No, Lewis, we shall never be able to requite his goodness to us. You are so kind in your last as to mention that if I should like to have anything fr. England you will try to procure it me; as for myself I want nothing thats worth the trouble of sending, but I have been asked several times to write to you for to send some English gloves for the women. Now if you could contrive to send a couple of dozen of ladies gloves you would not only please them but me too, for almost every day I am asked if I have wrote to you about them aprèsent je me suis acquitté de mes comission.

Lewis had now, at the age of seventeen, gone to Mr. Audibert, at Boulogne-sur-Mer, where the next letter is addressed.

To the same, at Boulogne.

Arnhem :
Nov. 28, 1783.

Your last gave me a great deal of pleasure to hear that you was well & that you like your situation. I suppose that by this time you are come from Dover. Here is another recruit come fresh from Scotland. I believe they will put him in the room next to mine for the two Brocks will not have him in their room any longer, he has been in their room ever since he has been here, he is a sad dirty dog, that is the greatest fault he has got, & he talks such broad Scotch that it is enough to make one die with laughing, so we are now five of us besides Scats, the Dutch boy. When you write give me some idea of your manner of living & how you spend your time & who are the people which compose Mr Audibert's family.

To the same, at Boulogne.

Arnhem :
Dec. 9, 1783.

I suppose this will find you at Boulogne & that you found a letter of mine there on your arrival. I thank you for the news you send me of our cousins marriage;[1] I thought it would soon be. You say that you will expect to find me as big as you next time you see me, in which I believe my dear Brother will be mistaken. I

---

[1] J. P. Fector. See above, letter of July 16.

get on very well with my companions; the Scotch boy is a queer fish, he won't wear a Robe de Chambre, no that he won't.

To the same, at Boulogne.

Arnhem :
9 Jan. 1784.

I suppose you have heard of the flying balls that are made at Paris & in France, pray have you seen any of them? I read in the French Newspaper that one was to go from Calais to Dover with two men inside of it, is it true or not? Methinks I should like to travel in the air so; if people find they take, I shall expect to see you come flying into Arnhem one of these frosty mornings. You don't know my dear brother how much I long to see you. I hope in a few months to have that pleasure, I wish you would come and fetch me when I leave Arnhem, do you think there is any likelihood you can. I am just beginning Book-keeping with Mr Gordon & I can assure you he keeps me at it, if I am lazy he always gives me you for an example. Mr Lee now occupys Bischoff's room to himself, he is now playing on the flute which is very agreeable to me as I can hear it very plain in my room. The Brocks & the Scot occupy the great room that we had when first we came, commonly called the Apple Kamer, they are a making a woeful noise at prest, I hear the Scotchman's pipes above the others, they are always a quarelling in that room about something or other, Mr Lee's melodious flute is quite drowned in their devilish noise. I remain avec beaucoup de sincerité votre affectionné frère.

To the same, at London.

Arnhem :
27 March, 1784.

I write to you at London because I think this will find you there as my Father says you are coming to town to see our brother William who I find is lately arrived in England. I expect you will answer this from London and let me know what my Father thinks about your coming to fetch me; I suppose that you will go back to Boulogne again for a few months. I long much to see my dear Father & you & brother William but I must take patience as my Father says. Let me hear from you soon for you well know what pleasure that gives me.

To the same, at London.

Arnhem :
7 May, 1784.

I find that our Father don't seem to relish your coming to fetch me so I have given up all thoughts of seeing you at Arnhem but I hope 'er long to have the pleasure of seeing my dear brother in England as the hour draws nigh for me to quit this country which I shall do with great pleasure. I long much to see us all together in the Friars.

I find by what you say that there is very curious things to be seen in London and I make no doubt but that you and William are great chess players. My Father says his house is going to be painted and that until that is done I can't come home, if you stay'd at London I should desire you to keep the painters close at it. Pray let me hear from you soon and send your letters directly to Arnhem for most of them that you write from Bou. goes first to London for there is wrote on the back 'mal envoyée à Londres' and are above two weeks a coming, I suppose you can hinder that.

To the same, at Boulogne.

Arnhem :
23 July, 1784.

It is now a long time since you have wrote to me, your last was dated if I remember right the 7th of May from London, I hope you will answer this soon after you receive it for indeed my dear brother I long very much to hear fr. you. William writes me word that the Frenchmen are mightily pleased with your horse and I make no doubt but you are also, knowing how fond you are of riding. If you don't quickly answer this I shall think Mad^{elle} Au. or some other young lady has taken possession of your heart for I know nothing else that can occasion such a long silence. It is now above a year since we have seen one another and that I find a long time for two people that have been parted for the first time of their lives, and I am sure you think the same. Mr Gavanon fait bien ses complimens à son ami Jean Louis & Mrs Lemaistre desires particularly to be remembered to you, the rest of the family send their compliments, I can assure you that the two first sing your praises very often which pleases me greatly and indeed I believe nobody could ever speak bad of your sweet temper.

The next letter is dated October 4, 1784, and announces that the writer is to leave Arnhem in two days' time for home; and on October 22 he writes from Austin Friars, his brother being still at Boulogne with the Audiberts :—

I arrived safe at London on the 11th of this month and left Arnhem 6th by which you may see I came very quick. I found Peter at Harwich at my disembarkment, and the next morning we set off in the Harwich Post Coach for London and found our dear Father in good health and Mr Fector[1] my uncle who went to Dover last week. I have not yet seen our brother William nor my cousin [James] Peter Fector nor his wife, they being at Dover ever since my arrival. Our dear Father is quite immersed in business but is in good health, you hardly know what pleasure your letters give him and therefore I wish you would write to him a little oftener for you well know how particular he is in that, and indeed it is what he naturally may expect from all of us when we are separated from him, I am sure my dear Lewis won't take this amiss from his brother. I found all new faces except Nanny and Peter on my arrival.

This is a great undertaking that my Father has commenced for our sakes and I hope we shall one of these days be able to compensate him which can only be done with a great deal of application from us. Saw the last air balloon very plain from the top of our house at Fulham, could see the two genuses at the bottom with the naked eye, but I remember you are an anti-balloonier so shall say no more about it.

To the same, at Boulogne.

London :
9 Nov., 1784.

Our brother William arrived the week before last in the Friars, I should hardly have known him anywhere else, he is so much altered, he is seldom at home. Mr J. P. Fector and lady arrived last friday here. I have not yet seen Mrs F. Went to see Mrs Siddons at Drury Lane with the Captain and Mr Floydson last Saturday, cannot say she answered my expectations but that I suppose because I am no judge of the matter.

[1] Peter Fector.

To the same, at Boulogne.

Friars :
18 Nov., 1784.

William is very well and all is blown over to all appearance between him and our Father which is as agreeable to me as to you. I cannot really tell you if my Father intends leaving you at Boulogne or no this winter, if I learn anything shall let you know depend upon it; as to your going to Paris I don't much think he would like it yet a while, but however I may think wrong and perhaps you may bring it about.

'L'air inflamable' is making great progress I find, but if your Frenchman at Calais is not quick he won't have the honour of being the first who will cross the sea, for they write from Dover that Mr Blanchard is making preparations at the Castle to fly over to your folks at Calais;[1] I wish I could be at either of the places to see one of them set off, you say you will never be tired of what I write to you about Balloons, you see I don't drop the subject; no, I hope that instead of dropping, the subject will rise still higher & I make no doubt but it will.

Our Father is in waiting this week at the London Assurance Mr Lane has & will dine with us every day in it he being in waiting with him. Mr Hurst comes twice a week to brush up my dancing which has great need of it and once a week I go with William to his house which is quite at t'other end of the town. I hear that a Dutch East India ship is recked [*sic*] off Boulogne and most of the crew perished; may be you may be able to comfort the few that remains as you talk the language for I should think there is very few of the French gentry at B. who can. My Father wants me to go to the riding school at Moorfields and I believe I shall, more for exercise & pleasure than to learn to ride for I think one may learn just as well on the road. How does your horse do? do not work him too much or else you'll make him lean and then he won't be better than the French bidet. You see I mix questions, answers, news, alltogether without any order. You'll make a special merchant I can see by the letter you wrote to Dover about business, it pleased my Father much.

---

[1] The ascent was made on January 7, 1785, when M. Blanchard, accompanied by Dr. Jefferies, successfully crossed the Channel, and descended near Guines.

To the same, at Boulogne.

London :
14 Dec., 1784.

I received your scrawl this afternoon and hope your next will be somewhat different, for I think those you receive from me deserve something better than your last. I should have taken care not to have let our Father have seen it, had you not mentioned it, for I am sure he would have been displeased to see you write in such a hurry. You well know, as well as me, how nice he is about his sons writing, and that when he sees a correct and well written letter from his Lewis nothing pleases him more ; and in that respect he is not to blame, for writing correct is the most useful thing of any in business. I hope you will forgive my troubling you with this long preamble which is chiefly as you may very well see for our Dear Parent to receive if possible still more satisfaction from you.

Our cousin W. F.[1] comes to town this week, he will lodge at his brother's house this time. I think my Father intends you shall stay at Boulogne this winter, but am not quite cirtain. I shall now conclude with wishing my dear Lewis a good night.

To the same, at Boulogne.

London :
21 Jan^y, 1785.

I received your two agreeable favours 17th and am much obliged to you for your pleasant discription of the balloon chace, which afforded William & me much mirth. Glad you received the glasses and pin, which was my chusing. You have I suppose also received the clothes by this time, they are Williams choice who has a pretty good taste for such things, as I imagine you know as well as myself. Our dear Father is, thank God in good health, but quite wrapped up in business, rather too much, for he don't take exercise enough. W. F. is gone back to Dover some time ago and is getting up another play.[2]

---

[1] William, youngest son of Peter Fector.

[2] A portrait of William Fector is given in the *European Magazine* for May, 1789. From the sketch which accompanies the portrait it would seem that he was entirely devoted to amateur theatrical performances. Beginning these in his father's house in Dover, he continued them on a larger scale in the room where the Dover Assemblies had been held, which he purchased and fitted up as a theatre. This, we are told, would contain 170 spectators, and was attended by his own servants in livery of blue-and-orange. The article from which these facts are taken gives a list of sixteen plays produced here by Fector, amongst them being the *Siege*

To the same, at Boulogne.
London :
7 May, 1785.

Am going to Fulham tomorrow, as also M^r & Mrs Fector,[1] and M^r & Mrs Lane, our Father, William etc. in short all the family. Mr J. P. F's chariot is as elegant a one almost as any in London. I believe your stay in France will not be very long, as our brother W. is going to leave us e'er long, and as soon as he does you will come to England I make no doubt. I do not know where, or in what regiment he is going.

To the same, at Boulogne.
London :
26 May, 1785.

As Mr Fector, the father, has intimated to our father that he thought your being at Dover during the absence of Mr J. M. F.[2] would not be amiss, and my father having nothing against it, you will soon now be at Dover, as I hear ; Mr J. M. F. sets off for his tour very soon. My father charges me however to tell you it is but upon condition that you do all possibly in your power towards the business, and that you don't spend your time idly while at Dover.

To the same, at Boulogne, but forwarded on to Dover.
London :
10 June, 1785.

I see that Mr John Fector had not yet arrived at Boulogne when you wrote, but by this time imagine he has been with you and communicated to you our Father's intention more fully than I did in my last to you respecting your leaving Boulogne and abode at Dover which I suppose you will not disapprove of in the least. My Father tells me to leave room in this for him to add a few lines which I am sure you will be very glad to find as you have not seen his dear hand for such a long time ; thank God, he is now recovered from his indisposition. Just going to Fulham with William. My Father has altered his mind and intends writing to you himself.

---

of Damascus, also mentioned in a later letter of Isaac Minet's ; to judge from the list, tragedy was his strong point. He went out of his mind, and died in 1805. A reference to Fector's theatre will be found in T. Rigden's *Historical Sketch of the Town of Dover* (Dover 1844), p. 164, where the performances are stated to have ceased in 1790.

[1] James Peter Fector. Mr. Lane was, perhaps, Thomas Bateman Lane, of Dover, father of Mrs. J. P. Fector.

[2] John Minet Fector, Peter Fector's eldest son, aged thirty-one in this year.

To the same, at Dover.

London :
22 June, 1785.

I am glad to find you are safe in England again. My brother Guillaume is at Fulham where he has been since Saturday, my father has paid for his commission in the 4th Regiment of foot but as yet have [*sic*] not received an answer from Ireland. I have spoke to my father about your keeping a horse at Dover and he begs you would not think of it while you remain there, and that you will sell your mare at Boulogne for as much as she will fetch. He begs you will keep to the Counting house and not run about for if he finds you do, you must not expect to stay long at Dover. My father desires me to add that he hopes to see you e'er long in London if he hears a good account of you from Dover, and then we will talk matters over but by no means to think of coming without his directions.

To the same, at Dover.

London :
1 July, 1785.

I rec^d your favour last Tuesday by which I find that your mare is safe at Dover again and also the reason for it, and my Father says that since you have got her there you may keep her if you choose, which I believe you will not hesitate much about. Your letter to my Father reached him this morning and he read it to me and desires me to tell you as above, but now that you have got a horse, to ride with moderation. Your dear Father is pretty well but the heat almost overcame him as it does a great many others, he desires his kindest love to you.

To the same, at Dover.

London :
12 July, 1785.

I am indeed very sorry for the death of young Sayer not so much on account of relationship [1] as the real friendship I bore him by being acquainted with him in Kent. He was cirtainly a very clever and good natured young man. It must have been very awkward to him to be destitute of all his relations during his

---

[1] William, son of Henrietta (sister of Hughes Minet, and wife of Thomas Sayer, of Eythorne), died in Paris on July 1. In Eythorne Church there is a monument to him.

sickness and in a country where I believe he could scarcely make himself understood.

W. Fector[1] set off yesterday morning for Tunbridge, and from thence he goes to Dover where I hope he will arrive safe. M. Gavanon[2] and Louis came to town yesterday afternoon, I suppose he will pay us a visit in the Fryars tomorrow or next day.

I wrote this yesterday, but the frank being full, deferred sending it. Mr Gavanon has since called on us, and dined here with Louis, I went with them afterwards to the Haymarket, they both asked very much after you. Mr Lane came about an hour ago to the Fector's where I was.

To the same, at Dover.

London :
27 July, 1785.

I suppose W. F. has received all he left here otherwise I should have heard from him. He made but a short stay with us this last time. I imagine he is very busy a getting up the Siege of Damascus & playing at cricket, n'est pas? I shall be much obliged to you, if when you see Cap. Rice, to ask him the name of his leather breeches maker as I know he is a very good one. I see some of your writing sometimes which makes me think you spend a good part of your time dans le comptoir. I begin to long very much to see you. I shall worry my father to let you come up to see us for a day or so if he don't do it without; he is at present pretty well, thank God, as is William.

To the same, at Dover.

London :
20 Aug., 1785.

Your last makes no mention of the question I want to know touchant les culottes de cuire, maybe you could not find an opportunity when Cap. Rice dined with you. I suppose you have received a letter from L. Gavanon, you make no mention of it, if you have, you should, in the mercantile manner accuse reception. Last week I rode with L. G. early in the morning to Fulham, showed him all about, and then breakfasted there; after that rode to Richmond to show him Richmond Hill, from thence to Kingston

---

[1] Third son of Peter Fector.
[2] The person with whom John Lewis and Isaac had been at Arnhem; Louis was his son.

JOHN LEWIS MINET

and to Hampton Court, saw the palace etc. and came back to dinner at Fulham. Apres dinné took him from Fulham across the country to Greenwich, showed the Hospital, drank tea there, and then in the evening came to town almost knocked up, although he would not own it, don't suppose he ever rode so far in a day before. William is at Guildford where he has been all this week, I suppose you have seen his name in the papers in the list of promotions. We none know when he will be called upon to join his regiment.

Vous pouvez compter que je ferai tout mon possible envers mon Père pour qu'il vous accorde permission de lui venir voir pour quelques jours à Londres, au moins il ne sera pas ma faute si vous ne venez point bientôt, je crois que nos cousins ici iront avant longtems à Douvres mais vous n'avez pas besoin d'en parler le premier.

These letters carry us on to August, 1785, when the correspondence ceases, though John Lewis Minet remained at Dover till 1788. In 1788, Isaac went abroad with a Mr. Francis Menet,[1] to make what would be called the Grand Tour, and I find four letters written to his brother in Austin Friars during this period, from which the following extracts are taken :—

To John Lewis Minet, at Austin Friars.

Geneva :
4 January, 1788.

I have yours which gave me great pleasure, it being the first news I have had since our departure which is now near four weeks. I am in daily expectation of hearing from my Father, however am

---

[1] Though the names are curiously similar, the Menets and Minets were in nowise connected. In speaking of the Loubiers in the last chapter (p. 159) the Menet family was mentioned, and I may add here a few particulars relating to it. A certain Nicolas Menet (married Marguerite Berson) was before 1600 living at Rozas, in the south of France, where his son François succeeded him. Another François of a later generation (married 1708, Marie Torras) was father of the Isabeau and Jeanne between whom the letters referred to in the last chapter passed. He had also a son, Jean François of Rozas. This Jean François had four sons, two of whom, at any rate, left France for the sake of their religion, Jean François, the elder, establishing himself in Turin as a silk merchant, while François, the younger, became Isaac Minet's travelling companion This François came to England in 1764, and was naturalised in 1766, but was also a citizen of Yverdun, in Switzerland (1771). He married Charlotte Albertine Achard, of Geneva, and had a daughter (Antoinette Marie, *d.* 1854) in Geneva, and a son (François) who lived in England, where he married Louise Cazenove, and his son, the Rev. John Menet, is the present vicar of Hockerill, co. Herts. Isaac Minet's friend, François, was a director of the French Protestant Hospital (12 April, 1780), but in the list of directors his name is misspelt Minet.

perfectly easy about his health by what you write me. I shall postpone writing to our dear parent till we return from Lausanne which will be in the course of a few days. After our return from Lausanne we shall stay here a week longer so that we reckon to leave Geneva for good by the 16th inst. when we shall direct our steps to Lyons. I like Geneva much am only afraid of getting 'une indigestion' there is so much good eating going forward, we have dined out every day for this week past. We went last Friday to a ball where I was very much entertained both with the company and dances; as to the first, the ladies in particular made me think I was in England both with regard to dress and beauty. The greater part of the gentlemen were English, among which was our prince Edward. Kiss my dear father for me. I am happier now I think you are with him.

To the same, at Austin Friars.

Lyons:
21st January, 1788.

We left Geneva the 17th and got to Lyons the next day in the evening. This town is one of the largest in France, and I believe one of the handsomest; the Hotel de Milan where we are is in the middle of a very noble square called la place des Terraux and the best inn we have met with yet. I acquitted you properly to our grandmother;[1] on my first introduction to her she said 'Ah! c'est mon petit fils Isaac, le seul qui m'a écrit.' She is indeed a very pleasant and worthy old lady, and I received very great satisfaction at seeing her, I assure you. We intend staying here five or six days more, and then shall bend our course direct south, and make our first stop at my fellow traveller's mother's relations in the Vivarais.

To the same, at Austin Friars.

Turin:
26 March, 1788.

You will have seen by my letter to my father of the failure of our intended plan of going to Genoa [from Nice]. It was very vexatious to us being obliged to put back to the port we came from after being at sea for many hours; as we saw no likelyhood of the

---

[1] Charlotte Henrietta Loubier, living at Lausanne, where her son-in-law, F. L. Debons, resided; she died there on the 16th November in this same year (1788).

wind's changing we resolved to turn our steps to this place where we arrived Saturday last in the evening, the fourth day after our departure from Nice. It took us one whole day to pass the Col de Tende as we were obliged to have the chaise taken to pieces and carried over it by men. We rode up it on mules and walked the greater part of the way down, it is almost incredible the vast quantity of snow that covers it, and there is but a very narrow path just broad enough for a mule. Some hours after us our chaise arrived with Maitre Francois, and before it was dark we had it put together ready to start the next morning. The village where we were obliged to sleep has but one Inn, by far the most blackguard place we have slept in yet, where by the bye we had a very good dish of frogs. The next morning early we were drawn by three mules (there being no post at this place) to Coni, where we found the regular post, and four horses ready in the street waiting, as we had sent Francois on before. In five or six hours we found ourselves in Turin, the roads being exceedingly good as well as the horses; they seem to understand travelling post much better in Italy than in France; we could not have come faster even in England. I was yesterday at the kings chapel where all the royal family were assembled to attend mass, the music was very fine indeed. Is Hastings tryal almost brought to a conclusion, and what turn does it take?

To the same, at Austin Friars.

Milan:
24 April, 1788.

I received your two letters, also one from my brother William; I return you both thanks, as very likely William may be with you now in town. I do not much wonder at my uncle's leaving the old house at Dover.[1] Have you seen much of our relation lately, M[r] D. Minet,[2] and are our cousins[3] at No. 11 on a sociable footing with them, as M[r] & M[rs] D. Minet called at their house a few days before my departure. We left Turin the 19th inst. and got to Milan the next day; I never saw a finer country anywhere, I could scarcely persuade myself I was out of England all the way, and the

---

[1] Peter Fector.
[2] Daniel Minet (*b.* 1729, *d.* 1790), who lived in Grosvenor Street, and at Bengeo, in Hertfordshire.
[3] James Peter Fector, who was living in Austin Friars from 1785 to 1789.

roads are full as good. Every body here keeps their carriage that is, all the merchants that can anyways afford it, which is not the case at Turin, where hardly anybody does but the nobility. I don't know if it was good policy letting the Major[1] ride the horse down to Bath that you bought for our dear father, as he rides very carelessly if I remember right, and may throw him down, though he would have had my black mare if he had not had the other, the less he rides any of our horses the better. I dare say you think so likewise. I am sorry to find that the major part of the Italian ladies do not talk French, I assure you there are a great many pretty women in this court and I often find myself at a loss by not talking Italian. We leave this town today for Bergamo, and from thence to Venice.

There are no more letters, but the journey must have extended to August, as we learn from a carefully-drawn-up statement of the cost of the expedition in Hughes Minet's hand, which it may be of interest to reproduce :—

```
1787.
Dec.  6.  So much paid Mr Francis Menet    .    . £43 . 10 . 0
  „   7.   6 .  6 . 0  cost of a pair of pistols.
          81 . 14 . 0  cost of a postchaise of Hatchett.
           1 . 15 . 0  cost of a writing apparatus.
          15 . 15 . 0  English money taken to Dover.
                      ─────────
         105 . 10 . 0  my son's moiety of which is  .  52 . 15 . 0
Aug. 22.  Paid Mr Menet, at his return to London
                       more   .        .      .    .  327 . 10 . 6
                                                     ─────────
                                                       423 . 15 . 6
Oct. 21.  Deduct so much I make good to my son
             (paying the like in money to Mr
             Menet for his ½) for my sons moiety
             of the evalued price of the postchaise
             I buy of them for 40l.    .    .   .      20 . 0 . 0
                                                     ─────────
          Total expense of my son's journey to Italy  403 . 15 . 6
```

This statement forms part of a most elaborate account drawn up by Hughes on the occasion of his son's coming of age in this year,

---

[1] ? His brother William; but see p. 178.

wherein Isaac is debited with the above total, against a credit of the rents of the house at Dover, which had been his (it will be remembered) since his uncle's (James Minet) death in 1774.

Isaac, the youngest son, being now of age, in the following June fresh articles of partnership were entered into, by which Peter Fector and Hughes Minet, and their respective sons, John Minet Fector and James Peter Fector, John Lewis Minet and Isaac Minet, were made partners;[1] and from this date till 1802 there is nothing to record.[2] William Minet was presumably with his regiment, the father with his two sons living partly at Fulham, and partly at 21 Austin Friars, where they devoted themselves to the business. Of the connexion of the two brothers with the business mention has been made in an earlier chapter, nor do we intend to touch upon this side of their life here, except to notice one pleasant outcome of their transactions, which survives to the benefit of this and future generations. The town of La Chaux-de-Fonds, lying high up in the Jura in the Canton of Neuchâtel, had a claim, under the will of a M. Amez-Droz, to a sum of money bequeathed to the town for charitable purposes, which claim, after a lawsuit of six years' duration carried on in the English courts, was successfully vindicated by the firm of Minet and Stride, as it then was, acting on behalf of the town. In recognition of this, the citizenship of the town was conferred upon Isaac Minet and his descendants, and this graceful act proved the foundation of a connexion with the Canton of Neuchâtel which has been strengthened in the friendships of each successive generation. The following is a transcript of the official grant:—

Lettre de Bourgeoisie.

Soit notoire à qui il appartiendra, présens et futurs, que par devant le notaire public et juré soussigné et en présence des témoins ci-bas nommés ont comparu les sieurs Louis Ducommun dit Verron, moderne, gouverneur de l'honorable communauté de la Chaux-de-

---

[1] The previous articles had included William, youngest son of Peter Fector, as a partner; but he is not mentioned in those of 1789. He died in 1803, and James Peter in 1804, so that after the latter date, till the end of the partnership, there were only two Fector partners, and practically only one, as Peter Fector, the father, owing to his great age, could take but little part in the business.

[2] It will be well to note here that John Lewis and Isaac were both citizens of Dover—the former admitted by purchase, August 1, 1788; the latter, by order of common assembly, September 23, 1825.

Fonds; David François Courvoisier-Clément, Capitaine de Milice moderne, Boursier de dite Commune; Félix Matthey, conseiller de Commune, Président de la louable Chambre de Charité de ce lieu, Charles François Ducommun dit-Boudry, Boursier de la dite Chambre et Henri Ducommun juge suppléant secrétaire des deux corporations, lesquels ont exposé que l'honorable Communauté de la Chaux-de-Fonds ayant pris en considération les soins généreux, bons conseils et bonne direction que Messieurs les membres de la maison de Commerce Minets et Stride de Londres ont donnés pendant plusieurs années au sujet du procès que la dite Communauté a eu à soutenir en Angleterre pour faire adjuger en faveur de la Chambre de Charité la rente qui lui a été léguée par défunt Monsieur Josué Amez-Droz, afin d'en faire un fond perpétuel dans ce lieu, et ne croyant pouvoir mieux exprimer les sentiments de sa vive gratitude que par la manifestation du désir de chacun de ses membres de s'attacher Messieurs Minets et Stride par des liens qui seraient aussi agréables que flatteurs pour les Corporations dont ils ont si bien soigné les intérêts, et perpétuer dans les générations futures le souvenir de leurs Bienfaits, elle aurait voté à l'unanimité de leur offrir la qualité de membres de la Communauté et de la Chambre de Charité de la Chaux-de-Fonds, ce que ces Messieurs ont accepté par leur lettre du trente Septembre 1824, et le Conseil d'Etat de Neuchâtel ayant par lettres Patentes en date du neuf Novembre dernier, délivrées au nom du Roi par Son Excellence Monsieur le Gouverneur de Zastrow, signées de Monsieur le Chancelier de Sandoz-de-Travers, et munies du grand sceau de l'Etat, accordé la Naturalité à chacun des trois membres de la dite Maison de Commerce, avec autorisation à la dite Communauté de les recevoir au nombre de ses membres et de leur en délivrer acte authentique.

En conséquence et dans le but que dessus, les dits sieurs cinq comparants déclarent et font savoir, qu'agissant par ordre exprès de la prédite Commune, en exécution de sa délibération du Douze Septembre de cette année : Ils reçoivent, agrègent et incorporent par le présent acte, Monsieur Isaac Minets, négociant à Londres, ainsi que tous ses descendans légitimes à perpétuité, aux nombre des communiers de la Chaux-de-Fonds et originaires de la Chambre de Charité de ce lieu, pour jouir de tous les droits, privilèges, astrictions, honneurs et avantages, dont jouissent et pourront jouir à l'avenir les autres membres des dites Corporations ; ce qu'ils accompagnent des vœux sincères de la Communauté pour la conservation, le bonheur et la prospérité de ses nouveaux membres, et ils promettent au nom qu'ils agissent de faire respecter et exécuter le présent acte envers et contre tous, en Jugement et dehors. Passé sous toutes autres clauses de droit et ratifié après lecture en l'Etude et par attouchement sur la main du dit Notaire, en présence des sieurs Frédéric Petitpierre de Couvet et Frédéric Louis Sandoz du Locle, les deux demeurant dans ce lieu, requis pour témoins, qui ont signé avec les sieurs comparants et le Notaire au pied de la minute suivant la Loi. A la Chaux-de-Fonds, le vingt-trois Décembre 1824.

(*Signé*) P.-J^e CUCHE, N^{re}.

Nous le Gouverneur et Lieutenant Général pour sa Majesté le Roi de Prusse, dans la Principauté de Neuchâtel et Valangin en Suisse ; Certifions que le sieur P.-J^e Cuche, qui a signé l'acte cidessus, est Notaire public et juré dans cet Etat, et qu'aux actes par lui expédiés en cette qualité pleine et entière foi est ajoutée tant en jugement qu'en dehors. Nous déclarons de plus que le papier timbré et le Contrôle ne sont pas en usage dans cet Etat et qu'il n'y a aucun Ministre public de la part d'aucune Puissance étrangère. Donné au Château de Neuchâtel, le 31 Décembre 1824.

Par ordre de S. E. Monsieur le Gouverneur,
Le Secrétaire du Conseil d'Etat,
(*Signé*) Jⁿ-AUG. DE MONTMOLLIN.

In 1802 Isaac married Susannah, daughter of Sir Charles Pole, Bart., an alliance which brought into the family a further strain of Huguenot blood, and one which in part was derived from the well-known Huguenot family of Bosanquet. The Poles were of Dutch origin, Mrs. Isaac Minet's grandfather having been born in Amsterdam ; and the original name of the family was Van Notten. After their emigration to England they were connected with the Dutch Church in Austin Friars.[1]

Two years later John Lewis Minet married a Miss Elizabeth

---

[1] See Table *N*. In the *Registers of the Dutch Reformed Church, Austin Friars* (ed. by W. J. C. Moens, Lymington, 1884, privately printed), will be found the entry of the burial of Susannah Minet's grandmother, Susanne Bosanquet (p. 149) ; grandfather (p. 155) ; and father and mother (p. 156). The same work gives a copy of the inscription on the tomb, with the shield of arms thereon (p. 176). A most elaborate Bosanquet pedigree has been drawn up by Mrs. Meyer ; a copy is in the British Museum library : *Genealogy of the Family of Bosanquet*, L. C. Meyer (Lond. 1877).

Morgan, and after his father's death, in 1813, resided at Hevers Wood, where he died in 1829, leaving no children. He lies with his father and brothers at Westerham.

Isaac, the youngest son, bought, in 1817, the estate of Baldwyns, near Dartford, in Kent, and after his retirement from business lived altogether there, devoting himself largely to local affairs. He served the office of high sheriff for Kent in 1827, and died suddenly at Maidstone, in 1839, whilst attending on the grand jury. His widow continued to reside at Baldwyns till her death, in 1869. She and her husband are also buried in Westerham churchyard. Baldwyns descended to their eldest son, Charles William, and on his death without male issue, in 1874, was sold. James Minet,[1] their younger and only other son, married Elizabeth, daughter of William Iggulden, and died in 1885, leaving a son, William.

To William, only son of James, and sixth in direct descent from Ambroise Minet of Cormont and of Calais, has fallen the task of gathering the scattered records of the family, and weaving them into a connected story. The work which Isaac began in 1737, and which William added to in 1751, another William, after an interval of one hundred and forty years, has taken in hand to continue. And now this record, 'which I, William Minet have had inclination to copy out and preserve for my owne and our family's satisfaction and handing it down to such of the family as may like or take pleasure in such innocent recreation,' is finished. Much more might have been written; what has been written might have been made more complete. Suffice it if what has been done serve to keep fresh the memory of men and women still held dear by us, their descendants, 'whose generations are ordained in this setting part of time.'

---

[1] James Minet took the surname of Lewis-Minet, in 1832, by Royal license, but seldom used the name Lewis, and then only as a Christian name. He is buried in the Paddington cemetery at Willesden.

APPENDICES

APPENDIX I

FACSIMILES OF THE AUTOGRAPHS OF AMBROISE MINET AND SIX OF HIS DESCENDANTS IN A DIRECT LINE

ambroise minet (1605–1675.)

Isa Minet (1660–1745.)

John Minet (1695–1771.)

Hughes Minet (1731–1813.)

Isaac Minet (1767–1839.)

James L. Minet (1807–1885.)

William Minet (1851 . . . .)

APPENDIX II

GENEALOGICAL TABLES

A SERIES of genealogical tables forms the framework on which a family history such as this must necessarily be built; for without these the reader would be unable to grasp the relation existing between the various members of the family. The relationships of a family whose history extends over two hundred and eighty years obviously cannot be given in a single table, and it has been a question of no little difficulty how best to group them; the principle finally followed will be better understood if prefaced by these few words of explanation.

Table *A* may be considered the main one, and shows the direct and unbroken line of descent from Ambroise Minet, the original ancestor, through Isaac, his fourth son, down to the present writer; this table also gives, in each generation, all the children of those through whom this direct descent is traced.

Tables *B* to *G* deal with the children of Ambroise other than Isaac. The first two are concerned with Thomas, eldest son of Ambroise, whose descendants form the eldest branch of the family, now, owing to the two marriages of Joseph Minet, divided into two; the elder being represented by John Cross Minet (Table *B*), the younger by William Brissault, John Brissault, and Charles Ernest Temple Minet (Table *C*). When this work was first undertaken I was unaware of the existence of any descendants of Thomas Minet; and when, by an accident during its prosecution, their existence was revealed, it was found on communicating with them that, apart from a vague tradition of French origin and of some early connexion with Dover, they were ignorant of the story of their ancestry.

Table *D* is again concerned with Thomas, and shows the descent of the Fectors through his daughter Mary. This has been given on account of the long business connexion of seventy-five years which existed between the Fectors and my own branch of the Minets.

Tables *E*, *F*, and *G* deal with the remaining children of Ambroise, of whom it may with some degree of certainty be affirmed that no descendants now exist.

APPENDIX II

The remaining tables (*H* to *O*) show the descent of the wives of six of the Minets in the main line of descent, and are arranged in the order of the generations into which they married; the first (*H*) gives all that it has been possible to ascertain of the family of Susanne de Haffrengue, wife of Ambroise Minet.

Tables *I* and *K* explain the two families of Sauchelle and de la Porte, from which was descended Marie Sauchelle, who married Isaac Minet; while the succeeding ones (*L*, *M*, *N*, and *O*) deal respectively with the ancestry of Alice Hughes, wife of John Minet, Mary Loubier, wife of Hughes Minet, Susannah Pole, wife of Isaac Minet, and Alice Evans, the first wife of William Minet; and here it may perhaps be noticed that, of these six alliances, one only failed to add something to the strain of Huguenot blood already running so strongly in the veins of the family.

As far as possible in the compiling of these tables, it has been my endeavour to arrive at accuracy by consulting such authorities as exist; and here, perhaps, those mainly relied on for dates and names may be mentioned :—

1. Family papers and records.

2. 'Registers of the Church at Guines,' forming the third volume of the publications of the Huguenot Society of London.

3. 'Registers of the Strangers' Church in Canterbury,' forming the fifth volume of the publications of the same Society.

4. 'Registers of the French Church at Dover,' printed by F. A. Crisp.

5. 'Registers of St. Dionys Backchurch,' printed by the Harleian Society.

6. 'Registers of the Cathedral Church at Canterbury,' printed by the same Society.

7. 'Registers of the Dutch Church, Austin Friars,' printed by W. J. C. Moens, F.S.A.

8. Registers of the Walloon Churches in Holland, transcribed and kept at Leyden.

9. Registers of St. Mary, Dover, and of Eythorne, Kent. Of the former, a transcript has been made by Mr. R. Hovenden, F.S.A., to whom I am much indebted for allowing me to consult it.

Notwithstanding all the care that has been used, many inaccuracies and many omissions yet remain, which further research would no doubt correct or supply. Undertaking such a work in the present day, we are at an immense advantage over our ancestors, both in being able to avail ourselves of authorities not within their reach, and in being inspired by a more scientific spirit; and nowhere does this appear more clearly than in a comparison recently made between these tables and a pedigree of the Minet family enrolled in the College of Heralds in *1799*. Future inquirers will, no doubt, be able to correct the tables now presented to them; but this may be with some certainty affirmed— that they will find less of error in them than the present writer has found in the document solemnly recorded in *1799*, and verified by the affidavit of Hughes Minet.

AMBROSE MINET,	= SUSANNE DE HAFFRENGUE,
b. 1613, at Cormont; d. July 16, 1679, at Calais.	b. 1626, at La Trésorerie; buried at St. Martin's-in-the-Fields, March 29, 1688. See H.

MARIE SAUCHELLE,	Jacob.	Stephen.	Mary.
b. Dec. 30, 1670, at Flushing; d. Nov. 30, 1738, at Dover; buried in St. Mary's. See I, K.	See G.	See G.	See G.

	Daniel, = Anna Maria Atkins,	William,
398, at n. 29, lin.	b. Nov. 18, 1699, at Dover; m. Dec. 17, 1728, in Chapel at Somerset House; d. May 12, 1730; buried in London, at St. Dionys Backchurch.	b. 1705; d. Nov. 22, 1743; buried at St. Dionys Backchurch, eldest daughter of Robert Atkins and Anne Bonnell, of Austin Friars, London, and More Place, Herts.	b. Dec. 8, 1703, at Dover; d. Jan. 18, 1767, in London; buried at St. Mary's, Dover.

ayer, ne, b. Sep. at	Four children, all d. young.	Daniel, = Rebecca Sturt,
		b. Oct. 22, 1729; d. Feb. 25, 1790; F.R.S., F.S.A.; buried at Bengeo, Herts, o.s.p.	daughter of ...Sturt, merchant, of Lisbon, and London later; d. 1819.

Three sons.

	ISAAC, = SUSANNAH POLE,
1831; m.	b. Nov. 10, 1767, St. Andrew's; m. Aug. 7, 1802, at Old Marylebone Church; d. March 14, 1839; buried at Westerham.	b. April 5, 1779; d. March 18, 1863, at Baldwyns, Dartford; buried at Westerham. See N.

tell, Lin- num- 29, un-	Frances Catherine, = Henry Anson Cartwright,	Millecent, = John Dixon Dyke,
	b. June 6, 1809; m. Aug. 11, 1841, at Dartford Church. d. at Exeter, Sept. 9, 1890.	b. Dec. 24, 1803; d. March 26, 1884, at Exeter.	b. Dec. 13, 1810; m. Feb. 10, 1836, at Dartford.	third son of Sir Percival Hart Dyke, Bart., of Lullingstone Castle, Kent; b. 1803; d. Aug. 1, 1885, at Glovers, Kent.
	See page 210.		See page 210.

WILLIAM, = (1) ALICE EVANS,
b. Sep. 13, 1851, at 19 Sussex Square, London; m. Sep. 26, 1882, at Abbots Langley.	b. July 9, 1856; d. March 13, 1887, in London; buried at Abbots Langley. See O.
	(2) July 10, 1889, MARY, dau. of Jos. Rayner, J.P., of Brighouse, co. Yorks, b. Aug. 3, 1855.

SUSAN,
b. March 3, 1884, at 47, Albion Street, London.

not within their reach, and in being inspired by a more scientific spirit; and nowhere does this appear more clearly than in a comparison recently made between these tables and a pedigree of the Minet family enrolled in the College of Heralds in 1799. Future inquirers will, no doubt, be able to correct the tables now presented to them; but this may be with some certainty affirmed—that they will find less of error in them than the present writer has found in the document solemnly recorded in 1799, and verified by the affidavit of Hughes Minet.

TABLE A.

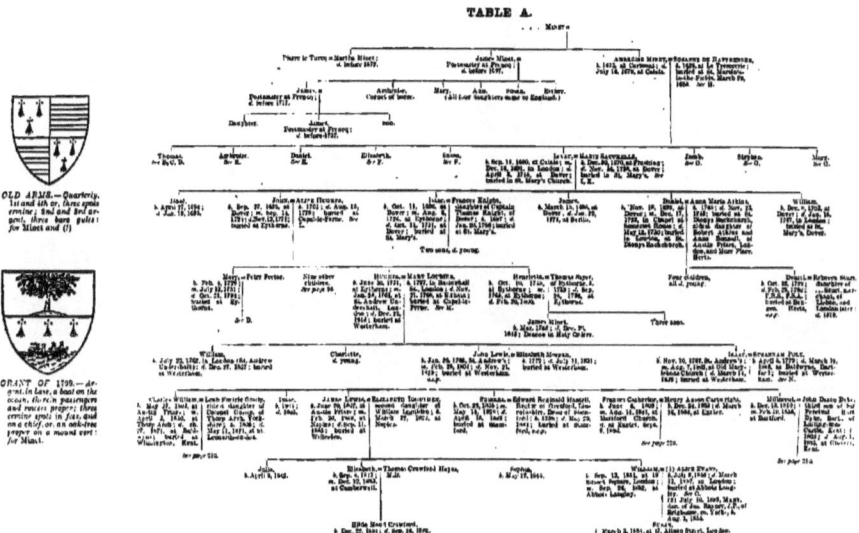

APPENDIX II

TABLE B.

Ambroise Minet = Susanne de Hafreugue.

Thomas, = Mary Gonhart,
b. 1648, Calais; m. Aug. 31, 1684, of Ardres; b. 1653; daughter of
Calais; d. May 29, 1698, Canterbury. Jacques Gonhart and Marie
Pluet; survived her husband.

Thomas, = Rebecca,
b. Sept. 14, 1684, dau. of John Winter,
Canterbury, of Dover.

Thomas, James = Josepha Maria Durpont, Susan Mary, = ... Woodruffe.
living abroad in 1767. of St. Michael's, Azores. living 1767.

Mary Isabel, Joseph, = (1) Anna Maria Mary Ann Victoria,
b. Aug. 26, 1762; bap. Ch. of b. March 19, 1766; bap. Ch. Barker, b. 1767; d. April 12, b. Nov. 21, 1767; bap. Ch. of
St. Sebastian, Ponte Delgada, of St. Catherine, Lisbon; 1868; bur. Charlton, Kent. St. Catherine, Lisbon; became sup.
St. Michael's. d. 1968; bur. at Charlton. (2) Elizabeth Brissault. S+ C. of a convent in Portugal.

Emily, Josepha Maria, Marianna, Joseph, = Amie Anne Lynch, Catherine, James,
b. Oct. 29, 1796; b. March 16, 1798; b. March 5, 1799; m. 1834; b. Aug. 7, 1800; dau. of Andrew Warthop, b. Oct. 27, 1801; b. March 14,
d. Feb. 1842; d. Oct. 29, 1876. d. 1855, s.p. =Rev. Herbert m. March 27, 1834; of Madeira, and West d. c. 1830. 1803;
= S. Wadeson. Temple, of Madeira, d. 1870. d. July 20, 1866. Lothian; b. Sep. 3, 1807. d. c. 1838.

Stephanie Beatrice, Mary Broughton, Amie,
b. Feb. 2, 1836; b. March 7, 1844. b. July 12,
d. 1857. 1847.

William, Susan Temple,
b. 1836, b. Feb. 19, 1837.
d. 1836. d. 1864.

Emily, John Crow, Francis,
b. Jan. 27, b. Sep. 18, 1839; b. Sep. 13, 1841,
1835. = Alice Vine Sworder. in N. S. Wales.

TABLE C.

Joseph Minet = Elizabeth Brissault.
S+ B. (see p. 40.)

William Brissault, = Eliza Arnold,
b. Oct. 16, 1810; m. March, 1840; b. July 12, 1811.
d. May 14, 1856.

Caroline = William, Fred. = Julia Evelina, Alfred Augelica Marianna Edith, Marianna Kate, Daniel St. Clair, = Elizabeth
Phœbe Bond, b. April 28, Dominic, b. Oct. 10, Higgins, Eliza, Augusta, b. Nov. 19, Elizabeth, b. Nov. 24, b. March 18, Rogus.
b. 1842. 1841; m. Oct. 10, 1842. m. July 29, b. July 2, b. June, 1846; 1847. 1850. 1851; m. 1892, 1855;
m. 1863; 1859. 1865. 1844. d. 1846. Ed. Hague. m. 1879.
d. July 23, 1870.

Alice Maud, William Frederick, Thomas Julia Ethel, Eva Angelica, Eleanor Mabel Margaret John Charles Ernest
Beatrice, b. 1862. Brissault, b. Sep. 7, 1860; Temple, b. June 7, 1866. b. July 2, 1867. Eliza, Julia, Kathleen, Brissault, Temple,
b. 1864; b. 1864. m. 1863. b. Aug. 14, b. 1866. b. 1861. b. 1863. b. 1864. b. 1867.
m. 1883, Charlotte 1865; m. 1890,
Ernest Eugenie Marie Ho-e
Searle. Ten-Breuck, Marie Ten-Breuck,
b. 1866. b. 1870.

Thomas Edward, Eugenie Henriette,
b. 1881. b. 1885.

Garrion,
b. 1884.

D D

THE HUGUENOT FAMILY OF MINET

TABLE D.

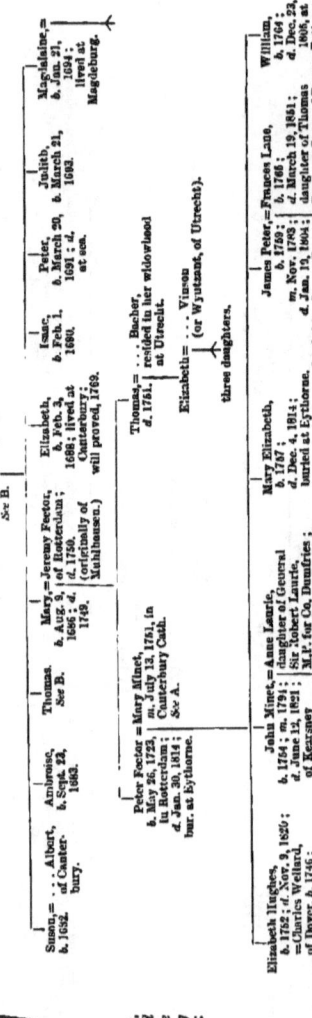

Vert, two doves in pale, argent, beaked and legged, gules, the upper one holding an olive-branch, or; for Fector.

APPENDIX II

TABLE E.

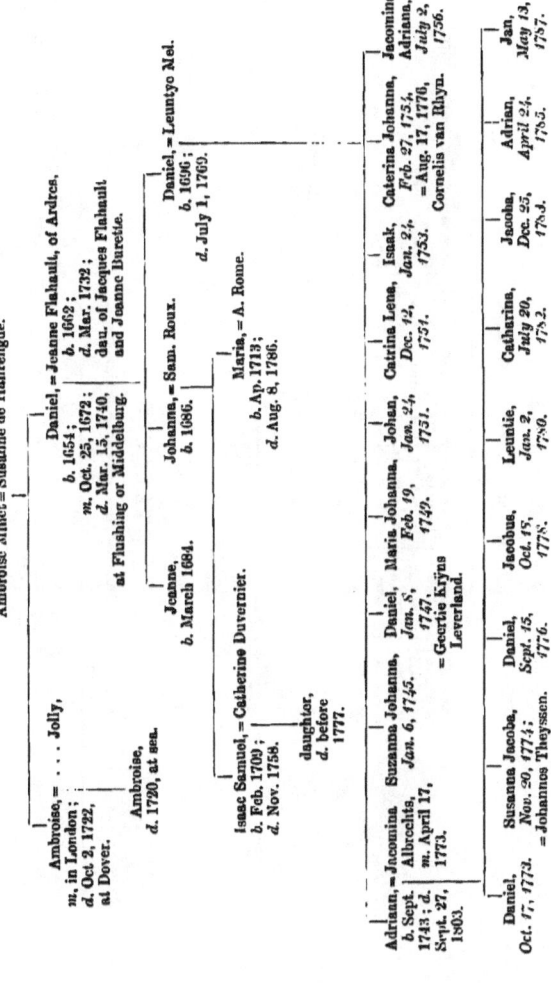

NOTE. The dates printed in italics in the above table are baptisms, and not births.

TABLE F.

Ambroise Minet = Susanne de Haffrengue.

- John Détries (1), = Elizabeth, = (2) Daniel Giles, of Oléron or   Suson, = Gregory Kerr, of Emmerich.
  of Andres;   b. 1656;   Bordeaux; b. 1657;   b. 1659;
  b. 1654;   d. Nov. 13,   m. Feb. 17, 1689, Dover;   m. April 21,
  m. Sept. 21, 1691; 1731, at   d. before 1690.   1690, at Dover;
  d. June 3, 1687, Dover.   d. 1691.
  at Dover.

  - Marie Francoise,   Suson,   Elizabeth Dina, = James de Rousselle, of Canterbury;
    b. at Andres,   b. at Andres,   b. Feb. 19, 1690;   d. 1775; will proved by
    Dec. 12, 1685;   July 15, 1683;   m. 1721;   Peter Fector.
    living 1767,   d. 1728,   o.s.p.
    at Dover.   at Dover.

TABLE G.

Ambroise Minet = Susanne de Haffrengue.

- Isaac = Marie Sauchelle,   Jacob,   Stephen,   Peter le Maistre, = Mary = Thos. Booth,
  See A.   b. Sept. 14, 1662; b. Sept. 24,   of Canterbury,   d. Dover;   m. 1715,
                              d. Sept. 20,   1664;   from St. Lo;   living 1726, at Canter-
                              1715, Dover.   d. Feb. 11,   m. Sept. 3, 1691; o.s.p.   bury;
                                                  1690, Dover.   d. July 22, 1712.   d. Mar. 1726.

APPENDIX II

TABLE H.—Descent of Susanne de Haffrengue, wife of Ambroise Minet.

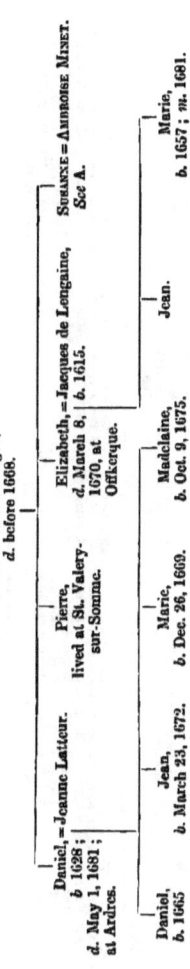

Etienne de Haffrengue (?).

Pierre de Haffrengue, d. before 1668.

- Daniel, = Jeanne Latteur.
  b 1628;
  d. May 1, 1681;
  at Ardres.
  - Jean, b. March 23, 1672.
  - Daniel, b. 1665
- Pierre, lived at St. Valery-sur-Somme.
  - Marie, b. Dec. 26, 1669.
- Elizabeth, = Jacques de Lenguine,
  d. March 8, b. 1615.
  1670, at
  Offkerque.
  - Madelaine, b. Oct. 9, 1675.
  - Jean.
- Susanne = Ambroise Minet.
  See A.
  - Marie, b. 1657; m. 1681.

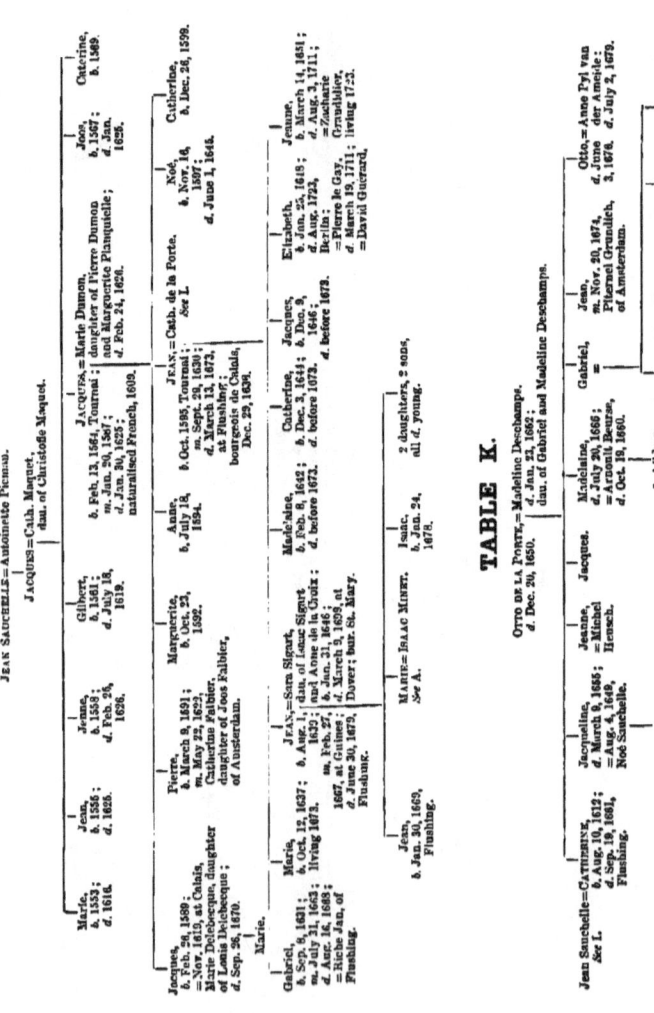

APPENDIX II 207

TABLE L.—Descent of Alice Hughes, wife of John Minet.

Hughes family fr. Wales.

Richard Hughes, *now represented by Sir F. Hughes, of East Bergholt, Suffolk.*

Captain WILLIAM YOUNG, = Alice ; . . . .
of Capel-le-Ferne,   d. at Eythorne,
d. at Madras, 1701.   æt. 95.

Henry Hughes (1), = ELIZABETH, = (2) William Veel, d. 1729 ;   Nicolas.   William,
of Deptford.   living   Comp. of Customs of Kent.   d. in Madagascar, 1701.
                    1745.

ALICE = JOHN MINET.   Amy,   Elizabeth = . . . Ridley.   Young,
See A.   living 1778.   bap. Aug. 10, 1708 ;
                                                            d. before 1753.

argent, a lion rampant, or : for Hughes.

TABLE M.—Descent of Mary Loubier, wife of Hugues Minet.

MATHIEU LOUBIER, = Marie Maytre.
of Nîmes.

John Louis, = Elizabeth Cazalet.
naturalised
in 1700.

ANTOINE, = Izabeau Vialat,   Henry, = Ippolyte   Mary = John Noguier,   Clauline = Etienne de Teissier,   Charles = Jane Bertin ;
of London ;   d. Dec. 1733.   of Lon-   Ann Duhur ;   of Lœils ;   Ilug. Ref. from   will proved
will proved   don ;   d. Nov. 4,   d. Dec. 24, 1753.   Languedoc.   1774.
Apr. 5, 1734.   will   1733 ; b.
                                proved   at Low
                                1753.   Layton.

John Louis ;   Charlotte = JOHN ANTONY ;   Elizabeth, = F. L. Deboss, of Lausanne ;   Charlotte, = James,   Stephen = Elizabeth.
b. 1700 ; d.   Henrietta,   m. 1734 ;   m. 1759 ;   d. cir. 1792.   b. Geneva ;
Feb. 19, 1767 ;   d. Nov. 16,   will proved   d. 1783.   d. before 1789.
= Magdelaine   1788, at   1745.
Berchere, b.   Lausanne.
1704 ; d. Ap. 30,
1767.

daughter = ... Doxat.

MARY = HUGUES MINET.   Antony,
See A.   d. 1744 (?).

D'argent, à un lion sortantd'un buisson: for Loubier.

TABLE N.—Descent of Susannah Pole, wife of Isaac Minet.

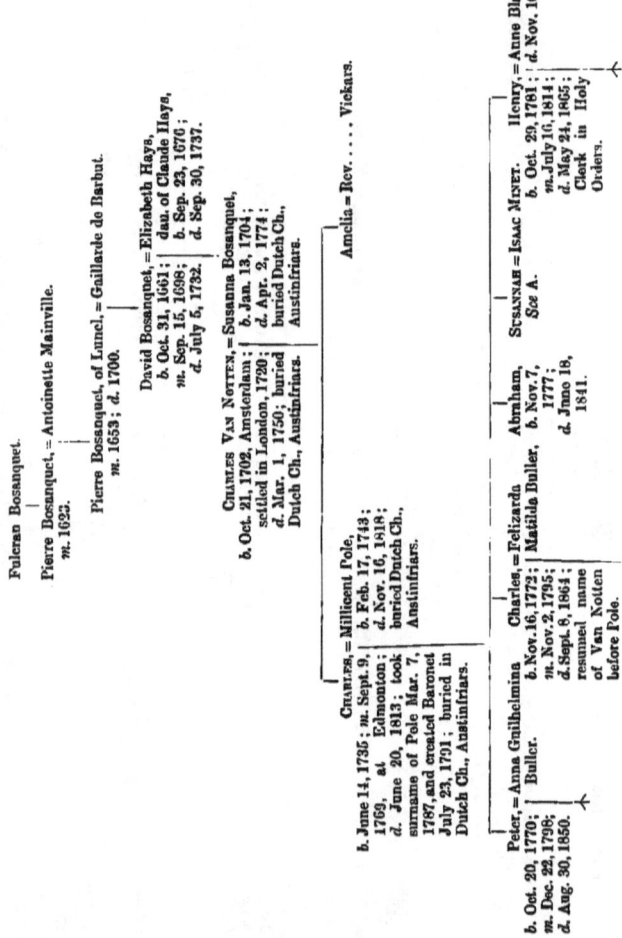

Fulcran Bossanquet.

Pierre Bossanquet, = Antoinette Mainville.
m. 1632.

Pierre Bossanquet, of Lunel, = Gaillarde de Barbut.
m. 1659; d. 1700.

David Bossanquet, = Elizabeth Hays,
b. Oct. 31, 1661;   dau. of Claude Hays,
m. Sep. 15, 1698;   b. Sep. 23, 1670;
d. July 5, 1732.   d. Sep. 30, 1737.

Charles Van Notten, = Susanna Bosanquet,
b. Oct. 21, 1702, Amsterdam;   b. Jan. 13, 1704;
settled in London, 1720;   d. Apr. 2, 1774;
                                buried Dutch Ch.,
                                Austinfriars.

Amelia = Rev..... Vickars.

Charles, = Millicent Pole,
b. June 14, 1735;   b. Feb. 17, 1743;
m. Sept. 9, 1769,   d. Nov. 16, 1818;
at Edmonton;   buried Dutch Ch.,
d. June 20, 1813;   Austinfriars.
took surname of Pole Mar. 7,
1787, and created Baronet
July 23, 1791; buried in
Dutch Ch., Austinfriars.

Susannah = Isaac Minet.
See A.

Peter, = Anna Guilhelmina Charles, = Felizarda   Abraham,   Henry, = Anne Blagrave,
b. Oct. 20, 1770; Buller. b. Nov. 16, 1772; Matilda Buller; b. Nov. 7, b. Oct. 29, 1781; d. Nov. 10, 1864.
m. Dec. 22, 1798;   m. Nov. 2, 1795;   1777;   m. July 16, 1814;
d. Aug. 30, 1850.   d. Sept. 8, 1864;   d. June 18, d. May 24, 1865;
                           resumed name   1841.   Clerk in Holy
                           of Van Notten   Orders.
                           before Pole.

Quarterly, 1st and 4th, argent, a chevron between three crescents gules, a mullet for difference: for Pole. 2nd and 3rd, quarterly: 1st and 4th, argent, four pallets azure; 2nd, or, a snake in pale, wavy, the upper half azure, the lower sable; 3rd, or, three crescents gules: for Van Notten.

TABLE O.—Descent of Alice Evans, wife of William Minet

Rice Evans = Hannah ...

Thomas, = Jane ...
b. June 19, 1716; m. Oct. 17, 1741.

Lewis, = Anne Norman.
b. Aug. 13, 1753; d. Nov. 19, 1827; M.A., F.R.S.

Arthur Benoni, = Anne Dickinson,
b. Mar. 25, 1781; m. June 17, 1819; dau. of Captain T. Dickinson, R.N.;
d. Nov. 8, 1851; Head Master of b. July 30, 1791; d. May 10, 1883;
Market Bosworth Gram. Sch. and Frances de Brissac.

Argent, a chevron between three elephants' heads, couped, sable: for Evans.

John, b. Nov. 17, 1822; m. Sept. 12, 1850; K.C.B., D.C.L., LL.D., F.M.S.	(1) Harriet Ann Dickinson, b. June 11, 1823; d. Jan. 1, 1858; buried at Abbots Langley. (2) Frances Phelps, b. Aug. 21, 1826; m. July 3, 1859; d. Sept. 22, 1890.	George, b. May 17, 1825; d. Jan. 25, 1847.	Emma, = John Waddington b. Sept. 13, Hubbard, 1829; b. July 10, 1823; m. Jan. 10, d. June 15, 1871. 1856.

			Harriot Ann. = Charles James b. Dec. 19, Longman, 1827; b. Apr. 14, m. July 15, 1880. 1852.
			See page 211.

Sebastian, = Elizabeth
b. Mar. 2, 1830; Goldney.
m. Apr. 6, 1858.

Sebastian, Frank,
b. Jan. 20, b. Aug. 9,
1859. 1862.

Emma, = H. S. Walker.
b. July 6, 1863;
m. Apr. 23, 1884;
d. July 20, 1891.

Anne, Arthur,
b. June 4, b. Jan. 3,
1820; 1832;
d. Feb. 19, d. Apr. 21,
1870. 1850.

Arthur John, = Margaret Lewis, = (1) Beryl Philip Norman, Alice = William Minet. Mary, George, Frances, Agatha.
b. July 8, Freeman, b. Feb. 15, May Ward, b. Dec. 13, See A. b. Oct. 25, b. Mar. 19, b. Jan. 12, 1862; m. Sept. b. Feb. 10, 1889.
1851; b. Oct. 17, 1853; b. May 23, 1854; 1860; 1859; m. June 1, 1892; 1, 1891, Wynnard
m. Sept. 19, 1848. m. Feb. 14, 1866; m. April 23, 1887, d. Apr. 20, 1865. Sarah Eleanora Hooper.
1878. 1884. d. Nov. 19, Ada Mary Gilbert Ronquette
1886; Dickinson.
= (2) Jan. 14, 1890,
Eva Fanny Bradford.

Alice Dorothy,
b. Feb. 16, 1892.

Arthur John, = Charlotte Marion Vigard.
b. Nov. 7, 1856;
m. July 10, 1888.

E.E.

I

Issue of Charles William Minet and Leah Fortrie Gossip.
(See Table A.)

1. FANNY CECILIA, *b.* at Rome, 3 Apr. 1831; *m.* 26 Sept. 1861, Robert Tubbs Nightingale Tubbs. He *d.* 26 July, 1891, *s.p.*
2. SUSAN MILLECENT, *b.* at Hevers Wood, co. Kent, 27 Aug. 1834; *m.* 31 Oct. 1864, General Sir Charles Dunbar Staveley, G.C.B., *b.* 18 Dec. 1817. *Issue:—*

   i. William Cathcart, *b.* 20 Sept. 1865.
   ii. Robert Napier, *b.* 5 Nov. 1866, *d.* 12 July, 1867.
   iii. Charles Russell, *b.* 5 Jan. 1868.
   iv. Rose, *b.* 29 Apr. 1869.
   v. Henry Collingwood, *b.* 5 July, 1871.
   vi. Arthur Godfrey, *b.* 24 Nov. 1872.
   vii. Cecil Minet, *b.* 3 Apr. 1874.
   viii. Leila, *b.* 9 Jan. 1878.
   ix. Susan, *b.* 28 Mar. 1882.

3. GERTRUDE, *b.* at Hevers Wood, co. Kent, 1 Sept. 1837, *d.* 4 Nov. 1872; *m.* 3 Feb. 1872, Thomas Godfrey Hatfeild. He died 19 Feb. 1882. *Issue:—*
   Gertrude, *b.* 4 Nov. 1872.
4. SOPHIA LOUISA, *b.* at Hevers Wood, co. Kent, 28 Apr. 1839, *d.* 18 Dec. 1855, *bur.* at Capel-le-Ferne.
5. GERALDINE HELENA, *b.* at Dover, 24 Jan. 1842.
6. GEORGINA EMMA, *b.* at Dresden, 21 Feb. 1846; *m.* 15 Feb. 1875, Henry Bethune Patton. *Issue:—*
   Bethune Minet, *b.* 6 Mar. 1876.
7. DELIA JANE, *b.* at Frankfort-on-Maine, 5 July, 1849; *m.* 17 Oct. 1871, Orfeur George Parker. *Issue:—*

   i. Robert George, *b.* 26 July, 1872.   ii. Owen Fortrie, *b.* 24 Aug. 1879.

II

Issue of Millecent Minet and John Dixon Dyke.
(See Table A.)

1. JOHN DIXON, *b.* 31 Oct. 1836.
2. EDWARD HART, *b.* 11 Nov. 1837.
3. HERBERT JENNER, *b.* 22 Jan. 1839, *d.* 30 May, 1868.
4. FREDERICK HOTHAM, *b.* 6 Feb. 1840; *m.* 20 Apr. 1871, Emily Thorndike. *Issue:—*

   i. Agnese Millicent, *b.* 21 Feb. 1872.   ii. Winifrid Amy, *b.* 1 Dec. 1881.

5. MILLICENT, *b.* 28 Apr. 1841.
6. CHARLES JAMES, *b.* 22 Apr. 1842, *d.* 5 July, 1886.
7. AUGUSTUS HART, *b.* 23 Mar. 1843, *d.* 21 Sept. 1889, *s.p.*; *m.* 8 July, 1884, Mercy Constance Cecilia Harris.
8. REGINALD HART, *b.* 15 Sept. 1844.
9. GEORGE HART, *b.* 21 Jan. 1847.
10. HENRY HART, *b.* 26 Mar. 1848; *m.* 10 Feb. 1886, Louisa Covey, who died 15 Dec. 1886, *s.p.*
11. JULIA, *b.* 2 Feb. 1851.
12. MATILDA, *b.* 17 Aug. 1853.

III

Issue of Frances Catherine Minet and Henry Anson Cartwright.
(See Table A.)

1. REGINALD, *b.* 15 May, 1842.
2. FRANCES ANNE, *b.* 1 Nov. 1844.
3. EMMELINE MARY, *b.* 30 May, 1846, *d.* 21 June, 1846.

4. MILLICENT VERNON, *b.* 13 Aug. 1847.
5. HUGH CHARLES VERNON, *b.* 19 Dec. 1848 ; *m.* 4 Mar. 1880, Mary Eliza Drake. *Issue :—*
    i. Reginald Henry Minet, *b.* 19 Apr. 1881.   ii. Una de Vere, *b.* 27 Nov. 1882.
                     iii. Emma Frances, *b.* 29 Feb. 1885.
6. SYDNEY POLE, *b.* 30 Jan. 1850.
7. MARY ANSON, *b.* 12 May, 1851.
8. NINA, *b.* 28 June, 1852.
9. HENRY ARTHUR, *b.* 17 July, 1853, *d.* 15 Dec. 1867.

IV

Issue of Harriet Ann Evans and Charles James Longman.
(See Table O.)

1. MARY, *b.* 29 Apr. 1881. | 3. SIBYL, *b.* 3 May, 1885.
2. WILLIAM, *b.* 14 Nov. 1882. | 4. FREDERICK, *b.* 9 May, 1890.

APPENDIX III

WILLS

1.—*Will of Isaac Minet, of Dover, died 8th April, 1745.*

I ISAAC MINET of Dover in the County of Kent being by the Grace of God in pretty good health and in perfect sound mind and memory and of the age of near eighty four years and uncertain of the time of my decease do in the name of God make this my last Will and Testament as followeth First I recommend my soul to the mercy of God through the merit of Jesus Christ the Saviour of the world and commit my body to be decently interred as my Executors hereafter named shall think fitt And as to my worldly goods which God hath blessed me with I do give and bequeath to my son John Minet Rector of the parish of Eythorn in Kent the sum of three thousand pounds of good and lawful money of Great Britain which sum of three thousand pounds shall six months after my decease by my executors or one of them be placed out at interest to the best advantage and the most security as may be possible to the liking and approbation of my said son John Minet and that the interest and profits arising from the same be duly paid to the said John Minet during all the time of his natural life and after his decease to Allix his wife for the maintenance of her and her children begotten by the said John Minet during her natural life and my will and intention is that after the death of the said John Minet and Alice his wife the said three thousand pounds shall be shared equally to such of the said children as shall be then alive and when any of the said children shall be disposed of either to prentices or settlement or marriage with consent of their parents such part of the principal of the said three thousand pounds may be allowed and given them as their said parent shall think reasonable And I do discharge acquit and forgive to my said son John Minet all such sums of money as he shall be indebted to me on any account whatsoever at the time of my decease Item I do give and bequeath to my son James Minet now at Berlin one thousand pounds which sum he hath already received and I do also give him the house I now live in together with the store house adjoining to it and the wharf and other premises belonging to my said house and also three houses situated on the Key near my said dwelling house now in the occupation of Henry Nethersole James Willis and Rooth Colbran all which houses and premises I hold by leases from the Right Honourable the Lord Warden of the Cinq Ports and assistants of Dover harbour I also give to my said son James Minet all the household goods and furniture belonging to my said dwelling house except the plate which I intend and order to be equally divided among my three sons John James and William Minet and I do also give to my said son James one half of all the Right and interest that I shall have at the time of my decease in any ship vessels or sloops Item I do give and bequeath to my son William Minet one thousand pounds and I also give him my store houses cellars gateway yard and all other premises belonging to the said storehouses which is part of the new buildings which I hold by Lease from the Lord Warden and Assistants of Dover harbour and also the other half of all the ships or vessells or parts of ships or vessells that I shall be possessed of at the time of my decease Item I do give and bequeath to my grandson Daniel Minet son of my son Daniel Minet deceased one thousand pounds of good and lawful money of Great Britain to be paid by my executors or one of them to his uncle William Minet In Trust for him the said Daniel one year after my decease on special condition that if he happens to dye and leave no issue of his body it shall not be in his power to dispose of the said sum of one thousand pounds my will and intention being in that case that the said sum of a thousand pounds shall be shared share alike among such children of my son John Minet as shall then be living Item I do give to my nephew Thomas Minet twenty guineas to my niece Mary Detirer twenty Guineas to my nephew Daniel Minet ten Guineas To Mary the wife of Jeremy Fector Elizabeth and Magdalen Minet each of them five guineas To Isaac Saml Roux and his sister each five guineas and also three guineas to Susanna Albert and to Mary Miller five guineas and to Mary Aldred and Sarah Pearce my servants each five guineas and to the poor I give ten pounds to be distributed by the Reverend Wm. Byrch in the manner he shall think fitt And my will and intention is that whatever my estate shall or may amount to more than the legacies in this my will and all my debts paid and the charge of my burial and probate of my will shall be equally divided among my three sons John James and William Minet and I do give to my grand daughter Mary Minet according to her Grand Mother Minet's desire the gold watch which was her said Grand Mother's and a gold equipage which was given her by the Dutchess of Marlborough and a brilliant ring I do give my gold watch to Hughes Minet my grandson Item I do make ordain and appoint my two sons James and William Minet the executors of this my will and Testament and I do by these presents revoke annull and make void and of no effect all former Wills and Testaments by me heretofore made and executed

In witness whereof I have hereunto set my hand and seal at Dover the 10th of Xber 1744 ISAAC MINET (L.S.)

Declared published signed and sealed in the Presence of
WM. BYRCH
PETER FECTOR

Memorandum that there is among my plate a silver tankard which my sister Mary Rooth did give to Mary the daughter of my son John Minet

Proved July 30, 1745.

2.—*Will of James Minet, of Berlin, died 29th January, 1774.*

Nous conseillers du Roi et greffier de la chambre Royale de Justice supérieure francaise sousignés en vertu du décret du 19 Sep. 1773 nous sommes transportés dans la maison de Mr James Kirkland située au triangle près de la Hausvogtey au Fredrickswerder où loge Mr James Minet of Doverpiere écuyer que nous avons trouvé jouissant d'une entière liberté d'esprit et d'entendement mais indisposé par son grand age aux fins de recevoir de lui sa declaration de dernière volunté laquelle il a faite et dictée de la manière suivante

1° Le dit Testateur donne et legue à son petit neveu Isaac Minet troisième fils de Mr Hughes Minet et son filleul la grande et belle maison qui lui appartient à dover comme immeuble paternel et toutes les autres maisons magazins caves et quais qui en dépendent et situés dans la même ville et généralement tous les immeubles qu'il possede tant au dit dover que dans quelqu'autre lieu de l'Angleterre et en cas que son dit petit neveu vint à mourir avant l'age de vingt un ans ou avant d'être marie ou sans laisser d'enfans en ces cas là il lui substitue son frère Guillaume dans tout le leg ci-dessus et si celui-ci ne parvenoit pas aussi au dit age il lui substitue son frère Jean Louis

2° Il donne et légue à l'église de la Dorothée Stadt de Berlin quatre cents ducats pour le soulagement des pauvres savoir deux cents ducats pour les pauvres François de cette ville et deux cents ducats pour les pauvres des Réformés allemands de la dite église de la Dorothée Stadt

3° Il donne et légue à l'église de douvres pour être employé à l'usage de ses pauvres vingt cinq guinées

4° Il donne et lègue à sa servante Marie Vincent cent ducats à son autre servante Anne Regine Engelfrieden vingt cinq ducats à son valet Joan vingt cinq ducats à son cocher Quirkel vingt ducats et à sa cuisinière qui se trouvera à son service au jour de son décès quinze ducats

5° Pour qui est de son corps le Testateur souhaite qu'on le depose dans le caveau de l'église de la ville neuve où sont deposés le pasteur Achard et le chevalier André Quithal

6° Quant à l'argent que le testateur a chez le banquier Neubronner et qui consiste selon la teneur de ses lettres de change du 1er Juillet 1773 à douze mois de date en quinze mille Rixdalers en or et quinze mille Rixdalers en argent courant de Brandenbourg ensemble trente mille Rixdalers qu'il lui a remis à raison de quatre pour cents d'Intérêts par an le dit Testateur veut qu'il transporte la dite créance de trente mille Rixdalers sur le compte de son neveu Mr Hughes Minet mais comme le Testateur a avancé cet argent au dit Sr Neubronner pour l'aider dans son commerce il veut et entend qu'il ne soit tenu à rembourser le dit capital que de la manière suivante savoir dix milles Rixdalers la première année après son décès dix mille Rixdalers la seconde et dix mille la troisième

7° Quant au reste de ses biens en quoi qu'ils puissent consister le dit

Testateur nomme et institue pour ses heritiers généraux et universels 1° Mr Hughes Minet son neveu 2° et 3° les deux soeurs germaines du dit Sʳ Hughes Minet et 4° Mr Daniel Minet neveu du dit Testateur pour se partager le tout en quatre portions égales

Le dit Testateur nomme pour son exécuteur testamentaire Mr Hughes Minet l'un des quatre héritiers ci-dessus et il veut et entend qu'il se mette en possession de tout ce qu'il delaissera dans la maison du Sʳ Kirklandt d'abord après son décès et en son absence Messieurs Kirklandt et Neubronner ou tel à qui le dit executeur testamentaire donnera sa procuration defendant expressement le dit Testateur toute mise de Scellé inventaire ou autre procédé de justice quelconque

C'est là son testament et disposition de dernière volonté qu'il nous a déclaré vouloir être ponctuellement executée après son décès voulant qu'il vaille soit comme testament codicille donation pour cause de mort ou telle autre disposition de la dernière volonté mieux authorisée par les loix defendant toute detraction de quarte Trebollianique Falcidie ou autre Et lecture ayant été faite à haute voix au dit Testateur par nous conseillers et greffiers sousignés il a declaré que c'etait là sa dernière volonté et a signé en notre présence avec apposition du sceau de ses armes et nous avons pareillement signé avec apposition du petit sceau de la justice supérieure Francaise—Fait et écrit à Berlin le 20 Sep. 1773

                                JAMES MINET   (L.S)
                                DE GAULTIER-ESTIENNE L.S
                                PIQUET *GREFFIER*   (L.S)

Proved Feb. 26, 1774.

3.—*Extracts from the Will of William Minet, of London, died January* 18, 1767.

His body to be interred near where his parents lie in St. Mary's, Dover.

To John Minet, his brother (with forgiveness of all debts) .	500*l.*
To Alice Minet, his sister-in-law	50
To Mary, his niece, wife of Peter Fector .	3,000
To Peter Fector	100
To the nearest akin of Henry Minet, son of John Minet, for his maintenance, per annum .	50
To Isaac and William Minet, his nephews, each	50
To Henrietta Sayer, daughter of John Minet .	3,000
'Unto my nephew Daniel Minet in confidence and trusting that if he dye without issue he will leave not only that sum, but all he may have left of his late father's estate and coming from our family, to such of them as may be living and that he may think most deserving and in need of it ; I do mean this as a recommendation only and not as a condition' (no sum is mentioned ; *see* later)	
To Mary Detrier, of Dover (*see* Table *F*) .	20

APPENDIX III

To Elizabeth Minet, of Canterbury (*see* Table *D*)	20*l*.
To Mary Woodruff (*see* Table *B*)	50
To Thomas Minet, 'late of Tetuan in Barbary' (*see* Table *B*)	50
To James Minet, 'now of Lisbon,' with forgiveness in these two latter cases of all debts (*see* Table *B*)	50
To John Jacques Descottes, of Copenhagen	50
To Susannah De la Court, 'second cousin to my late mother'	50
To Elizabeth, her daughter, 'being an honest, diligent and dutiful young woman'	100
To Bernard, her son, with forgiveness of debts	20
To Daniel Dabbadie, of Brentford, with forgiveness of debt he and his father, Francis, owed	20
To 'My good friend, a most able and skilful physician who has practised physic in the most successful humane and honorable way Dr Herman Bernard of London'	100
To James De Roussell, of Canterbury, 'as a token of my esteem for him and his regard and friendship to my relations' (*see* Table *F*)	25
To Henry Farley, 'clerk of our contoir at Dover'	50
To Lewis Peter Hume	300
To William Eidsforth, cellarman	600
To Alice Styles, servant	400
To Thomas, her son, 'whom I have employed in the business'	200
To Margaret, wife of Peter Hume, servant-maid	300
To John Wilkinson, deputy cellarman	50
To the poor of the French Church in Threadneedle Street	100
To the Directors of the French Hospital near St. Luke's	100
To the charity school in Westminster, for the education of poor children of French refugees, Protestants	50
To the poor of St. Mary and St. James, Dover	100

'With regard to my private books, letters, papers, and writings relating to family or other concerns I do very much recommend and desire they may be put up into chests under locks and keys, the keys sealed up and directed to my brother James Minet of Berlin to be delivered to him if he comes to England. But if my brother does not come over then my nephew Hughes Minet only may inspect and burn them, and I do in a very perticular manner recommend that they may not be sent abroad nor never be exposed to be, nor fall into the hands of any other family, or into strange hands. In the case of my said nephew's death I desire my other executors to destroy them without inspection.'[1]

[1] It may be permitted at this lapse of time, and to one who has endeavoured to collect the traditions of the family, to regret that this direction was carried out.

'And Whereas I did agree with my brother James Minet that the old family mansion house at Dover should be pulled down and that a new house should be built on the same ground at the pier at Dover, he and myself to pay one half of the said house, to compleat a good creditable family mansion house for the name and carrying on of the trade & commerce; all of which has been done in a very costly useful and creditable manner about the year 1750, and the whole paid for by us. We did agree that the said house should become our joint property during our lifetime, and should in case of either of our deaths become the property of the survivor of us; but if it does please God that my brother James shall die before me' the house is left to Hughes Minet, and, failing him, to Peter Fector, with strict injunction that the name of the firm is always to commence with that of 'Minet.'

The one-half share in the Dover business is next dealt with, and after realisation, is to form part of the general estate.

A sum of 5,000*l.* is bequeathed to trustees, to be applied in the purchase of lands of inheritance for Hughes Minet.

Capel Church farm is devised to James Minet for life, and after his death to Hughes Minet in tail, with remainder to Daniel Minet.

'All the residue of my personal estate I do give unto my beloved brother James Minet in the firm hopes and confidence that if his health will permit him he will come and reside in England, and that he will not alienate any part of my estate from our family. And I do direct that after his death the said residuum of my estate be divided into three parts,' one-third to go to Daniel Minet, one-third to Hughes, and one-third to Peter Fector, in the case of the latter third the condition as to the name of the firm being again repeated.

Then follows a legacy of 200*l.* a year to his brother John, and the appointment of three executors—James and Hughes Minet, and John Dolignon. The amount of the legacy to Daniel Minet, omitted in the earlier part of the will, is named as 5,000*l.*, and Daniel is added as trustee for the 5,000*l.* left for Hughes' benefit.

'And finally I the said testator William Minet to this my last Will and Testament written on eleven pages foregone in this book, and this latter part on the twelfth page the whole of my own handwriting, with my signature on the left hand corner of every page and of which there is no copy or duplicate and unto which I have set my hand and seal this fourteenth day of October in the year of our Lord one thousand seven hundred and sixty five.

(*Signed*) WILLIAM MINET.

'*Witnesses*, STEPHEN HALL, partner with Sir Jos. Hankay & Co., JAMES GORDON, Seedsman in Fenchurch Street, GEORGE GARTHORNE, clerk to Sir Jos. Hankay & Co.'

By a codicil which is unsigned and undated, the farm at Hayes, in Middlesex, for the purchase of which the testator had agreed with John Dodd, is left to James Minet for life, and after his death to Hughes and Daniel. To Mary, wife of Peter Fector, a further sum of 2,000*l.* is left, in consideration of which the legacy of one-third of the residue to Peter Fector is revoked; and the residue is divided equally between Hughes and Daniel. Henrietta Sayer receives a further 1,000*l*., and various additions are made to some of the other legacies.

The following is a note made by Hughes Minet on his uncle William's will:—

'Memo. Mr William Minet died on Sunday the 18th day of January 1767. His will is dated the 14th of October 1765. His codicil (in his own handwriting) refers to the date of the will and to the will itself, but is neither signed or dated. Both the said will and the said codicil were proven by Hughes Minet and John Dolignon on the 9th of February 1767. Mr James Minet (who came from Berlin a little while before) proved the said will on the 4th of August, 1767, following, he putt the executors (that is his nephew H. M.) to great difficulty by delaying his jorney to England so long. After said Mr James Minet's death, Hughes Minet and John Dolignon proved the new probate (a nuncupatory codicil being obtained) on the 5th of March 1775.

'Memo. Mr James Minet died at Berlin on the 29th day of January 1774. Mr John Dolignon was buried at Cheshunt 12 November 1776, so he died a few days before that.'

4.—*Extracts from the Will of Hughes Minet, died December* 23, 1813.

Dated September 19, 1811; proved February 15, 1814.

'I desire to be buried in the churchyard of the parish wherein I shall happen to die, neither unless my executors shall have any valid reason respecting themselves to the contrary, do I wish that any monument, tablet, or any other device or contrivance of that kind, beyond a "hic jacet" in wood be inscribed to me or erected on my account.'

Capel Sole farm (inherited from his mother) he devises to his son William; and as to Capel Church farm, in which he had a life-interest under William Minet's will, 'I remind my son William that I consider the same a devise direct from me since I had undoubted evidence and cirtain assurance that he purchased the farm for me after his brother James death, and that he was under an engagement to my late mother to devise the farm to me absolutely that I might add the same to her adjoining farm Capel-sole, and this I am cirtain of, notwithstanding my uncle as well in this as in many other instances confusedly expressed his meaning in his will.'

The farms at Hayes, in Middlesex, and the land at Brasted, in Kent, are devised to John Lewis Minet, and the land at Camberwell to Isaac Minet.

'Whereas my late uncle James Minet godfather of Isaac Minet in respect to the memory of his, my late uncle's father gave him the name of Isaac and did on that account and in preference bequeath to him his dwelling house in Dover in order that the family name might be the better perpetuated in a house of business there, I actuated by the same motives' bequeath everything at Dover to Isaac.

Various legacies of no interest follow, and John Lewis and Isaac, his sons, are appointed executors.

APPENDIX IV

INSCRIPTIONS TAKEN FROM MONUMENTS OF THE MINET FAMILY

1.—*Isaac and Mary Minet.*

Inscription on a tombstone in the nave of St. Mary's Church, Dover, which vanished in the restoration of 1844:—

> HERE LIETH THE BODY OF
> MARY
> THE WIFE OF MR ISAAC MINET
> WHO DIED Y^E 30TH NOV. 1738 AGED 68 YEARS
> "IN HOPE OF A BLESSED RESURRECTION."
>
> HERE LIETH THE BODY OF
> MR ISAAC MINET
> MERCHANT
> HE WAS BORN AT CALAIS THE 15TH OF SEP. 1660
> FROM WHENCE BEING PERSECUTED FOR THE SAKE OF
> THE PROTESTANT RELIGION HE FLED TO THIS PLACE
> FOR REFUGE, 1686.
> HE HAD BY MARY HIS WIFE FIVE SONS, JOHN, ISAAC,
> JAMES, DANIEL, & WILLIAM
> HE DIED Y^E 8TH AP. 1745
> "THE MEMORY OF THE JUST IS BLESSED"

2.—*Isaac, Mary, Isaac, Jr., Frances, and William Minet.*

Inscription on a monument in St. Mary's Church, Dover, which, on the restoration in 1844, was removed from the north to the south aisle, where it still remains:—

> NEAR THIS PLACE ARE DEPOSITED
> THE REMAINS OF
> MR ISAAC MINET
> OF THIS TOWN MERCHANT
> WHO DIED 8 APRIL 1745 ÆTAT 85 YEARS
> AND OF MARY HIS WIFE
> WHO DIED 30 NOV 1738 ÆTAT 68 YEARS
> BY WHOM HE HAD FIVE SONS
> JOHN ISAAC JAMES DANIEL WILLIAM
> LIKEWISE THE REMAINS OF
> MR ISAAC MINET J^R
> OF THIS TOWN MERCHANT
> SON OF THE SAID MR ISAAC MINET
> WHO DIED 11 OCT 1731 ÆTAT 35 YEARS
> AND OF FRANCES HIS WIFE
> WHO DIED 20 JAN 1766 ÆTAT 69 YEARS
> AND OF
> MR WILLIAM MINET
> OF LONDON MERCHANT
> WHO DIED A BACHELOR THE 18 JAN 1767
> ÆTATIS 63 YEARS.

3.—*John Minet.*

Inscription on a monument in the south chancel wall of Eythorne Church, Kent:—

HIC JACET
JOHANNES MINET A.M.
RECTOR ECCLESIÆ EVTHORNE
EXPECTANS RESURRECTIONEM
OBIIT 13 NOV
A. CHR. NAT. 1771
ANNO ÆTAT 77

4.—*John Minet, Peter and Mary Fector, and others.*

Inscription on a stone in the north aisle of Eythorne Church, Kent:—

IN A VAULT BENEATH THIS STONE
LIE DEPOSITED THE MORTAL REMAINS OF
THE REV^D JOHN MINET
WHO DIED 13TH NOV. 1771 AGED 77 YEARS
HAVING BEEN RECTOR OF THIS PARISH
NEARLY 50 YEARS.
ALSO OF **PETER FECTOR** ESQ^{RE}
OF DOVER AND OF THIS PARISH
WHO DIED 30 JAN 1814
AGED 90 YEARS
ALSO OF **MARY FECTOR** HIS WIFE
DAUGHTER OF THE ABOVE REV^D J. MINET
WHO DIED 21ST OCT 1794 AGED 66
ALSO OF THE UNDERMENTIONED CHILDREN OF
THE ABOVE PETER AND MARY FECTOR
VIZ **WILLIAM FECTOR** ESQ^{RE}
WHO DIED 23RD DEC. 1805 AGED 41 YEARS
MARY ELIZABETH FECTOR
WHO DIED 4TH DEC. 1814 AGED 57 YEARS
ALSO OF **ELIZABETH HUGHES WELLARD**
WIFE OF CHARLES WELLARD ESQ^{RE}
OF DOVER.

5.—*Alice and Mary Minet.*

Inscription on a tablet in the south wall of Capel-le-Ferne Church, Kent:—

TO THE MEMORY OF
ALICE MINET
WIDOW OF THE REV^D JOHN MINET
RECTOR OF EYTHORNE
WHO DIED 15 AUGUST 1778
AGED 77 YEARS
ALSO OF **MARY MINET**
WIFE OF HUGHES MINET OF LONDON ESQ^{RE}
WHO DIED 21 NOVEMBER 1768
AGED 31 YEARS

THE HUGUENOT FAMILY OF MINET

6.—Daniel Minet.

Inscription on a tablet in the north wall of Bengeo Church, Herts:—

SACRED TO THE MEMORY OF
DANIEL MINET F.R.S.
WHO TO A WELL CULTIVATED MIND ADDED
THE CHARACTER OF A SINCERE CHRISTIAN
AND A GENEROUS BENEFACTOR TO THE POOR
LAMENTED BY HIS NUMEROUS FRIENDS
HE DEPARTED THIS LIFE THE 25TH OF FEBRUARY
1790 AGED 61
THIS MONUMENT HIS AFFLICTED WIDOW
CAUSED TO BE ERECTED AS A SMALL PLEDGE
OF HER AFFECTION.

7.—Hughes Minet.

Inscription on a monument in Westerham Church, Kent:—

IN A VAULT IN THE CHURCHYARD
NEARLY BEHIND THIS MONUMENT
ARE DEPOSITED THE REMAINS OF
HUGHES MINET ESQ^{RE}
WHO DIED AT HIS RESIDENCE IN THIS PARISH
DECEMBER 23 1813 IN THE 83RD YEAR OF HIS AGE
HE WAS THE SON OF THE REV^D JOHN MINET M.A.
RECTOR OF EYTHORNE, KENT. WHOSE ANCESTORS
BEING PROTESTANTS FLED FROM FRANCE
ON THE REVOCATION OF THE EDICT OF NANTES
IN 1685, AND SETTLED AT DOVER WHERE THEY
ESTABLISHED A MERCANTILE HOUSE WHICH
HAS CONTINUED IN THE FAMILY TILL THE PRESENT TIME
HE MARRIED MARY (A DAUGHTER AND COHEIRESS OF
ANTHONY LOUBIER ESQ^{RE}) WHO DIED 21 NOVEMBER 1768
AND IS INTERRED AT CAPEL-LE-FERNE IN THIS
COUNTY, BY WHOM HE HAS LEFT ISSUE
THREE SONS WHO ERECT THIS TABLET AS A
TRIBUTE OF FILIAL RESPECT TO THE MEMORY OF AN
AFFECTIONATE AND GREATLY REVERED FATHER
AND A MOST UPRIGHT LIBERAL AND CHARITABLE MAN

8.—William Minet.

Inscription on a monument in Westerham Church, Kent:—

TO THE MEMORY OF
LIEU^T-GENERAL WILLIAM MINET
OF DOVINGDON, HERTS
ELDEST SON OF HUGHES MINET ESQ^R
WHO AFTER 40 YEARS SPENT IN THE SERVICE
OF HIS KING AND COUNTRY
DEPARTED THIS LIFE 27TH DECEMBER 1827
IN THE 66TH YEAR OF HIS AGE

APPENDIX IV

9.—*John Lewis and Elizabeth Minet.*

Inscription on a monument in Westerham Church, Kent :—

IN MEMORY OF
JOHN LEWIS MINET ESQʀᴇ
OF HEVERS WOOD IN THIS COUNTY
SECOND SON OF HUGHES MINET ESQʀᴇ
THIS TABLET IS INSCRIBED
BY HIS WIDOW
DIED 21 NOVEMBER 1829
IN THE 64ᵀᴴ YEAR OF HIS AGE
ELIZABETH MINET
WIDOW OF JOHN LEWIS MINET
DIED 11ᵀᴴ JULY 1831
IN THE 59ᵀᴴ YEAR
OF HER AGE

10.—*Isaac and Susannah Minet.*

Inscription on a monument in Westerham Church, Kent :—

SACRED
TO THE MEMORY OF
ISAAC MINET ESQʀᴇ
OF BALDWYNS, IN THIS COUNTY
DIED MARCH 14ᵀᴴ 1839
IN THE 72ᴺᴰ YEAR OF HIS AGE
HE SERVED THE OFFICE OF
HIGH SHERRIFF FOR THIS COUNTY
IN THE YEAR 1827
ALSO OF **SUSANNAH**
WIDOW OF THE ABOVE
DIED MARCH 15ᵀᴴ 1869
IN THE 90ᵀᴴ YEAR OF HER AGE

APPENDIX V

DEEDS RELATING TO LA TRÉSORERIE

THE following deeds, as interesting in themselves, and more especially as relating to the Wimille Haffrengues and the Trésorerie, I have thought it worth while to set out in full. From them it would appear that the Trésorerie had descended from Pierre de Haffrengue to his two sons, Daniel and Pierre, who had let it to one Pierre Coze, who was habitually behindhand with his rent. The first document, of February 7, 1668, is a statement of account between the landlords and tenant, made up to November 11, 1667, wherein, after making certain allowances and deductions for money spent in repairs, Pierre Coze is shown as owing a considerable balance. On this document is endorsed a memorandum of May 6, 1668, by which certain further allowances are credited to the tenant; but the exact amount of these is not specified. A further endorsement of October 18, 1669, shows an increased amount as then owing by Coze. Another endorsement, of October 26, 1669, shows that a part of the debt had then been paid. The last note, apparently meant to be signed by Coze, but which is not so signed, and which, moreover, has no date, is an acknowledgment of continuing indebtedness. It will be noticed that it is in the memorandum of October 26, 1669, that the payment is stated to have been made at the Converserie.

The next document (of March 9, 1689) is evidence that Daniel and Pierre Haffrengue had fled from the country on the Revocation, as they no longer appear as landlords, their place being taken by the Commissioner of the escheated land. There is no other evidence of their flight, nor is it known in any way where they escaped to. Coze was evidently still an unsatisfactory tenant, and the Commissioner was not as long-suffering as his former landlords, for though a much smaller sum was now owing, an execution had been put in, to relieve himself from which Coze, with his son as surety, had agreed to give this bond. These strong measures seem to have succeeded, and the balance was finally cleared off, with a further sum due for costs, by June 10 following. This last document is very much damaged, and some portions of it are undecipherable. Both the documents have come into the possession of M. Landrin, through whose courtesy it is that I am able to reproduce them here.

Deed of February 7, 1668.

'Ce jourdhuy septiesme jour de Feb^r mil six cens soix^e huict Jacqueline du Pré f$\tilde{e}$ de Pierre Coze et Louis Coze son fils occupeurs de la maison de Daniel de Haffreingue et Pierre de Haffreingue situé en la parroise de Wimille ont ce jourdhuy f^t compte ansemble auecq led^t Daniel de Haffreingue pour vn terme de la jouissance de lad^{te} maison occupé par led^t Coze escheu à la St Martin[1] d$\breve{e}$r, montant à la sol de deux cens quattre vingt dix liures, par leq^l compte appert led^t Coze avoir paié la sol de cent dixhuict liures onze sols trois deniers dvne part pour les causes contenue par le memoire et partij dud^t Coze tant pour rediffication desd^t battim^t que paim^{ns} f^{ts} pour matereaux, coõ aussy la sol de trente nœuf liures quattre sols porté par quitt^{ce}, le tout faisant ansemble la sol de cent cincq^{te} sept liures quinze sols trois deniers ; de sorte que led^t Coze se trouue redebuable de la sol de cent trente deux liures quattre sols nœuf deniers[2] pour led^t terme escheu à lad^{te} St Martin : sauf neantmoins sy

---

[1] The more usual quarter days were Easter, St. John, St. Remi, and Christmas. St. Martin falls on November 11, and is the half-quarter day.

[2] 12 deniers = 1 sol, 20 solls = 1 livre ; so

             *l.*118 11 3 paid
               39   4 0 allowed
              157 15 3 total paid and allowed
              132   4 9 balance due
            *l.*290   0 0 rent for one quarter—*i.e.* 1,160 livres a year.

led^t Coze rapporte cy apres aultre acquict que ceulx de ce jourdhuy represente il luy en sera tenue compte; cõe aussy ne luy a esté deduicte auscune choze pour la leué des deniers roiaulx de ceste pñte anne, ce quy a esté f^{te} sans aulcune choze desroger au bail a ferme desd^{ts} immeubles: f^t les jours et an susd^{ts}. Les memoires et quitt^{ces} de ce faisant mention ont esté delaissés es mains dud^t Coze.

'Signe et paraphe de Robert le Jessin pour lapsens dud^t Pierre de Haffreingue pour y avoir recours sy besoingt est en cas derreur

'DANIEL DE HAFFRENGUE.
'LOUIS COZE.'

First Endorsement.

'Et le six^{me} jour de May aud^t an mil six cens soix^{te} huict Pierre de Haffreingue desnomé en ces pñts estant aud^t Wimille a procedé a la reuision du pñt compte par laq^{lle} a icelluy agréé et agréé et en augmentaõn dicelt pour lobmission dy avoir apporté quattre busseaux daueine a la petite mesure paié au Seig^r de Lesmond par la quitt^{ce} dud^t Bennet sen recepuoir [son receveur] pour lanné 1667 il a accordé et accorde cõe aussy Jeanne Latteur fē de Mr Daniel de Haffreingue quil soit passé en compte cincq^{te} quatre sols aud^t Coze en deduction de lad^t sõl de cent trente deux liures quatre sols nœuf deniers, cõe aussye leur desduire les tailles s mentionné, et le tout sur les quittances et acquits quils representerent par cy apres; et les memoires et quittances resultant du pñt compte ont este remis es mains desd^{ts} de Haffreingue.

'PIERRE HAFFRENGUE.
'JENNE LATTEUR.'

Second Endorsement.

'Le dixhuict^{me} jour d'Octobre mil six cens soix^e nœuf Pierre de Haffreingue et Jeanne Latteur fē de Daniel de Haffreingue ont f^{ts} compte auecq Pierre Coze leur fermier pour tous les paim^{ts} par luy f^{ts} en leur acquits et pour partie de rediffication sans quittances, paim^{ts} de taille et gñallemt pour toute choze jusque a ce jour, compris le compte cy deu^t f^t entre les parties, led^t Coze sest trouué estre encore redebuat vers lesd^s de Haffreingue de la sõl de quatre cens quatre vingt liures sur le restast de ces termes, compris celluy de la Sr Jean dēr pour raison de son fermage lesq^{ls} quittances ont esté pñtemt remis es mains desd^{ts} de Haffreingue, en tesmoigñ de quoy ils ont signé

'PIERRE COZE.   'PIERRE DE HAFFRENGUE.
'JENNE LATTEUR.'

Third Endorsement.

'Ce vint sixesme octobre 1669 Pierre Coze a baillé a nostre aquy a la Converserie cinquant liure et soisant et onze liures quy a fay promesse lesquelle seront deduit sur ce cont cy

'de plus six liur . . . .   'P. DE HAFFRENGUE.
'a baille a ma soeur . . . .   'JENNE LATTEUR.'

Fourth Endorsement.

'Je suis redeuable a Daniel Haffrengue la somme de cent cinquante six liure pour sa par.

'Et a Pierre de Haffrengue la some de cent trente quattre liure des contez pour sa par.'

Deed of March 9, 1689.

'Pardeuant les notaires royaux resident a Boulogne soubsignez est comparu Pierre Coze laboureur dem^t a Wimille lequel a recogneu estre redeuable vers Antoine Guerard dem^t a Bout commissaire estaby a la saisie . . . . . des terres de la maison nommée la Tresorerie en la paroisse dud Wimille de la Somme de cent cincq liures pour loiers de partie desd terres tout compte jusques et compris ce terme de la Mimars prochaine dernier (*sic*) de ses jouissances, sur laquelle somme ayant payé comptant trente liures reste deub soixante quinze liures, laquelle somme il s'oblige solidement auecq L[ouis] Coze son fils laboureur dem^t a Auding[hem] la caution comparaissant aussi . . . . en dedans trois semaines de ajourdhuy, et ce par les voyes que led Guerard pourroit estre contraint, en consideraõn de quoy led Guerard a donné et donne main levée [1] de l'execũon de deux vaches executées sur led Pierre Coze, laquelle execution demeurera neantmoins en estat pour la sureté dud payement. En foy dequoy ils ont signé aud Bout le neufies Mars mvj^e quattre vingt neuf sans prejudice des fraix sauf ceux deub au req^t auquel ils ont estés paiée

'SOMERARD.

'Et le dix^{me} de juin aud an est comparu pard lesd^{ts} no^{res} led G[ue]rar denomé . . . dessus leq^l . . . . as receu comptant dud Pierre Coze la somme de soix [ante qui]nze liures requis cy dessus oultre vingt cincq . . . . pour la . . . . . led G[ue]rar fay absolue quittance et . . . . . est . . . . qu'il appartiendra, en foy dequoy il a siné a Boulon . .

'SOMERARD.'

APPENDIX VI

THE CUPS OF THE CHURCH OF GUÎNES

THE following extracts from the Tanner MS. in the Bodleian Library, at Oxford, refer to the two silver cups formerly the property of the Church at Guînes, but which, on the destruction of that Church, were brought to Dover. The appeal to the Archbishop of Canterbury seems to have been successful, as the cups remained at Dover. It is not clear from the document whither the books had gone, or who had been guilty of the 'fraudulent subtilty'; but one of them—the book of accounts of the Guînes Church—has survived, and is now in the possession of M. Landrin, of Guînes.

[1] 'Main-levée est un acte qui détruit une saisie ou une opposition, soit qu'il soit consenti par la partie, soit qu'il soit prononcé en Justice. Ainsi, bailler main levée est lever et ôter l'autorité de Justice apposé sur la chose saisie, et en rendre au saisi la libre jouissance, telle qu'il l'avait avant la saisie' (C. J. de Ferrière, *Dict. de Droit et de Pratique*. Paris, 1758, *s.v.* Main-levée).

The story of the two cups is somewhat curious. The first we hear of them is in the extract from White Kennet's diary quoted on page 12, in which he mentions seeing them used on Sunday, October 8, 1682. On the scattering of the congregation of Guines in 1686 the cups, with the linen, were, by order of the Guines Consistory, removed to Dover, whither the majority of the congregation had escaped. A minority, however, had taken refuge in Zealand, where they had joined the already-existing church at Cadzand; whereupon arose questionings as to which body represented the former Church of Guines, and therefore had the right to the cups.

As early as 1686 the Church at Cadzand had evidently made some claim to the possession of these cups, and in October of that year we find the representatives of the Dover Church stating their case to Archbishop Sancroft in the following memorial :—

May it Please your Grace

We are obliged (by the request of the Heads of the families who haue took refuge in this Towne) to haue recourse to your fauorable protection, to represent to your Grace their just complaints, and defence against the proceedings of some particular persons of the Church of Callais retired into Zealand, The Case in short is this, The Church of Callais haueing been destroyed the Elders of itt thinking to saue what might belong to itt did send hither the Cups and Linnen which serued att the Communion, with order to keep them and to make use of them in our Church, By the same orders, My Lord, we should haue receiued and kept here The Books of the Church, but by a fraudulent subtilty others were sent us in their roome, which we were obliged to restore: These Heads of families, whereof ours complaine, haue the said books in their keeping, we can be content they should remaine there, and do not ask for them. But they demand of us the Cups and Linnen aforementioned and that in a way altogether unworthy of Christians and Brethren by letters filled with injuries calumnies & threatnings against which we haue made no other opposition then our Patience, Reseruing our selves in case of Necessity to haue recourse to you for justice My Lord, under whose protection Diuine Prouidence hath placed us, in our dispersion by the persecution in France: All the fauour we beg of your Grace in this occasion is only that your Grace would haue the goodness to vindicate the Heads of our Families in the design they haue to keep for the service of our Church the said Cups and Linnen; we declareing in their behalf My Lord that they pretend nothing of propriety therein and that they will most willingly render them to the Church of Callais, unto which the whole belongs, so soon as it shal please God to re-establish the same That your Grace would please to interpose your authority to put a stop to those scandalous proceedings of their party, who haue all that belonged to the said Church, Except those Cups and Linnen, which they threaten to gett whateuer it may cost them, though they do not make the Thirtieth Part of the Church of Callais, Notwithstanding which Let them remaine in peaceable possession of all which they haue, we ask nothing of

G G

them But withall most humbly beseech your Grace that the Cups and linnen which we haue may remaine here with us, they being so necessary for our celebrating the holy Communion. We are with all possible Respect,

My Lord,
Your Graces
Most humble and most obedient Seruants the
Pastor and Elders of the French Church att Dover.
S. DE LEBECQUE minister
ISAAC DE LA CROIX
CHARLES JOHNSON [1]

Dover The 14 October 1686.

Endorsed:—Conc. ye coīon-plate &c of ye Dover-French.

Accompanying the memorial was the following statement of facts:—

Nous soussinés Chefs de famille de l'Église Protestante cy devant recueillie au Bourg de Guisnes pour convaincre de nullité les prétentions que nos frères de l'Eglise de Catzan s'attribuent aux coupes de lad[ite] Eglise lesquelles sont présentement en cette ville, nous disons :—

Premièrement que les dittes coupes apartiennent a l'Église de Guisnes que Dieu poura restablir vn jour par sa grace, a laquelle pour lors elles doivent estre restituées, de manière qu'aucuns particuliers de cette Église la n'y peuvent justement pretendre droit sous pretexte qu'ils sont nombre et qu'ils forment vn corps par ce que ce n'est plus l'Église de Guisnes mais vne tres petite partie de icelle ; c'est pourquoy nous estimons que les coupes sont vn depost sacré auquel on ne peut attenter comme proprietaire sans encourir le blasme d'une manifeste vsurpation, et nous croyons ce depost seurement entre nous pour en rendre en temps et lieu aussy bon comte que pouroit faire l'Église de Catzan. Secondement que nous sommes non seulement en pouvoir mais aussy en obligation de les garder veu les ordres exprés que nous en avous receûs de l'Église de Guisnes reduitte pour lors a quelque anciens Diacre et particuliers des Principaux qui avoient charachtere et autorite pour en disposer comme ils ont fait, au deffaut d'un plus grand nombre.

En troisieme lieu que l'Église de Catzan se faissant l'Église de Guisnes elle doit faire soumission aux loix de la Discipline et Synodes des Eglises de France dont la pratique constant a esté de faire transferer a l'Église la plus voisine ce qui apartenoit a celle qui estoit destricte ; or sans contradit la nostre est la plus voisine de celle de Guisnes et par consequent ce que nous pouvons avoir entre nos mains qui luy apartienne doit demeurer a nostre garde : et pour cette raison nous avons a demander a Messrs nos frères de Catzan les livres de la Bibliothèque dont le Catalogue qui nous est resté pour tout bien est chargé du Recipiste de Monsieur Trouiller leur Pasteur comme nous le justifirons en temps et lieu ; fondés d'autant mieux a leur faire cette demande que nous avons esté expressément chargée par les anciens et Diacre

---

[1] Bodleian Library, Oxford. Tanner MS. 92, fo. 96.

restans pours lors de toute l'Eglise, de retirer et de garder les dits livres ce que nous sommes encore pretes de justifier devant qui il apartiendra.

En dernier lieu nous dissons contre ce que ces Messieurs peuvent alleguer qu'ils ont le plus grand nombre de leur costé, que tous ce qu'ils sont en leur troupeau ils sont de l'Eglise de Guisnes, nous disons que cela ne fait rien pour leurs pretentions contre nos deffences ; parce que nous formons vn corps aussy bien qu'eux ; autant parfait en ses parties que s'il estoit plus nombreux, que si ces messieurs sont tous de l'Église de Guisnes, tout ce que nous sommes aussy de refugiés ici sommes de la mesme Église, nous adioustons que si leur Eglise est si nombreuse elle ait d'autant plus en estat de faire la despence de deux coupes pour la Communion, surtout veu qu'elle n'est point chargée de la subsistance de son pasteur commes nous sommes ici de celle du nostre, non seulement du nostre mais aussy des ministres Anglois et de plus des pauvres Anglois dont quelques vns de nous sont taxés a plus de 65ᵘ par an.

Tout ce que dessus bien prouvé et bien entendu veu nos justes deffences nous formons oposition a ce que les dittes coupes soyent rendues au Consistoire de l'Église de Catzan priant pour cet effet celuy qui en est presentement depositaire de ne l'en point d'essaisir a nostre preiudice, fait le present arresté et signé.[1]

(*No signatures in the original.*)

Whether by virtue of possession, or as the result of some interference on the part of the Archbishop, is not known, but the cups remained at Dover ; though two years later a fresh attempt was made to recover possession of them for Catzan. On October 17, 1688, we read in the minutes of the Church at Dover :—

Le sieur Jacques Cassel sestant pñte a cette compagnie porteur d'une procuration en sou nom a luy adresséc par nos freres de l'eglise de Cazan pour demander de leur part les couppes nappes et deux serviettes de l'eglise de Calais au frere Isaac de La Croix aquy ils ont esté envoyez par ordre du consistoire de la ditte eglise de Calais, ce qu'ayant communiquez a nos chefs de famille cy devant membre de cette eglise la (sans en prendre quand a nous aucune aultre connoissance) les dits chefs de famille ont fait opposition pr ecrit q̃ nous avous a ce que les dits effets fussent remis es mains dudit sr Cassel, et ont requis le dit frere de La Croix de les garder jusques a ce qu'il en soit reglez aultrement; de quoy en avous octroyez audit de La Croix afin dy avoir recours quant besoin sera et de ce qu'il a esté affert par le dit frere de La Croix de remettre les dit couppes et linges entre les mains de quy les dits chefs de familles auroient trouvez le plus aproppos.

S. DE LE BECQUE.   SIMON CONIET.
ISAAC DE LA CROIX.   DAVID LE CANDEL.

The minutes contain nothing further ; but evidently this attempt was as unsuccessful as the first, as in 1736, after the Church had ceased to exist, the cups with the linen—which, if it was the same, must indeed have been 'fort usé'—remained in the possession of Isaac Minet.

[1] *Ibid.* fo. 94.

The books of the Church of Guines, by which was probably meant the Registers and the book of the Consistory minutes, had apparently, we gather from the memorial of 1686, gone to Catzan; of the books, one has again returned, curiously enough, to Guines, where it is now, in the safe keeping of M. Landrin.

One would much wish to know the history of the cups and of the books of the Dover Church, which remained with Isaac Minet in 1736. The books—that is, the Registers and Minute Book of Dover—were, certainly as late as 1784, still in the possession of the family, as in that year M. de la Chaumelle returned them to Hughes Minet after borrowing them for purposes of research. This appears from a letter which accompanied them on their return to Hughes, and which still remains with them. From that time until recently, when Mr. F. A. Crisp acquired them, their fate is unknown. Did they by any chance remain in the Bank, whence, on the clearance which in 1867 restored to the Minets their own manuscript, they emerged, to pass unrecognised into some dealer's hands?

The cups were probably kept by Isaac in the Bank vaults, and as to the fate that has befallen them one can only conjecture. They may have been taken by his son James to Berlin, or William may have removed them to London; or, again, they may have remained at Dover. One thing only is certain—no mention of them is ever made by any Minet after 1736.

APPENDIX VII

UNIDENTIFIED MINETS

THE name of Minet does not seem to be at all a common one in England, but in the course of the researches undertaken in connexion with this work a few instances of its occurrence have been met with which it has been impossible to identify, or to connect in any way with the family treated of in the foregoing pages. With the hope that some future historian of the family may meet with more success than the present writer, these instances are here collected, with notes of the places where they were found.

The first consists of a group of baptisms of the children of what, from the dates, must be the two families of Andries and Andreas Minet; but whether the latter was son of the former there is nothing to show. From the fact of their being members of the Dutch Church in Austin Friars, one may reasonably infer that they came from Holland, and search in the admirable Leyden Index to the Registers of the Low Countries might perhaps throw some light on them. The entries are as follows:—

    10 Oct. 1648 Minet, Jonas   f. Andries
    1 Nov. 1649 ,,   Susanna f.   ,,
    27 Feb. 1651 ,,   Sara f.   ,,
    20 Mar. 1681 ,,   Elizabeth f. Andreas & Sara
    17 Jun. 1683 ,,   Joseph f. Andreas Zalr. & Sara Van de Velde.[1]

---

[1] *Registers of the Dutch Reformed Church, Austin Friars*, ed. by W. J. C. Moens, p. 51. Lymington, 1884.

APPENDIX VII

The deaths of three of the five children whose baptisms have just been given are found entered in the Registers of Saint Dionys Backchurch :—

    1650. Aug. 8. Susanna Minett, dau. of Andrew Minett
    "   "   15. Jonas   "   son of   "   "
    1683. Ap. 12. Elizabeth   "   dau. of   "   "
                                        buried in North Yard.[1]

The Registers of St. John's Church, Dublin, make us acquainted with a second family of Minets, about which I have to confess my utter ignorance. The Christian names, though Scriptural, are not those in use among the Calais Minets. These are the entries :—

    Minet, Caleb   born 10 Feb $168\frac{2}{3}$
    "   Joshua   "   24 Mar $168\frac{4}{5}$
    "   Sarah   "   11 July 1691
    "   Thomas   "   25 Sep 1694
          (Marriage)
    Thomas Minet to Mary Minet 30 July 1679.[2]

Stepney gives yet another instance of the name in the entry in the parish registers of the baptism, on September 2, 1699, of Susanna, daughter of Frederick Minet, of Whitrow (in Stepney), weaver, and Susan, his wife ; here, again, Frederick is a Christian name quite unknown in our branch.[3]

The Winter Exhibition at the Grosvenor Gallery in 1884 provided another puzzle, yet unsolved, in the shape of a picture of a Mrs. Minet, painted by Gainsborough, probably about 1775. This portrait was then the property of Mr. C. Bischoffsheim, who was good enough to inform me that on the back of the picture was a slip of paper stating that Mrs. Minet was the wife of the British Consul at Athens, and that the picture was painted as the companion to one of Mr. Minet ; Mr. Bischoffsheim had bought the picture about the year 1870, but did not know where the companion portrait was. The picture has been engraved. I have not been able to find any record of the English Consuls at Athens at that date, the archives of the Consulate not going back so far ; and, moreover, the age of the lady, which would be about forty-five, does not correspond with that of any Mrs. Minet of our branch then alive, so that the originals of the Gainsborough portraits must remain in the list of unidentified Minets.

A François Minet is given in the list of Directors of the Hospital for Poor French Protestants (ed. 1876), but this is a misprint for François Menet, who was the companion of Isaac Minet in his tour in 1788.[4]

[1] 'The Reister Booke of Saynte De'nis Backchurch Parishe' (Harleian Soc. publications, *Registers*, vol. iii.).
[2] *Proc. of the Huguenot Soc. of London*, i. 332, 335
[3] I owe the knowledge of this fact to my friend, Mr. J. W. Hardy, F.S.A.
[4] See page 189.

INDEX OF PERSONS AND PLACES

N.B.—*The prefixes de, l', &c., being used or omitted arbitrarily in the original documents, names in which they occur should be also looked for under their respective initial letters.*

ABREE, J., 74
Achard, Charlotte Albertine, 189
────── Pasteur, 213
Agnew, David C. A., 58
Aigues Mortes, 159
Aimery, Isaac, 27, 70
────── Marie, 26, 27
Albert, —, 38 ; see Table D
────── Mrs., 129, 212
Albrechts, — ; see Table E
Aldred, Mary, 212
Alkham, 95, 96
Amboy, 177
Amez-Droz, Josué, 193, 194
Amiens, 113
Amsterdam, 64, 82, 86, 111, 113, 195
Andres, 42
Anna, 92
Ardres, 2, 7, 22, 42, 43, 44, 45, 46, 51, 62
Arnhem, 178, 179, 183
Arnold, Eliza ; see Table C
Arras, 113
Astle, T., 110
Atkins, Anna Maria, 108 ; see Table A
────── Edward, 109
────── Kinsey, 109
────── Robert, 108
Audibert, —, 179, 180
Audinghem, 224
Aumont, Duc d', 108
Austin Friars, 149, 150, 152, 164, 191, 193
Axel, 44
Ayloffe, J., 110
Azores, 40

BACHER ; see Table D
Backen, Wm. Bonham, 138
Baldwyns, 196
Ball, Capt., 127
Bance, —, 27, 28
Barker, Anna Maria, 40 ; see Table B

Barrington, S., 152
Bayley, F., 11 ; see Table D
Bazeley, Capt., 134, 140
Beachy Head, 65
Bengeo, 110, 170, 191
Benn, Capt. Hans, 140
Benoist, 113
Berchère, —, 161 ; see Table M
Bergues, 96
Berlin, 94, 95, 102, 103, 104, 106
Bernard, Dr., 73
────── Hennan, 215
Berson, Margueritte, 189
Bertin ; see Table M
Beurre, Jacqueline, 26
Beurse, Arnoult, 83, 87 ; see Table K
────── Francois, 83, 92
────── Gabriel, 83
────── Guillaume, 83
────── Madelaine, 83
────── Marie, 83
Bigland, R., Richmond Herald, 171
Billingsley, John, 66, 96
────── Mrs., 70
Birch, — ; see Byrch
Bischoff, —, 181
Bischoffsheim, C., 228
Blagrave ; see Table N
Blanchard, —, 184
Blanet, Jacques, 81
Blindston, Capt., 67
Bocket, T., 168
Bod, T., 79
Bolver, J., 72
Bolwerk, Gerard, 65
Bond, Caroline Phœbe ; see Table C
Bonhôte, Fred. ; see Table C
Bonnell, Anne, 108
Bordeaux, 45
Border, T. G., 79
Bosanquet, 195 ; see Table N
Boston, New, 176

BOU

Boulogne, 8, 13, 15, 179, 183, 184, 186, 224
——— Bishop of; see le Tonnelier de Breteuil
Bourdet, Mr., 13
Bovingdon, 178
Bowles, Tobias, 108
Boyes, Sir Wm., 68
Boyket, Capt. Wm., 64
Boyton, —, 6
Bradford; see Table O
Bradley, Thos., 67, 68, 69, 72, 73
Brander, Jons, 64
Brasted; see Hevers Wood
Brissault, Anne Angelica, 40
——— Elizabeth, 40; see Table C
——— Esther, 40
——— John, 40
——— Mary, 40
——— William, 40
Brock, —, 180
Browne, John, 96
Brulefer, Elizabeth, 51
Brunswick, 177
Bruyeres, Hy.; see Table D
Buck, Jno., 28
Buller; see Table N
Bulwark Rock, Dover, 34
Burette, Jeanne, 42
Byrch, William, 73, 74, 135, 212

CADZAND, 57, 225, 226, 227
Calais, 2, 6, 7, 8, 10, 11, 12, 13, 19, 20, 21, 24, 39, 42, 45, 46, 48, 50, 51, 53, 65, 66, 80, 81, 85, 88, 89, 90, 92, 97, 102, 104, 196
——— Street, 162
Camberwell, 162, 217
Campbell, Lord, 66
Campredon, David, 53, 56, 95, 96, 110
Canterbury, 38, 39, 46, 49, 51, 52, 68, 70, 157
——— Archbishop of, 57, 224, 225
——— Cathedral, 137, 157
Capel-le-Ferne, 96, 100, 162, 216, 217
Carlisle, Bishop of, 110
Carrel, Etienne, 25
Cartwright, 210; see Table A
Cason, John, 97
Cassel, Jacques, 25, 38, 227
——— Marie, 21
Cazalet, Eliz.; see Table M
Cazenove, Louise, 189
Charlton, 56
Charnell, John, 111, 112
Charost, Amand, Duc de, 25
Chauvel, J., 73

DEG

Chauvelin, 29
Chaux-de-Fonds, La, 193, 195
Clermont; see Cormont
Clinton, Sir Hy., 177
Coetlogon, Denis Claude, 68
Colbran, F., 120
——— R., 74, 120, 121, 123, 127, 139, 140, 212
Coldridge, 56
Colin, Pierre, 88
Collin, Gabriel, 57
Collins, —, 72
Colliot, Wm., 115
Coni, 191
Coniet, Simon, 227
Conilliette, Isaac, 56
Coppen, Marie, 38
Coquet, Simon, 14
Cormont, 7, 8, 9, 10, 16, 115, 196
——— Street, 162
Cossart, —, 120
Cottin, John, 108
Courtebourne, Marquis de, 25
Courvoisier, Clement D., 194
Cove of Cork, 176
Covey, L., 210
Coze, Louis, 223, 224
——— Pierre, 16, 221, 222, 223, 224
Cramers, Wm., 84
Crisp, F. A., 51, 58, 173, 199, 228
Croisic, 63
Crommelin, Dan., 131
Cross, Dr., 96
Cruche, P. J., 195

DABBADIE, Dan., 215
Dale, —, 96
Dalglish, John, 67, 73, 74
——— Mrs., 69
Darras, J. M., 115
Dauling, John, 95, 96, 100
Deal, 65, 131
de Barbut; see Table N
de Bavre, 171
Debons, Mrs., 179
——— F. L., 190
de Bussavent, Claude, 25, 29
de Butler, —, 157
de Cashel, James, 28
de Castillon, M., 107
de Couvet, F. Petitpierre, 195
de Fays, Susanne, 38
de Gaultier, Estienne, 214
de Glarge, Cornils, 87
'Degrave,' The, 100, 101
de Guines, M., 107

Degulhon, 57
de Haffrengue; see Table H
─────── Anne, 15
─────── Charles, 15
─────── Claude, 15
─────── Daniel, 7, 15, 16, 22, 221, 222, 223, 224
─────── Etienne, 15
─────── Jean, 16
─────── Jehan, 14, 15
─────── Leon, 15
─────── Madelon, 14, 15, 16
─────── Marie, 15
─────── Peter, 7, 13, 15, 16, 221, 222, 223, 224
─────── Philippe, 14, 15, 16
─────── Prudence, 13
─────── Samuel, 15
─────── Susanne, 7, 8, 12, 13, 15, 16, 37, 42, 44, 48, 172
de Hane, Jacob, 36, 54
de Haut, David, 58
de Joffré, René, 29
de Jormeaux, Antoinette, 90, 93
de la Court, Bernard, 215
─────── Elizabeth, 215
─────── Susanna, 215
de la Croix, Anne, 14
─────── Charles, 90, 93
─────── Isaac, 45, 54, 56, 226, 227
─────── Marie, 26, 91
─────── Pierre, 14
─────── Susanne, 89, 90
de la Hode, ─, 13
de la Marre, Anne, 36
de la Porte; see Table K
─────── Catherine, 83, 86, 88
─────── Gabriel, 83, 84, 91
─────── Jacqueline, 83, 87
─────── Jacques, 87, 88
─────── Jean, 84, 86
─────── Jeanne, 86, 87
─────── Madelaine, 85, 86
─────── Marie, 84
─────── Otto, 83, 85, 86, 91, 92
─────── Susanne, 84
de la Salle, ─, 108
de le Becque, Jeanne, 36
─────── Louis, 26, 36, 56, 82
─────── Marie, 86; see Table I
─────── Solomon, 45, 51, 52, 56, 82, 226, 227
Delemar, Jacques, 38
de Lengaigne; see Table H
de l'Epinoy, Pigault, 20
de Lescluze, Jacob, 45
Deprez, ─, 38

Deprez, Susanne, 38
de Rousselle, James, 46, 137, 138, 215; see Table F
de St. Martin, Armand Jean, Sieur de Fréthun, 89
─────── Henri, 89
─────── Susanne Louise, 89
Desbionuille, Elizabeth, 16
Deschamps, Gabriel, 86
─────── Madelaine, 83, 86
─────── Nicolas, 83, 86
Descottes, J. J., 215
de Senlecque, Jacques, 15
─────── Jean, 15
─────── Suson, 15
Destrier, Jean, 31, 32, 33, 44, 45, 46
─────── Marie Francoise, 44, 45, 46, 70, 71, 72, 120, 130, 135, 212, 214
─────── Pierre, 44, 45
─────── Susan, 44, 45, 46
de Teissier; see Table M
de Thosse, Francois, 25
de Vaux, Simon, 11
Devinck, Benjamin, 67, 68
─────── William, 68
de Zastrow, Gouverneur, 194
d'Hoye, Judith, 10
─────── Samuel, 29
Dickinson; see Tables D, O
Dieppe, 111
Doctors' Commons, 97, 140
Dodd, John, 216
Dolignon, John, 163, 216, 217
Dorotheenstädtische Kirche, 105, 213
Dorset, Duke of, 59
Dover, 2, 3, 5, 11, 12, 21, 24, 39, 42, 46, 47, 48, 49, 50, 52, 53, 57, 58, 59, 61, 66, 67, 73, 93, 95, 103, 105, 106, 114, 186, 193, 224, 225, 228
─── Castle, 99
─── French Church at, 54 et seq.
─── Mayor of, 58, 162
Down, Mary, 61
Dowse, ─, 79
Doxat; see Table M
Drake, M. E., 211
Drury, Robert, 100, 101
du Bois, Cardinal, 108
─────── Mr., 120, 125
Dubue; see Table M
Duc, ─, 125
Ducommun, Chas. Francois, 194
─────── Henri, 194
─────── Louis, 193
Dumolin, ─, 91
Dumon, Marie, 81, 88
─────── Pierre, 81

H H

DUN

Dundas, Lieut.-Gen., 178
Dunkirk, 92
Dunstan, Jos., 33
du Ponsue, Antoinette, 80
Dupont, Francis, 115
du Pré, Jacqueline, 222
Durant, —, 96
Duriez, Jonas, 21, 26, 27, 31, 36
——— Samuel, 53
Durpont, Josepha Maria, 40; see Table D
Dutch East India Co., 63
Duvernier; see Table E
Dyke, 210; see Table A
Dyvedon; see Yverdon

EATON, William, 24, 50
Edborough, Rich., 97, 98
Edes, —, 79
Edward, Prince, 190
Eidsforth, Wm., 215
Elcocks, —, 135
Emery; see Aimery
Emmerich, 48
Engelfrieden, Anne R., 213
Enkhuysen, 64
Essex, Earl of, 68
——— Lady, 68
Etaples, 8, 115
Evans, 211; see Table O
——— Hy., 90
Evrard, Marie, 36
Ewell, 96
Eyghes, Jean, 86
Eythorne, 2, 5, 96, 97, 98, 99, 101, 150, 155, 170

FALBIER, Caterine, 82
——— Joos, 82; see Table I
Fannet, Pierre, 60, 102
Farley, Hy., 215
Fayal, 40
Fector; see Table D. *Where no page number is affixed to a name, it will be found only in the Table.*
——— A. J. Laurie
——— Anne Elizabeth
——— Caroline, 76
——— Charlotte Mary
——— Elizabeth
——— Elizabeth Hughes, 219
——— Emma
——— James Peter, 179, 183, 186, 191, 193
——— Jeremy, 41, 62, 113, 118, 120, 124, 128, 212
——— John Minet, 41, 150, 166, 174, 186, 193

GOV

Fector, Mary, 118, 120, 150, 159, 212, 219
——— Mary Elizabeth, 219
——— Minet
——— Peter, 3, 5, 39, 41, 46, 62, 66, 70, 72, 74, 100, 103, 113, 115, Chap. viii. *passim*, 157, 159, 162, 174, 183, 191, 193, 212, 214, 219
——— Peter Lane
——— Thomas
——— William, 185, 188, 193, 219
Fenchurch Street, 116, 149, 157
Flahault, Anne, 14, 43
——— Jacques, 42
——— Jeanne, 42, 43
Flanders, 47
Floydson, —, 183
Flushing, 26, 43, 44, 52, 53, 81, 82, 85, 86, 88, 90, 91
Folkestone, 65, 131
Fontainebleau, 62
Fouet, Pierre, 53
Fountain's Farm, 177
Framery, Pierre, 15
Franc; see Frencq
Francomme, Jean, 55
Franklyn; see Stephens
Freeman; see Table O
French Protestant Hospital, 189, 215, 229
Frencq, 7, 9, 26, 115
Fulham, 164, 166, 186, 193
Furnes, 90, 92
Furness, Sir Robert, 96

GARTHORNE Geo., 216
Gatou, Daniel, 91
Gavanon, Mr., 178, 182, 188
——— Louis, 179, 188
Gay, Goddard, 74
——— Mrs., 70
Gibson, Capt. Chas., 61, 110
Giles, Daniel, 45, 46, 60; see Table F
——— Elizabeth Dina, 45, 46
Girod, Estienne, 54
——— Gabriel, 54
——— J. Jacques, 54
Glover, —, 161
Goldney; see Table O
Gordon, —, 181
——— Eliz., 115
——— Jas., 216
Gorkum, 85
Gossip, L. F.; see Table A
Goubard, Jacques, 37
——— Jonas, 37
——— Marie, 37, 38
Govers, Corniles, 92

INDEX

Grandidier, Zacherie, 61, 94, 103, 108
Grandsire, Madame, 68
——— Magdelaine, 68
Gravelines, 32
Gravesend Bay, 176
Gray, Dr., 68
Groundicb, Piternel, 84
Guérard, Antoine, 224
——— David, 94, 103
Guérin, Peter, 59
Gueulle, Jacob, 14
Guines, 10, 11, 12, 14, 19, 20, 42, 43, 92, 224, 225, 226, 228
Gunman, Capt., 67
——— Madame, 70

HAGEN, Ed.; see Table C
Halifax, 176
Hall, —, 67
——— Stephen, 216
Hardwicke, Ld. Chanc., 2, 66, 110, 116
Harris, M. C. C., 210
Harvey, Rich., 96
Hatfeild, G., 210
——— T. G., 210
Haudeguemp, Jean, 42
Hayes, 164, 216, 217; see Tables A, N
Hays, Claude, 26, 91
——— James, 26, 31, 36, 53, 60, 89, 103
——— John, 26, 31
——— Marie, 89, 91
——— Robert, 53, 92
——— Scribe, 89
Headborough; see Edborough
Heard, Isaac, Principal King of Arms, 170
Hebert, Anne, 40
——— Mary, 40
——— Mary Anne, 40
——— Nicolas, 40
Herbault, Joseph, 15
Hervieu, Jean, 92
Heusch, Michel, 86, 87
Hevers Wood, 167, 196, 217
Higgins; see Table C
Hodgson, Cuthbert, 74
Holland, John, 58
Hollingbury, Col., 58, 67, 74
Hoogstad, Capt. Jacob, 64
Hooper, Wynard; see Table O
Horse Guards, Oxford Regt. of, 47
Hovenden, R., 199
Hubbard; see Table O
Hughes, Alice, 98, 99, 100, 101
——— Elizabeth, 99, 100, 101
——— Henry, 101
Hughes; see Table L

Huitmille; see Wimille
Hume, L. P., 215
——— Margaret, 215
Huot, Elias, 104, 105
Hurdis, Harriet, 165
——— James, 165
——— James Henry, 165
——— John Lewis, 165
Hurst, —, 184

IGGULDEN, Eliz., 196
——— Wm., 196

JAMES, —, 59
James II., 56
Jan, Riche, 87, 91
Jersey, Lady, 67
Joan, 213
Johnson, J., 140
——— C., 226
Jolly, —, 41
Jones, Counsellor, 66
——— Mrs., 70
Jovet, Susanne, 36

KENNET, White, 11, 42, 225
Kerr, Gregory, 48, 54
Kingsbridge, 177
Kirkland, Jas., 213, 214
Knatchbull, Sir Ed., 162
Knight, Frances, 102, 218
——— Thos., 102
Knott, John, 67
Knowles, Capt., 132

LA CHAUSSÉE, 29
la Converserie, 14, 16
Lafarce, Solomon, 32
la Haye, 14
Lamb, Isaac, 61, 67, 110
Lambe, James, 67, 96
Lambert, Sir John, 108
Lambeth, 96, 97, 162
Lambrecht, —, 87
Lamens, Catherine, 35
Landrin, C., 11, 14, 16, 30, 222, 224, 228
Lane, Frances, 179; see Table D
——— Thos. Bateman, 184, 186, 188
L'Aoust, Thos., 86, 87
la Petite Walde, 33, 46
Larnes, Madame, 91
la Trésorerie, 7, 8, 13, 14, 16, 221

LAT

Latteur, Jeanne, 16, 22, 223
—— Susanne, 14, 16
Laurie, the Rev. Sir J. R. L. Emilius, Bart., 41 ; see Table D
—— Mrs., 75
Lavaure, —, 96
le Beauclerc, Louis, 88
le Candel, David, 227
le Duc, —, 26
—— Pierre, 89
Lee, —, 181
Lefebvre, F., 14, 26
le Gay, Pierre, 60, 94, 95, 103, 105
le Heup ; see le Keux
le Jessin, Rob., 223
le Keux, —, 56, 57
le Maire, Abraham, 26, 31, 36, 103
le Maistre, Pierre, 38, 49, 60
—— Mrs., 182
le Quesne, Marie, 45
Lernoult, Adrian, 26, 31, 35, 36, 89, 90, 152
—— Elizabeth, 90
—— Margaret, 90, 152
—— Mary, 90
Lescott, Paul, 55
Lesmond, Seigneur de, 223
le Tonnelier de Breteuil, Claude, 19, 25, 51
———————— Francois, 19, 20
le Turcq, Marie, 8, 26
—— Pierre, 8 ; see Table A
Leverland ; see Table E
Lille, 83, 85
Lingo, James, 28, 32
Lisbon, 40, 63
Lock, Thomas ; Clarenceux, 170
Lodowick, John, 68
Lombart, 160
London, 47, 52, 53, 84, 95, 96, 97, 103, 114
—— Assurance Corporation, 116, 139, 160, 184
Long Island, 177
Longman, 211 ; see Table O
Loubier ; see Table M. *Where no page number is affixed to a name, it will be found only in the Table.*
—————— Antoine, 160
—————— Charles
—————— Charlotte
—————— Charlotte Henrietta, 190
—————— Clodine
—————— Elizabeth
—————— Henry, 160
—————— John Antony, 146, 159
—————— John Lewis, 160, 161
—————— Mary, 159, 162
—————— Matthieu
—————— Susanne, 159, 160

MIN

Louis XIV., 2, 65
—— XV., 62, 157
Lovel, Chas., 67
Lower Hardres, 99, 132
Lydden Spouts, 131
Lynch, Dr., 70, 72, 73, 127, 130
Lyon, Jno., 68

MACQUEEN, Jno., 61, 68, 96
Mactier, A. ; see Table D
Madeira, 40
Madras, 100
Magnus, —, 135
Mainville ; see Table N
Mantell, Ed. Reginald ; see Table A
—— Susan, 76
Maquet, Caterine, 80
—— Christofle, 80
Marcq, 20, 46
Maréchal, André, 30, 31
Margate, 104
Marlay, Col. ; see Table D
Marlborough, Duchess of, 212
—————— Duke of, 132
Marsh, Col., 65, 96
Matson, Christopher, 68
—— Gen. E. ; see Table D
—— Henry, 67, 68
—— John, 73, 74
—— Nathaniel, 67
Matthey, Felix, 194
Maxted, Ed., 96
Maytre, Marie ; see Table M
Mel ; see Table E
Menet, Francois, 189, 192, 229
—— Isabeau, 159, 189
—— Jean Francois, 189
—— Jeanne, 160, 189
—— John, 189
—— Nicolas, 189
Meyer, L. C., 195
Middelburg, 44, 80, 81, 83, 84, 85
Miller, Mary, 212
Milles, Jer., 110
Minault, 171
Minet ; see Tables A to G. *Where no page number is affixed to a name, it will be found only in the Tables.*
—— Adrian
—— Alice, 98, 211, 214, 219
—— Alice Gertrude
—— Ambroise, 2, 7, 8, 9, 10, 11, 12, 16, 23, 34, 37, 38, 41, 42, 43, 44, 47, 48, 50, 51, 52, 60, 61, 196
—— Andreas, 228, 229
—— Andries, 228

INDEX

Minet Angelica Eliza
—— Ann, 7
—— Anna Maria, 108, 109
—— Annie
—— Caleb, 229
—— Caterina Johanna
—— Caterina Lena
—— Catherina
—— Catherine
—— Charles Ernest Temple
—— Charles William, 101, 151, 175, 196
—— Charlotte
—— Daniel, 8, 22, 24, 37, 41, 42, 43, 44, 46, 50, 51, 52, 60, 61, 62, 69, 70, 79, 94, 97, 108, 109, 111, 114, 125, 138, 139, 163, 164, 191, 212, 214, 216, 217, 220
—— Daniel Sinclair
—— Delia Jane, 210
—— Edith
—— Eleanor Eliza
—— Elizabeth, 8, 32, 38, 41, 43, 44, 45, 46, 52, 60, 61, 98, 102, 212, 215, 221, 228, 229
—— Emily
—— Esther, 7, 9
—— Fanny Cecilia, 210
—— Frances Catherine
—— Francis
—— Frederick, 229
—— Georgina Emma, 210
—— Geraldine Helena, 210
—— Gertrude, 210
—— Henrietta, 98, 99, 130, 214, 217
—— Henry, 98, 99, 214
—— Hughes, 5, 39, 62, 98, 99, 100, 101, 105, 107, 114, 115, Chaps. viii. ix. *passim* 178, 192, 193, 212, 213, 214, 215, 216, 217, 220, 228
—— Isaac, 1, 2, 3, 4, 6, 7, 8, 9, 10, 13, 18, 21, 24, 37, 38, 39, 42, 46, 47, Chap. v. *passim*, 88, 89, 94, 95, 98, 99, 103, 112, 114, 139, 140, 150, 151, 157, 170, 175, 193, 194, 211, 213, 217, 218, 221, 227, 228
—— Isaac Knight, 102
—— Isaak
—— Jacob, 8, 34, 38, 46, 51, 52, 62
—— Jacoba
—— Jacomina Adriana
—— James, 7, 8, 9, 10, 39, 40, 60, 69, 94, 98, 103, 104, 105, 115, 127, 151, 163, 170, 211, 212, 213, 215, 216, 217, 228
—— James Lewis, 1, 6, 9, 75, 76, 153, 167, 196
—— Jan
—— Jeanne, 43
—— Johanna

Minet, John, 2, 5, 60, 69, 70, 72, 73, 95, 96, 98, 99, 102, 103, 122, 127, 135, 154, 155, 156, 157, 164, 211, 214, 218
—— John Brissault
—— John Cross
—— John Lewis, 150, 152, 166, 167, 174, 175, Chap. x *passim*, 213, 217, 221
—— Jonas, 228, 229
—— Joseph, 40, 228
—— Josepha Maria
—— Joshua, 229
—— Judith, 38
—— Julia
—— Julia Evelina
—— Kate
—— Leuntie
—— Mabel Julia
—— Magdelaine, 38, 212
—— Margaret Kathleen
—— Maria Johanna
—— Marianna
—— Marianna Augusta
—— Marianna Elizabeth
—— Martha, 8, 9, 26,
—— Mary, 4, 5, 7, 8, 34, 38, 39, 41, 48, 60, 62, 78, 93, 94, 98, 99, 103, 113, 118, 125, 127, 136, 137, 138, 150, 159, 162, 213, 214, 215, 216, 218, 219, 229
—— Mary Anne Victoria, 40
—— Mary Broughton
—— Mary Isabel, 40
—— Maud
—— Millecent
—— Peter, 10, 38, 115
—— Robert, 10
—— Sara, 228, 229
—— Sophia
—— Sophia Louisa, 210
—— Stephanie Beatrice
—— Stephen, 8, 23, 28, 31, 34, 42, 47, 48, 51, 52, 95, 150
—— Susan, 7, 8, 34, 37, 38, 39, 41, 48, 61, 129, 164, 221, 228, 229
—— Susan Millecent, 210
—— Susanna Jacoba
—— Susanna Johanna
—— Susanne, 9, 22, 38, 43
—— Thomas, 8, 37, 38, 39, 41, 44, 50, 51, 60, 61, 62, 95, 118, 120, 130, 132, 135, 136, 137, 212, 215, 229
—— William, 2, 3, 4, 5, 10, 39, 40, 60, 62, 69, 70, 72, 77, 78, 98, 99, 100, 101, 103, 105, 109, 110, 111, 112, 115, Chap. viii. *passim*, 157, 160, 161, 163, 176, 177, 178, 182, 184, 189, 192, 212, 217, 218, 220, 228
—— William Brissault

MIN

Minet & Fector, 47, 54, 62, 147
—— William, and Company, 141, 147
Minot, 171
Miol, Lewis, 149, 152
Mire, Robert, 57
Mitchel, —, 107
Moens, W. J. C., 195, 199, 228
Montmartel, Paris de, 108
Montreuille, 8, 9
Morell, F., 110
Morgan, Elizabeth, 166, 175, 195
Mulhausen, 118
Murray ; see Table D
Myatt's Fields, 162

NATIONAL PROVINCIAL BANK, 5, 150
Nérac, Treaty of, 20
Nethersole, Hy., 212
Neubronner, —, 214
Neuchâtel en Boulonnais, 13
Newcastle, Duke of, 110, 116
Newendam, 113
Newiar, Susanne, 53
Newman, Mrs., 166
Newport Street, Long Acre, 42, 52
New York, 177
Nieuport, 41, 43, 48, 92
Noguier ; see Table M
Norman, Anne ; see Table O

'OLD BANK,' The, 151
Oléron, Ile d', 46
Oliver, Capt., 100
Olmius, Herman, 90, 152
—— John Ludovic, 152
—— Margaret, 90, 152
Orange, Prince of ; see William III.
Orsec, Capt., 64
Ostcapel, 84
Ostend, 92, 102
Otto, Mrs., 130
Oxenden, —, 56
Oxford Regiment of Horse Guards, 47

PAIEN, E., 56
Papillon, —, 96
Parent, James, 65
Parker, O. G., 210
Paskall, John, 64, 65
Patton, H. B., 210
Pearce, Sara, 212
Peck, Dr., 68, 69
Peltier, Jean, 38
Pemble, Dr., 96

ROU

Penny, Solomon, 57
Perche, Jacques, 55
—— Mrs., 70
Peterborough, Bishop of ; see Kennet
Petitpierre ; see de Couvet
Phelps ; see Table O
Picinan, Antoinette, 80
—— Baudar, 80, 81 ; see Table I
Pier House, 151, 159
Pilart, Daniel, 35, 37, 44
—— Madelaine, 26, 90
—— Marie, 37
—— Sara, 25
Pillans, Thos., 111
Piquet, 214
Pitt, John, 101
Planquielle, Marguerite, 81
Ploetmel, 68
Poitiers, Bishop of, 57
Pole, Sir Chas., Bart., 164, 195
—— Susannah, 164, 175, 195
Ponfade ; see Poujade
Ponton, André, 31
Porré, Michel, 89
—— Pierre, 63
Portsmouth, 64
Poujade, —, 57
Poultny, John, 72
Primrose, —, 64
Pybus, Capt., 132

QUANDALLE, Mary, 115
Quebec, 178
Quirkel, —, 213
Quithal, André, 213

RAOULT, Curé, 21
Rayner, Jno. ; see Table A
Ready, Storer, 165
Regan, Elizabeth ; see Table C
Regnier, Marie, 38
—— Susanne, 38
Rice, Capt., 188
—— E. R. ; see Table D
Richards, Elizabeth, 21, 50
—————— Patience, 21, 24, 50
—————— William, 21, 24, 50
Ridley, Capt., 132
Rollin, Jacques, 92
Rome, A. ; see Table E
Rooth, Thos., 49, 97, 104
Rotterdam, 41, 104, 111, 113
Rouquette, S. E. ; see Table E
Roussier, Isaac, 37
Roussillion, Isaac, 36

ROU

Roussillion, Pierre, 36
Roux, Sam., 212 ; see Table E
Rye, 65

SAENDAM, 113
St. Andrew Undershaft, 162
St. Catherine's College, Cambridge, 95
St. James', Dover, 215
St. Martin's-in-the-Fields, 7, 8, 52
St. Mary, Dover, 93, 102, 117, 170, 215
St. Michael's, 40
St. Ubes, 63
St. Valéry-sur-Somme, 7
Samson, Capt., 126, 133
Sandford, Lieut.-Gen. Ed., 177
Sandoz, Louis, 195
Sandoz-de-travers, —, 194
Sandy Hook, 176
Sardier, —, 179
Sauchelle ; see Table I
——— Anne, 82
——— Caterine, 80, 82, 86, 87, 92
——— Catrina, 92
——— Elizabeth, 60, 78, 85, 87, 88, 93, 94, 95, 103, 104
——— Gabriel, 86, 87
——— Gilbert, 80, 86
——— Isaac, 93
——— Jacques, 26, 80, 81, 82, 86, 87
——— Jean, 53, 78, 80, 81, 82, 85, 86, 87, 88, 89, 90, 91, 93, 95, 173
——— Jeanne, 61, 82, 88, 103, 108
——— Jenne, 80, 81, 85, 87, 92, 94
——— Johan, 82
——— Joos, 80, 86
——— Madelaine, 86, 87
——— Marguerite, 82
——— Marie, 38, 52, 53, 54, 60, 68, 77, 80, 82, 85, 86, 87, 88, 91, 93
——— Noé, 82, 83, 84, 86, 92
——— Pierre, 10, 82, 86
——— Robert, 92, 93
Savoye, Église de la, 56
Sayer, James Minet, 165, 166
——— William, 187
——— see Table A
Scorcewska, Countess, 107
Searle, Ernest ; see Table C
Sétuval, 63
Sharp, Gregory, 110
Sheerness, 64
Sheppardswell, 56, 96
Siddons, Mrs., 183
Sigart, François, 89, 90, 91
——— Isaac, 26, 31, 36, 60, 89, 90, 91, 92, 93, 95, 102, 103

VAN

Sigart, Marie, 26, 53, 90, 91, 92
——— Sara, 53, 60, 89, 90, 91, 92, 95
——— Susanne, 89
Sloane, Sir H., 116
Slodden, John, 67
Somerard, —, 224
Souchey, —, 14
Spitalfields, 40
——— Artillery Church, 53
Stamper, R., 152
Stanley, Elizabeth, 38
Staten Island, 176
Staveley, Sir C. D. S., 210
Stephens & Franklyn, 111, 113
Stock, Susanne, 45
Stockwood, —, 96
Stride, J., 150
——— L, 152
Stringer, Capt. G., 135
Sturt, Rebecca ; see Table A
Styles, Alice, 215
——— Thos., 215
Sulzer, —, 106
Summerson's Ferry, 176
Sworder, Alice Vise ; see Table B
Sy, Sara, 89

TALLARD, Marshal, 108
Temple, H. H. ; see Table B
Ten-Brenck ; see Table C
Tergou, 113
Tetuan, 40
Theyssen, J. ; see Table E
Thiébault, Dieudonné, 106
Thomas, J., 153
Thorndike, E., 210
Threadneedle St., Church of, 9, 109. 215
Torras, Marie, 189
Tournai, 88
Tricotel, Pierre, 89, 90
Trouillart, —, 11, 38, 226
Tubbs, R. T. N., 210
Turner, Wm., 96, 97

UNDERDOWN, V., 74, 140

VAILLANT, V. J., 9, 171
Valla ; see Vatta
van der Ameide, Anne Pyl, 85, 91
van der Velde, 228
van Notten ; see Table N
van Rhyn ; see Table E
van Teylingen, Susanne, 93

VAN

Vanthune, Catherine, 33, 44, 45, 46, 52
van Wanbeck, Johan, 84
—————— Maximilian, 84, 93
—————— Sara, 84
Vatta, Marie, 22
Veel, Elizabeth, 74
——— Wm., 67, 98, 99
——— Young, 101
Vialat, Izabeau ; see Table M
Vickers ; see Table N
Vincent, Marie, 213
Vinson ; see Wynzant
Vizard ; see Table O
Vroom, Capt. Wm., 64

WAAL, 85
Wake, Archbishop, 96
Walker ; see Table O
Wandsworth, Church of, 57
Ward ; see Table O
Wardrop ; see Table B
Wellard ; see Table D
Wessels, —, 179
Westerham, 166, 175, 178, 196
Westfield, Wm., 64
Westminster, French School, 215
White, —, 131

ZEA

Wickenden, Robt., 67
Wilkins, Dr., 96
Wilkinson, Jno., 215
William III., 47
Willis, Jas., 212
Wilmott, Sam., 97, 98
Wimille, 7, 13, 16, 222, 223, 224
Winell, —, 58
Winter, John, 38
——— Rebecca, 38
Wise, Dr., 96
Woodruffe ; see Table B
Wright, Oliver, 100
Wroth, Sir Henry, 172
Wynzant ; see Table D

YORK Island, 177
——— Philip, 66, 96
Young, Alice, 98
——— E., 152
——— Elizabeth, 98, 101
——— R., 152
——— William, 98, 100, 101
Yule, Col., 101
Yverdon, 36

ZEALAND, 8, 225

www.ingramcontent.com/pod-product-compliance
Lightning Source LLC
Chambersburg PA
CBHW031342230426
43670CB00006B/410